STEALING
REMBRANDTS

STEALING REMBRANDTS

THE UNTOLD STORIES OF NOTORIOUS ART HEISTS

Anthony M. Amore
and
Tom Mashberg

palgrave
macmillan

First published in 2011 by
PALGRAVE MACMILLAN®
in the United States—a division of St. Martin's Press LLC,
175 Fifth Avenue, New York, NY 10010.

Where this book is distributed in the UK, Europe and the rest of the world,
this is by Palgrave Macmillan, a division of Macmillan Publishers Limited,
registered in England, company number 785998, of Houndmills,
Basingstoke, Hampshire RG21 6XS.

Palgrave Macmillan is the global academic imprint of the above companies
and has companies and representatives throughout the world.

Palgrave® and Macmillan® are registered trademarks in the United States,
the United Kingdom, Europe and other countries.

ISBN: 978–0–230–10853–0

Library of Congress Cataloging-in-Publication Data

Amore, Anthony M.
    Stealing Rembrandts : the untold stories of notorious art heists / Anthony M.
  Amore, Tom Mashberg.
       p. cm.
    Includes bibliographical references and index.
    ISBN 978–0–230–10853–0 (hardback)
       1. Art thefts. 2. Theft from museums. 3. Rembrandt Harmenszoon van
  Rijn, 1606–1669. I. Mashberg, Tom. II. Title. III. Title: Untold stories of
  notorious art heists.

N8795.A46 2011
364.16'287599492—dc22   2010049196

A catalogue record of the book is available from the British Library.

Design by Newgen Imaging Systems (P) Ltd., Chennai, India.

First edition: July 2011

10 9 8 7 6 5 4 3

Printed in the United States of America.

For Gabriela and Alessandra.

This book cannot hold the words I'd need
to describe how much I love you.
—A. A.

To my mother, Francesca Lack
—T. M.

CONTENTS

AUTHORS' FOREWORDS

AN INVESTIGATOR'S JOURNEY

A Rembrandt is the jewel of most any museum's collection, and its loss can be a staggering blow. When I joined the Isabella Stewart Gardner Museum (ISGM) in Boston as security director in the fall of 2005, I made it my mission to recover the 13 works of art, including three Rembrandts, stolen in the dead of night on March 18, 1990. Today, it remains the greatest unsolved art heist in the world, and the unsurpassed Rembrandt van Rijn is at the heart of it. More than one seasoned investigator told me that, to find the art, I would have to "eat, sleep, and drink" the case and experience heartbreaks along the way. They were certainly right. For me, part of it included studying the extensive modern history of Rembrandt heists.

Of course, my first duty as security director was to shore up the safety of the entire Gardner collection. Because of the theft, many had accused the ISGM of lax security. I quickly found not only that this was unfair, but that the standards, personnel, and technology at the Gardner were at least as good—and usually better—than those in place at other institutions. I was gratified to find that the leadership and staff at the museum, from Executive Director Anne Hawley and the museum's trustees, to the conservators, archivists, and gallery guards, were committed to giving me the tools, support, and funds necessary to ensure the security of Mrs. Gardner's amazing possessions. The ISGM now features robust and cutting-edge safeguards, and even as it expands into the 2010s with a bold new wing, I believe it is prepared for the security challenges of today and the future.

Having seen to it that the museum was a sanctuary as well as a showplace for its art, antiquities, and other great artifacts, I directed my attention to the recovery of the stolen works. It is in my nature to become obsessed with a mission, diving headfirst into all available literature, talking to all those with a connection to a case, and reaching out to experts and law enforcement officers.

My quest began with a reexamination of all aspects of the Gardner theft and the years of subsequent investigation. This meant gathering and analyzing every pertinent document received or created by the museum over a 15-year period. I informed the director that I would need all her files, notes, and correspondence related to the theft, and I told the museum's staff that anything they retained on the matter was to be handed over to me. Everyone was eager to comply, and I found that the museum's records on the theft and the 13 stolen items—the vital data of the case—had been carefully maintained.

I spent months reading thousands of pages of leads, theories, letters, articles, memorandums, court papers, and other materials. I built a database of the information contained in these records. Names, dates, addresses, phone numbers, email addresses, vehicle information, birth dates, death dates—all this had to be catalogued to ensure that no detail, however small, would be overlooked. This method continues to serve me well in comparing old information to newer leads.

The next major undertaking was gathering intelligence from current and retired law enforcement sources of good repute—those familiar with the case and those experienced in the worlds of local and international art crime. Equally necessary was interviewing knowledgeable members of the criminal underworld as well as their families, friends, and associates. I also sought out the journalists who have made a study of the case, among them my coauthor, Tom Mashberg.

Another pivotal step in my investigation of this 20-year puzzle was researching how art criminals operate, their method, or MO. Combining the intelligence I gathered and the reams of information available online and in the memories of old art experts, I examined crimes that bore even the slightest resemblance to the Gardner case. I searched through decades of newspaper records, using the Boston Public Library as well as the archives at major local and national newspapers. I had many burning questions. For instance, because the Gardner thieves had dressed as police officers to trick a security guard into granting them entry, I wanted to know what other crimes were committed in Boston by men disguised in police uniforms, or in any uniforms. I also wanted to study robbery methods that were completely different from the Gardner robbery—this would let me rule out certain criminals and keep a tighter focus.

One of the more intriguing characteristics of the Gardner heist is that two of the stolen paintings, *The Storm on the Sea of Galilee* (1633) and *A Lady and Gentleman in Black* (1633), both by Rembrandt, were cut from their frames. When an artist paints, the canvas is held taut by a stretcher, and that stretcher is then packed inside the frame. In this theft, both the stretchers and frames were left lying on the museum floor. Why had the thieves done this? Was it because the frames and stretchers, all combined, were too heavy to carry out? Possibly, but there were two thieves on hand, both described by the guards as young and healthy, and they spent a leisurely 81 minutes in the museum. They had all the time they needed to carry away the paintings rather than commit what can be described only as a witless act of desecration: slicing two Rembrandt canvases from their stretchers. Why risk irreparable damage? Were they so unschooled as to imagine they could manhandle the canvases without wreaking destruction on the paintings? That alone is a key insight into the culprits. Thieves schooled in art would have done no such thing. Moreover, the robbers anticipated that they were going to cut some paintings from their frames. Why else would they have brought along an instrument that was sharp and sturdy enough to slice through stiff, varnished paint and linen canvas? Two other major art thefts in Massachusetts (both involving Rembrandts, as the following chapters will show) were pulled off more than 15 years before the Gardner crime without anyone resorting to cutting canvases. Why do so now? Had these thieves learned their lessons in theft outside Massachusetts? Was this their first art crime?

To answer these questions, I needed to examine art thefts spanning the globe and learn how common it was for paintings to be cut or removed from their frames, both before and since 1990. That examination led me to obscure art thefts committed in a similar fashion. I set out to learn whether this act was some form of signature, a telltale or forensic clue much like those left behind by repeat killers.

This kind of analysis is akin to the initial investigation conducted by a homicide detective. Aside from the obvious questions (e.g., victim's identity, manner, and time of death), the detective has to consider the whole scene to get a jump on the identity of the perpetrator. When a murder victim is found still wearing an expensive watch or carrying a wallet full of money, robbery seems an unlikely motive. Similarly, items not stolen during a museum heist tell an investigator important things about the thieves. In the great majority of thefts, it has quickly become clear, the thieves were not art experts and had no shopping lists. This is because they often bypass works by great artists whose names may not be known in every household—Rubens, Titian, Tintoretto—yet whose works might be far more valuable than the small Rembrandt or Picasso or Manet they decide to remove. Or because they take a piece by an Old Master that is less significant than others by the same artist that hang nearby. Such missteps by thieves are routine. Assuming that doing so means the robbers had a strict shopping list rather than a case of cluelessness could easily throw investigators off-track.

It did not take me long to learn that the sheer number of thefts of paintings from museums, even if narrowed to just the United States, was overwhelming. I also quickly learned that it was not unusual for paintings to be cut or removed from their frames before a getaway. But far more striking was the number of Rembrandt works stolen in the past century. Art theft is notoriously underreported, so it is not possible to say exactly how many such robberies have taken place. But our careful calculations show that about 80 different Rembrandt works have been stolen worldwide during the past 100 years. (For a listing, see page 205.) They include three items from the Gardner Museum and the *Guinness Book of World Records* holder for "most oft-stolen painting in the world," *Jacob de Gheyn III* (1632). Known as the "Takeaway Rembrandt" (and discussed in Chapter 3), it has been filched four separate times. Clearly, it was time to examine this criminal sub-specialty. Could an answer to the Gardner mystery rest among the details of those many other Rembrandt crimes?

Thefts of Rembrandts have occurred in an endless variety of ways, and will no doubt continue for decades to come. The International Foundation for Art Research's quarterly journal lists an etching stolen from Hilligoss Galleries in Chicago in 2007, *Adam and Eve* (1638), as the most recent Rembrandt work to make our list. (In 2010, the best-selling novel *The Rembrandt Affair*, by Daniel Silva, featured a well-researched plot revolving around a stolen Rembrandt. Clearly such crimes are growing in legend.) Beyond sheer numbers, though, research shows that the rationales behind the thefts, and the manner in which the items were recovered or returned, are as novel as the ways in which they were taken. To a large extent, Rembrandt's works are not so much stolen as kidnapped—or "art-napped"—with some sort of extortion, reward, or ransom in mind.

With this as my backdrop, in 2008 I contacted my future coauthor, Tom Mashberg, a veteran investigative reporter who worked for the *Boston Herald* from 1994 until 2010. Mashberg had first investigated the Gardner crime in 1997, and in the course of his reporting, a well-known New England art thief, Myles J. Connor Jr. (Chapter 6), told him that he was the "inspiration" behind the crime. (Connor was in prison when the robbery took place, a fairly impenetrable alibi. By "inspiration," he meant that his own tentative plans to rob the Gardner were carried out by some of his cohorts.) In the course of his reporting, Mashberg was famously taken by car to an undisclosed warehouse location, where he was shown what appeared to be *The Storm on the Sea of Galilee*, from the Gardner trove. I had read accounts of how his unnamed escort held the rolled painting before Mashberg and allowed it to unfurl for a brief examination in the dark by flashlight. No one knows for certain if the item was real, and for good reason. There's not an art expert alive who would make a positive identification of a painting based on a few seconds of observation in the dark with nothing but the beam of a flashlight. We may never know what Mashberg saw that night. Based on what I've learned about the structure of *The Storm* and its well-varnished canvas, however, I lean toward its not being the Gardner's painting. But I'll always be nagged by the fact that Mashberg asked to see *The Storm* and was very shortly thereafter granted his request. And there are other significant but confidential clues obtained by Mashberg that strongly suggest he was on the right track. During the often frustrating 14 years that Mashberg spent on and off the story as a news reporter, he has been careful to keep the public accurately informed without jeopardizing the investigation. That is one reason why I am collaborating with him here.

This book is not a detailed look at the theft of three Rembrandts and ten other items (including a rare Vermeer) from the Isabella Stewart Gardner Museum in 1990. Though I have every confidence those great works will be recovered, we cannot yet say why the art was stolen, by whom, or how it will be brought home. For those and other important reasons, the Gardner tale must wait to be told. But that crime inspired the research leading to this intriguing and surprising catalogue of Rembrandt heists.

Our goal here is to enlighten, educate, and entertain anyone interested in the crime of art theft and in the life and works of Rembrandt Harmenszoon van Rijn (July 15, 1606–October 4, 1669). Rembrandt's paintings, drawings, and prints are numerous enough to have been scattered around the globe. There are Rembrandts in more than half the 50 states. They appear in major international landmark collections and in smaller, parochial museums and galleries on six continents. Many are, of course, in private hands. As such, they will always attract the attention of crooks from every walk of life. Each Rembrandt case carries a wealth of information that will help when investigators race to solve the next such heist and gives me critical insights into how we will recover the Gardner artworks. One thing is certain: To track down a stolen Rembrandt, one must be as exacting as the artist himself.

—*A.A.*

A REPORTER'S JOURNEY

Newsmen and newswomen are a lucky breed. We get to chat with people who own Rembrandts one minute and interview the criminals who steal them the next. It allows for a well-rounded picture of art theft and helps make up for the fact that a major collector could dump our entire annual salaries on an etching the size of a postage stamp.

In 1997, I spotted a small item in the *Boston Herald*, where I was working as an investigative reporter. It announced that the Isabella Stewart Gardner Museum would increase its reward for the return of 13 stolen items from $1 million to $5 million. Like many who read it, my reaction was, "Wait, they're still missing?"

The ISGM had been robbed seven years earlier. The case prompted a torrent of coverage that within a year slowed to a trickle. Surely there must be some fresh news? After all, three Rembrandts and a Vermeer had been taken, paintings worth $300 million by some accounts. Admittedly I knew little about Vermeer. But Rembrandt? Now that was a headline name.

I mentioned this odd business to my editor, a matter-of-fact veteran of the news trade. Chewing on a toothpick and gazing at the ceiling, he said: "Looks like you need to become an expert on art theft."

Nearly 15 years later, I am still trying to learn about this widespread and byzantine criminal specialty, but I have made some progress. I have interviewed enough museum officials and masterpiece owners to realize that their love of art is fierce and genuine, even if their ability to secure it is wanting. And I have spoken with enough art thieves to know that they are not all brutes and philistines, but, like the famed bank robber Willie Sutton, are simply in it for the money. You will hear many of their voices here and gain insights into their way of thinking. You'll read about the petty thief who was suddenly the cock of the walk in jail because his nickname became "Rembrandt," and you will also see that art thieves have been far better at accruing prison time than wealth.

The major goal of our book is to give specialists and general readers a revealing and accurate understanding of this costly and sordid global racket. There are enough interviews with thieves, owners, victims, investigators, and others to make it interesting, perhaps even compelling. And if Anthony Amore and I have done our job right, it is also a useful guide for those in the business of preventing, investigating, studying, and solving art heists. Too much mythology and not enough fact surround these acts, and we have tried to debunk the fallacies and paint as true a picture as we can. As you will see, our first chapter takes a skeptical look at one of the most cherished theories about art crime. The bulk of the book backs up our thesis by giving readers the stories behind a multitude of notorious crimes in which stolen art is the common thread.

Our book has a second important goal: to tell people about the great Rembrandt—who he was, why he painted what he did, and why his works are such constant targets. We do this by explaining as often and as specifically as we can how and why a particular stolen Rembrandt came into being. Think of it as background reporting. As a newsman, this has led me to believe that Rembrandt would have been a great journalist. His "beat" was seventeenth-century Holland, the Dutch "Golden Age," and he covered it with the same zeal and tenacity one sees in the works of George Orwell, Ida Tarbell, Matthew Brady, and Ernie Pyle. The difference, of course, is that his coverage was in the form of hand-crafted images, not words or photos. Rembrandt turned down a lucrative offer to become a court-sponsored painter and to ply his trade solely among the nobles and bishops of Europe. Instead, he lived a boisterous and gritty urban life and drew and etched hundreds of images of contemporary customs and events.

Rembrandt immortalized almost everything he saw. Hangings, parades, trade ships, men and women laboring in the sun and cold, children frolicking, sick people begging, bodies being autopsied, old ladies leaning on windowsills gossiping, and food vendors offering up pancakes along the streets. Rembrandt showed how bucolic yet ramshackle life was for Dutch hay farmers and livestock owners living on the banks of sea-level waterways. He drew or painted the West Africans who arrived in Amsterdam in the 1600s and the manner in which an ox was butchered and a brain dissected. We have all this and much more to visualize today because Rembrandt had the vital traits found in all good journalists and chroniclers: endless curiosity, a fine eye for detail, and an intense desire to explain what he saw or learned to a wide public. His work should inspire any reporter to do better—to be more detailed, more accurate, more observant, less predictable. I defer to the great scholars of Rembrandt, many listed in our bibliography, for the educated, discerning, and nuanced views of his life, his art, and his impact. But speaking as a layman and a newsman, I will say that learning about this astonishing man, so much more than an iconic name in the highbrow arena of art, was one of the great pleasures that came with writing this book.

Rembrandt died grief-stricken and barely solvent, having lost the people and property he loved. He was buried in Amsterdam's Westerkerk Church, but the exact location of his tomb is unknown. Today he is immortal. A stirring finale to a fascinating story. Or, as we newspeople might say, a good "kicker."

—*T.M.*

STEALING
REMBRANDTS

Why Rembrandt?

It seems hard to fathom that works by one of history's greatest artists, the Dutch master Rembrandt van Rijn, have routinely been stolen over the past 100 years. How can items of such astonishing value and relative scarcity so often fall prey to criminals, both the petty and the sophisticated? There are two overriding reasons: For decades museums, galleries, and individuals oversaw these precious items with a laxity bordering on negligence; and the iconic status of the Rembrandt name makes gunning for his paintings an irresistible impulse.

Even those with little background in fine arts—and that includes most criminals—are impressed when standing before a Rembrandt. His name is a catchphrase, used nowadays to market tooth whitener and art supplies, and the prices for his works are assumed to be in the tens of millions. Such prestige is well deserved. Rembrandt's compositions depict every imaginable human emotion—joy, anger, sadness, shame—with singular clarity. His paintings, drawings, and etchings show the full kaleidoscope of seventeenth-century Dutch life, from the most privileged citizens to the most wretched—even the dead.

(No detail escaped him. In an etching depicting the tale of the Good Samaritan, Rembrandt features, in great detail, a mutt squatting to relieve itself as the main scene unfolds.) The artist led an unusual, operatic life and left an indelible legacy, bequeathing images from his age. That confluence of fame, worth, and genius attracts not just fans but thieves, not just the curious but the avaricious.

It compounds matters that Rembrandt was among the most prolific masters of all time, working in three mediums: oil paintings, drawings, and etchings on metal. Many of his works have been lost, particularly the drawings. But estimates put his total extant production at 2,000 pieces. Scholars have spent more than 100 years authenticating and reauthenticating his works, using every available tool of modern technology (chemical tests, microscopes, spectroscopes, imaging devices), and the tallies have varied widely over time. In 1911, when just about anything old and Dutch (or even Flemish) was called a Rembrandt, Henri Rochefort, a French connoisseur, warned Americans in the *New York Times* that "very few of the 2,500 'Rembrandts'" said to be in the United States then were genuine.[1] In 1968, art historian Walter Wallace estimated that "as many as 2,300 of Rembrandt's works survive and have thus far been identified—some 600 paintings, 1,400 drawings and 300 etchings."[2] Today, Dutch and American scholars agree on the following minimum numbers: about 300 paintings, 700 drawings, and 80 metal plates from which Rembrandt printed etchings. Adding to the puzzle is the fact that the metal plates were used multiple times to create prints, making it somewhat difficult to know if a surviving print was run off the presses by Rembrandt himself (which would significantly heighten its value) rather than by someone else after his death. Today, as many as 6,000 impressions attributed to Rembrandt could be in existence. For counting, cataloguing, and theft purposes, they number as Rembrandts as well.

By contrast, there are no more than 36 known paintings by Johannes Vermeer, whose name today has acquired its own mythic stature, and none of his drawings or sketches survive.

In addition, Rembrandt was heavily imitated and copied in his day, and after his death, by exceptional artists, many of them his former colleagues and students. Works attributed to him have frequently been reclassified as those done by an apprentice or copyist. The painting *Landscape with an Obelisk* (1638) was purchased as a Rembrandt at the turn of the twentieth century by the famed Boston art collector Isabella Stewart Gardner and in 1984, it was reattributed to a Rembrandt disciple, Govaert Flinck.[3] (In 1990, it was stolen.) Conversely, in October 2010, the Museum Boijmans Van Beuningen in Rotterdam, Holland, became the happy owner of a painting reclassified as a Rembrandt. The painting *Tobias and His Wife* (1659) had been attributed to one of the master's pupils, Barent Fabritius, until a Dutch professor, Ernst van de Wetering, chairman of the authoritative Rembrandt Research Project, examined it and declared it authentic. The work was swiftly relocated from a drab reception area to the museum proper. Its value soared from $110,000 to $11 million.

Regardless of the exact tally, no one disputes that Rembrandt left behind more great works of art than any of his contemporaries. Consequently, there are enough confirmed Rembrandts to ensure that almost every big-name museum and many smaller institutions have at least one. (Many more are in the hands of art dealers and private collectors.) Yet there are few enough to make all Rembrandts inordinately valuable and criminally tempting. Rembrandts have not quite garnered the stratospheric auction prices—$80 million to $140 million—for superstar artists like Vincent van Gogh, Paul Cézanne, and Pablo Picasso. In the past decade, however, several Rembrandts have fetched record sums for Old Master works. These include *Portrait of a Man with Arms Akimbo* (1658), which went for $33.2 million at auction in 2009 (Columbia University had sold it for $1 million in 1974), and *Portrait of Aeltje Uylenburgh, Aged 62* (1632), which was purchased in 2000 for $27.5 million and resold in 2006 for $31 million.

Even a possible Rembrandt can entice millionaires. In 2007, a painting dubbed "the mock Rembrandt" by the British press (*The Young Rembrandt as Democrates the Laughing Philosopher*) sold for $3 million at auction in Cirencester, England. And it bears noting that not all Rembrandt sales are locks. Portrait of a Man in a Red Doublet (1633) was on sale in Maastricht, Holland, in 2006 for $26 million, but was withdrawn when no buyer emerged. It was eventually sold to a private collector for an undisclosed amount. A life-sized Rembrandt,

Minerva in Her Study (1635), has failed to attract a buyer willing to pay its owner, a Manhattan art dealer, the $46 million asking price.

*   *   *

None of this madness would have seemed entirely strange to Rembrandt, who is one of history's first market-oriented impresarios. While art crime was relatively unknown in his day, a mad scramble to own works by big names exploded just as he was coming of age. The post-Renaissance rise of the merchant classes in Northern Europe meant commissions were no longer the province of the church and nobility. Rembrandt tapped into that new demand. At his peak, he oversaw a workshop filled with ambitious, paying apprentices and enjoyed life as a wheeler-dealer and free spender (habits that ultimately wrecked him). In the 1630s, "Rembrandt Inc.," churned out portraits at an assembly-line rate. The master himself produced 54 of the works in one two-year stretch while launching a significant etching and printmaking operation on the side. Dutch art collectors wanted to cover their walls with scenes from real life rather than the typical saints and biblical tales. These Calvinists and Mennonites venerated industriousness and invention over idleness and leisure. While most Europeans shunned visual representations of men and women sweating and toiling, the Dutch embraced the genre. They sought out pictures of tailors, cobblers, kettle makers, artisans, grindstones, and blacksmiths, all depicted laboring amid their workaday machinery and mess. Paintings and prints of such scenes were affordable and plentiful and showed the fullest range of city life—from dockworkers, mendicants, and foreign travelers to physicians, children, and dogs. As a complete, ambitious, and prolific professional artist, Rembrandt could do it all. The result is that today, there is much by him left to admire, and much left to steal.

*   *   *

As with authenticating his works, confirming Rembrandt thefts is a tricky matter. Some items were stolen because they were believed to be Rembrandts at the time of the crime, but are no longer listed as authentic (see Chapter 4, *Man Leaning on a Sill,* and Chapter 8, *Portrait of a Rabbi*). Other stolen "Rembrandts" have been missing for too long to face proper modern scrutiny and attribution. Some of his works may have been lost or misplaced but were registered as stolen, and some thefts may never have been noticed or reported. More than 100 years of news clippings, police reports, and museum files reveal thefts that were resolved immediately and cases that have never been closed. The best estimates of actual thefts are as follows:

	Works Registered as Stolen	*Works Recovered since 2000*
England	3	2
Germany	6	0
Sweden	2	2
Switzerland	2	2
Unknown	59	2
USA	22	2
Italy	1	0

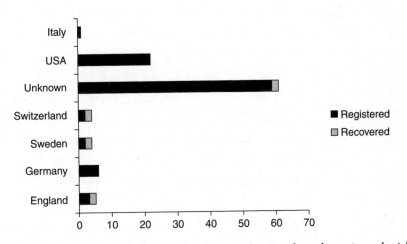

Source: From the Art Loss Register database. Stolen Rembrandts registered with it between the years 2000 to 2010.

The chart shows that whatever the final tally, Rembrandt is in the category of Pablo Picasso—the most stolen artist in history—in terms of works robbed. Picasso's body of original pieces is put at 20,000, and according to the reputable London-based Art Loss Register, some 550 of his works, including paintings, lithographs, drawings, and ceramics, were missing and presumed to be stolen as of 2011. That number excludes the many dozens of Picassos that were stolen and recovered. Still, with around 80 verifiable thefts on his balance sheet, Rembrandt also stands apart. This is why studying robberies of his works offers such insight into the enormous, perpetual, and fluid world of art crime and the people behind it.

No matter how abundant the targets, stealing art is difficult. So how do Rembrandt thieves do it? The simple answer is: however they can. Methods include daring entries into and escapes from well-guarded museums, bumbling snatches by unschooled hoodlums, wily ruses, messy smash and grabs, surprise attacks, and, of course, violence. Each Rembrandt crime, dissected and reverse-engineered, provides museum and law enforcement officials with vital lessons on securing their collections and recovering lost items. Despite fanciful portrayals on film, art theft has rarely been the stuff of suave iconoclasts or mystifying technology. Many of the basic techniques used a century ago—most commonly, taking advantage of security weaknesses—are employed by thieves today. It might strike Rembrandt himself as ironic that the majority of his thefts involve duping or circumventing the people assigned to watch over his art. His great masterpiece *The Night Watch* (1642) portrays the men in charge of guarding Amsterdam by night as a gaggle of dandified and half-cocked musketeers, rather than as redoubtable sentries. Rembrandt had tapped into something of primal importance when it comes to security at any level. Guards, patrollers, watchmen, security officers, and the like are most vulnerable when they are overconfident, half-prepared, relaxed, or predictable. Thieves understand this intuitively. They are always on the lookout for the soft underbelly of any security system. And as Rembrandt himself exposed, it is all too human to let one's guard down after many quiet, uneventful days and nights.

CHAPTER ONE

There Is No "Dr. No"

Few crimes appear as far beyond the reach of the average person as an art heist. It is little wonder, then, that the most enduring myth attached to the thefts of famous paintings centers on what we call the "Dr. No Fallacy." This is the notion that a sinister and elusive tycoon has masterminded and commissioned a museum robbery; has employed professional, technologically brilliant thieves to carry out the crime; and has provided his specialists with a strict "shopping list" based on his refined sensibilities. The art ends up in the mystery mogul's private lair, appreciated only by him.

Simple research shows that the Dr. No myth began with an iconic moment in the 1962 James Bond film of that name. Bond (played by Sean Connery) is shown with Dr. Julius No (portrayed by Joseph Wiseman) strolling past Francisco Goya's stolen *Duke of Wellington* (c. 1812–1814) portrait while deep inside No's hidden headquarters. Bond does a double-take as he passes what he instantly recognizes to be the purloined painting and mutters, "So that's where it went." Goya's portrait of the general who vanquished Napoleon Bonaparte (himself an art plunderer of note[1]) at Waterloo in 1815 had been stolen from London's National Gallery a few months before filming began. Its late inclusion as a gag line in the film, by script assistant Johanna Harwood, (who received a screenplay credit for *Dr. No*), has helped propagate an enduring misconception about just who commits art theft. This mythical uber-rich "connoisseur thief" has cropped up in movies such as *The Thomas Crown Affair* (1999), *Entrapment* (1999; Sean Connery is himself the "Dr. No"-like figure in this film), *Hudson Hawk* (1991), and the forgettable *Art Heist* (2004). He has been the focus of endless speculation and grudging admiration, and even psychoanalyzed as a "wealthy fetishist" who seeks out stolen art "that only he can contemplate and appreciate."[2] If only we could meet him.

The reality is far more grimy and far less romantic. By and large, our research shows, major art theft is committed by common criminals associated with local crime rings. They are not lone-wolf specialists nor "made" men in the Mafia, Yakuza, or a similarly insidious criminal organization. Rather, they are part of what law enforcement calls "disorganized crime." They are most often petty offenders involved in all sorts of thievery, with only tenuous connections to criminal syndicates. Generally they are burglars and break-in artists whose résumés might feature armored-car robberies, small-time bank jobs, home invasions, and drug dealing. They bear no resemblance to Hollywood actors like Pierce Brosnan or Sean Connery, and they skulk about in every city around the globe. And since there are museums or important art collections in any good-sized city, the fact that art is so often the target of their banditry should come as no surprise. Any time high-value items, uneven security, public access, and opportunistic criminals are thrown together, theft ensues.

Still, when art is stolen, there is an irresistible tendency to insert high intrigue into the drama. Goya's *Wellington* was stolen from the National Gallery at the height of the Cold War, prompting the Soviet newspaper *Izvestia* to drum up a "capitalistic plot." The Russian government urged Scotland Yard's investigators to look into the private collections of North and South American millionaires. They couldn't have been more off the mark. The painting was stolen by a pudgy, penny-pinching English national, Kempton Bunton, who was upset with the British government's decision to spend £140,000 (about $3.4 million in 2011 dollars) on the Goya while he was charged a licensing fee to watch BBC television. Acting on security information that he teased out of unwitting gallery guards, Bunton slipped into the museum by climbing through a loosened bathroom window at an hour when intrusion-detection alarms were turned off. He carried his prize out the same loo window. The painting's 1965 recovery was as un-Hollywood as the crime itself: Unable to force the government to eliminate the television licensing fee, Bunton simply gave *Wellington* back, leaving it at the luggage office at Birmingham New Street Station in London. Adding to his unexciting profile as an international man of mystery, Bunton turned himself in to the authorities even though investigators had discounted him as a suspect, figuring that at 61 he was too old to accomplish the deed. In a cheeky letter to police before his surrender, Bunton referred grimly to the Goya as "three-pennyworth of old Spanish firewood," giving British newspapers some incendiary headline material.[3] Yet he could barely get himself arrested because the London police had bought so heavily into the concept of a globetrotting art felon with cultured tastes.

Overblown notions about art heists predate the days of James Bond and similar forms of popular culture. History is filled with mistaken theories that posit grandiose or nefarious plots to purloin great works. Two examples from the early twentieth century stand out. On July 1, 1911, in what was seen as a test of the Anglo-French alliance of the day, Germany sent a gunboat to the port of Agadir in Morocco, North Africa. This move became the catalyst for what was dubbed the "Second Moroccan Crisis," a French colonial brushfire. Seven weeks later, with the flare-up still burning through the diplomatic corridors of Europe, Da Vinci's *Mona Lisa* disappeared from the walls of the Louvre in Paris.

Intricate theories abounded over who had taken the world's best-known painting. A German journalist declared the loss not a theft but a contrivance by the French government to divert attention from the imperialist troubles in Morocco. The truth was far more mundane: The *Mona Lisa* had been lifted by a housepainter, Vincenzo Peruggia, who had worked as a contractor at the Louvre installing glass over paintings. His motive? To return the masterpiece to his—and Da Vinci's—home country of Italy.

Another illustration of the heedless rush to point to art theft as a major conspiratorial act comes from the United States. In 1955, authorities at the Brooklyn Museum in New York discovered that eight rare silver figurines had been stolen. Puzzled by how and why they were taken, police told the public that the theft was "a perfect crime" committed by cunning international pros. Imagine the embarrassment when the NYPD and museum officials learned that the figurines had fallen prey to two 14-year-old boys with the bright idea of pocketing some unusual-looking toys. Cases like this explain why many in the security business embrace the axiom, "The first version of the story you hear is always wrong."

Works by Rembrandt have not been spared such knee-jerk hype. In April 1938, British police flooded ports and airfields after a Rembrandt and four other treasures were stolen from a castle in Kent. The Rembrandt had been bought from Russia's State Hermitage Museum by Sir Edmund Davis during Stalin's rule, and Davis had recently declined to lend it to the Dutch government. The heated theories of international machinations and melodrama were doused five weeks later, when some of the art turned up in the hands of a run-of-the-mill London fence. That early experience hardly taught the Brits a lesson. At the start of 2000, when Cézanne's *Auvers-sur-Oise* (1880) was robbed from the Ashmolean Museum at Oxford University, a cry went up in the British press that it had been "stolen to order" by a baronial villain eager to enjoy the $10 million painting in selfish isolation. It is, alas, still missing. In April 2010, a lively episode of *The Simpsons* was spun from the notion that the evil Mr. Burns was in misanthropic possession of two stolen Rembrandts, including *The Storm on the Sea of Galilee* (1633) from the Isabella

Stewart Gardner Museum in Boston. Our research highlights how many of these cherished theories, concocted legends, and amusing myths have been debunked.

AN AGE-OLD ACT OF PLUNDER

High-value art theft is nearly as old as art itself. Early civilizations plundered enemy treasures with imperious disregard for cultural worth, while individual thieves always found ways to pilfer the finer heirlooms of their neighbors or societies. In antiquity, the Babylonians ransacked King Solomon's Temple in Jerusalem and took away the Ark of the Covenant. Consider it a very early masterpiece heist. Greece's greatest sculptures, paintings, and tapestries arrived in Rome as booty centuries before the birth of Jesus—and the great orator Cicero lamented this pillaging in his orations at the time.[4] In 1934, the destructive theft of two fifteenth-century panels from Jan van Eyck's legendary *Altarpiece* at Saint Bavo Cathedral in Ghent, Belgium, showed how a single determined criminal could wreak his own sort of cultural and religious havoc. Some 460 years before the Ghent robbery, Polish pirates in the Mediterranean stole the triptych *Last Judgment*, by Hans Memling, as it was being shipped from Bruges, Belgium, to Florence's Medici Chapel. It has resided in Gdansk, Poland, ever since. Pirates of a different sort infiltrated the Gardner Museum in 1990 and made off with 13 artworks that, a generation later, remain a sort of buried treasure for modern times.

History's roster is as endless as it is strange. The Nazis uprooted countless masterpieces from France, Italy, Austria, and elsewhere during World War II, including Rembrandts. They crated them up and sent them by rail to Berlin, for Hitler and Göring to swap and drool over. These depravities are known collectively as "the Rape of Europa." In 1994, Lynn H. Nicholas wrote *The Rape of Europa*, which won the National Book Critics Award and later became the basis for the 2006 documentary, of the same name, that was released to great acclaim. For a taut Hollywood war movie on the topic, see *The Train* (1964), starring Burt Lancaster.) Some 1,900 years before the Third Reich, the forces of Emperor Titus Flavius sacked the Jewish Temple in Jerusalem and organized the orderly removal of its treasures for a triumphal procession through Rome (the scene is immortalized in stone on a Roman arch viewable to this day). And art theft cannot be discussed without reference to the innumerable instances in which one nation's antiquities have become another nation's curios and museum pieces. The Elgin Marbles—prized sculptures from ancient Greece—were brazenly shipped off to England in the early 1800s by Ambassador Thomas Bruce, the earl of Elgin. They remain in the British Museum, but the Greeks want them back. In 2006, tarred with the brush of cultural imperialism, the Metropolitan Museum of Art in New York and the J. Paul Getty Museum in Los Angeles agreed to return dozens of ancient marbles, bronzes, frescoes, and vases to Greece and Italy. Egyptians, Peruvians, and Native Americans, among others, today rightly resent and continue to challenge the imperialistic raidings of their vaults and tombs for all manner of glittering artifacts. Clearly, art theft is as much a spoil of war, conquest, or colonialism as it is an act of grand larceny or petty crime. Some thieving nations have treated stolen art with reverence and others have melted it down for the gold. The same holds true for individual criminals. Some will care for a heisted Rembrandt with a peculiar form of veneration. Others will cut it from a frame, roll it in a tube, and toss it in a car trunk.

Effectively, art theft can never be stopped. It is too enticing, too easy, and too potentially lucrative. Fine arts, jewels, and antiques always appreciate in value. Witness the sale in May 2010 of Pablo Picasso's *Nude, Green Leaves and Bust*, which fetched $106.5 million at Christie's New York auction house, the most money ever paid for a painting. The purchase price was more than $25 million above Christie's estimate—this despite a severe recession. Three months earlier, a sculpture by Swiss artist Alberto Giacometti, *Walking Man I*, sold for £65 million ($103.7 million) at Sotheby's auction house, making it the record-holder for a sculpture. Sotheby's had estimated the Giacometti's worth at £12–£18 million, making *Man* quite a piece of investment property.

It is not very surprising, then, that just ten days after the Picasso sale, more than $100 million in paintings by Picasso, Henri Matisse, and Amedeo Modigliani were stolen from the Paris Museum of Modern Art through the embarrassingly simple expediencies of a smashed window and a faulty security system. (In this case, the frames also were left behind.) Just a day later, a private collector in the south of France was beaten and hogtied while his lone Picasso was taken. Criminologists classify such crimes as essentially copycat cases arising from the media attention surrounding the initial robbery. They help demonstrate that art capers are utterly commonplace—so much so that it is clear even to minor-league criminals that they do not require a sophisticated crime ring or a wealthy backer to pull off.

Why is art theft worthy of concern? The Federal Bureau of Investigation estimates that theft, fraud, looting, and trafficking in stolen art and antiquities are crimes that surpass $6 billion a year in value. It is widely recognized that trafficking in illicit art ranks with drugs, weapons, and money laundering in its global pervasiveness. The international Art Loss Register, which maintains an enormous private database of artistic loot, records 170,000 missing pieces around the world. Along with Rembrandt and Picasso, the list includes names like Cézanne, Van Gogh, Vermeer, Rubens, and Titian. Large-scale art theft tends to become international news. This happened after the Baghdad Museum was looted in March and April 2003, at the onset of the Iraq War, and when *The Scream* was stolen in Norway in 1994 (another version of the Edvard Munch painting was stolen in 2004). But it's rarely the loss of the irreplaceable pieces that is lamented or treated as highly newsworthy. Rather, it is the dollar figure attributed to the spoils that grabs the headlines and the popular imagination.

Consider again the 2010 theft from the Paris Museum of Modern Art. Americans awoke that day to the following bulletin from the Paris bureau of the Associated Press: "Lone Thief Steals $600 Million in Art From Paris Museum." The story generated a great deal of coverage in the week after the heist, even though most people would be hard-pressed to conjure up a mental image of Picasso's *The Pigeon with the Peas,* or Matisse's *Pastoral,* both of which went missing. When did the story finally calm down? After officials in Paris announced that the estimated value was in fact closer to $100 million. The initial reports were off by a mere half-billion dollars. But in the world of art-heist coverage, being wrong by that immense amount is considered "in the ballpark." It's art, after all—a commodity few understand or control. Assigning a dollar value to art is by nature an act of conjecture. In an age when instantly grabbing the "eyeballs" of the public is the only way for the news media to survive, there are few better ploys for drawing rapid attention than tossing about figures like $100 million or "a half-billion."

Let us set aside for now the truism that no thief could ever hope to gain that kind of money from the ransom or resale of stolen art. (In the coming chapters we will show what forms of tribute do, in fact, change hands when fabled paintings are recovered.) It is the freedom to attach almost any sum to the value of an art heist that makes the act a unique crime in the public consciousness. Drug seizures also prompt huge dollar estimates as law enforcement officials strive to give the goods a "street value." But a street value for ounces of pot and kilograms of heroin does exist. Art has no real street value. And how many onlookers can identify or empathize with the holders of high art and their missing treasures or lost fortunes? Few indeed.

To illustrate the point, ask yourself: How many people have heard of Edgar Degas's *Cortège Aux Environs de Florence*? It's a good bet few could pick it out of a lineup or recognize it on someone's wall. Yet it is a piece by a famed Impressionist stolen in the biggest property crime of all time—the Gardner Museum heist. As museum officials note, any piece lost from the Isabella Stewart Gardner collection leaves a hole in the "collective piece of art" that is the museum. Thus, its removal undermines a generous legacy meant to be shared with any individual who cares to visit the institution. It also robs the public of the particular beauty and resonance of the lost item. And in many cases it robs posterity of a vital glimpse into the human past. Today, we take for granted the terabytes of images that depict how we live from every angle. But the ability to record historical and personal scenes on a mass scale is less than two centuries old. Art and artifacts predating this era is all we have to help us visualize how our ancestors lived and saw the world. When that cultural heritage is depleted even by one work, all suffer the loss. Although many may feel otherwise, art theft is never a victimless crime.

Some onlookers even applaud art theft as a type of class warfare. When an item valued in the millions is stolen, especially one viewed as unattainable, inaccessible, even incomprehensible, or seen as the exclusive province of the rich and snobbish, sympathy rarely carries the day. Instead, a very visceral sense of admiration can take hold, and a twisted and false Robin Hood–like mystique is attached to the robbery. As if the art has been somehow "liberated" from the hands of the privileged and is now back, for better or worse, in the public realm. The absurdity of this is self-evident whenever art is taken from a museum, given that museums great and small represent the most earnest form of public sharing. But when it is taken from a private owner, the dismissive attitude is just as corrosive. People who can afford great art are by and large good caretakers. They often build climate-controlled chambers, maintain relationships with top-level conservators, and use professionals to move and store their items. In 2006, art collector and casino magnate Steve Wynn accidentally put his elbow through a Picasso he was planning to sell for $139 million (*Le Rêve* [1932]). Wynn spared no cost repairing the painting. Scotland's 10th Duke of Buccleuch and 12th Duke of Queensberry, Richard Walter John Montagu Douglas Scott, unwillingly removed a great Rembrandt, *Portrait of an Old Woman Reading* (1655), from the walls of his publicly accessible Drumlanrig Castle in Galloway in 2003. He chose to lock it safely away in a climate-controlled vault after another of his important paintings, Da Vinci's *Madonna with the Yarnwinder* (1501), was stolen by thieves disguised as tourists. He also offered a $200,000 reward for the return of the Da Vinci, which was at last recovered in Glasgow in 2007. It might be hard to feel empathy for a multimillionaire Scotsman with two duchies and six names, but the duke was so stricken by the devious (and discourteous) theft that he suffered several years of poor health and died before the *Madonna*'s reappearance. The men implicated in the theft were hardly art aficionados or Robin Hood's Merry Men. They had threatened to destroy the Da Vinci if they were not paid $10 million in extortion money.

Arts writer Marc Spiegel insightfully summed up the enduring appeal of the "Dr. No" fallacy in the New York-based *Art + Auction* magazine in March 2004: "Certainly the idea of some shadowy mastermind amassing a premier collection through commissioned thefts has plenty of panache. The fact that it resonates so well with the public might give the art world cause to reflect on what the public's perception of collector scruples may be." There is little doubt that the public views super-affluent owners of great artworks with more than a touch of envy and enmity. Yet Steve Wynn and the Duke of Buccleuch had the wherewithal to safeguard and restore the works they owned, to become preservers as well as possessors. There is little hope that art stolen hastily and destructively from museums or great residences by career criminals will be handled with the delicacy and scientific care required to keep it safe either briefly or in perpetuity.

MURKY MOTIVES

In the modern era, famous works of stolen art are frequently recovered. Nearly all the Rembrandts written about in this book were located and returned. Art theft experts like former FBI agent Robert K. Wittman have found that the recovery or return of stolen art follows an odd pattern: If a stolen piece is not recovered quickly, a generation may pass before it resurfaces. This is due in part to expiring statutes of limitation, the deaths of those involved in the crime, or the hope that any investigation will have been filed away in a cold-case drawer, making return a risk-free endeavor. But the main reason is as simple as supply and demand. In this all-seeing and instantaneous age, there is no real market for stolen masterpieces. They are quite simply too famous to sell.

Art theft garners far more attention and publicity than its recovery. This is not solely due to superficial or distracted media coverage. Frequently, confidentiality is the key to recovery, and details surrounding the who and why of the theft are never released as part of the bargain for restitution. In the mid-1980s, two paintings were stolen from the Longfellow House in Cambridge, Massachusetts—a portrait of George Washington by Jane Stuart (artist Gilbert Stuart's daughter) and a painting titled *The Nuremberg Market* by Jules Achille Noel. Because the Longfellow House served as the quarters and command center for General Washington during the Revolutionary War, it is a national historic site and is managed by the National Park Service. Thus the theft of those two pieces constituted a federal crime.

Nearly ten years after the robbery, the art was recovered by the FBI. However, according to information obtained by the authors through a Freedom of Information Act request, the identity of the culprits was never disclosed, even between the federal agencies involved. The FBI entered into a memorandum of agreement with the Park Service requiring, among other things, that "any artwork recovered as a result of this agreement will not be put on public display for minimum [*sic*] of three months after the date of recovery by the NPS." Penciled in after this stipulation were these handwritten terms: "Nor will there be any media release for a minimum of three months."[5] Clearly this was intended to protect the identities of the thieves (or informants) and the terms and methodology of the recovery. (It also served to obscure what must be a damned good tale of intrigue.) In another example from Massachusetts's rather infamous history of art crime, a $50,000 portrait of Benjamin Franklin (1785) by French artist Joseph-Siffred Duplessis was stolen from the central branch of the Boston Public Library on Good Friday, 1990. Although the painting was recovered, only the details of the initial theft were reported in the press. Information about how the painting was returned to the

BPL exists only in the elusive memories of some of the staffers still employed there 21 years later.

So much secrecy might suggest that many art thefts and subsequent recoveries are intended to set in motion and then camouflage a cynical political or prosecutorial deal, one too distasteful to make public. In the past century, though, only two known thefts stand out as having been driven by such motives. One involves the heist of a Rembrandt on loan to the Boston Museum of Fine Arts from the Paine family of Massachusetts, which was returned to the museum in exchange for a more lenient prison sentence for the thief. The perpetrator was Myles J. Connor Jr. of Milton, Massachusetts, and his story is detailed in Chapter 6. The other occurred in April 1974, when a gang led by a well-to-do Irish Republican Army sympathizer, Rose Dugdale, violently stole 19 masterworks from the collection of Sir Alfred Beit at the Russborough House near Dublin. (Beit was pistol-whipped, and he and his wife were bound and gagged during the assault.) The IRA wasn't seeking ransom money. It wanted to use the paintings as leverage to obtain the release of jailed confederates. The plan collapsed 11 days later when Irish police recovered all 19 paintings—among them a Rubens and a Vermeer, but no Rembrandt—from a rented cottage in Cork.

There has been much talk in recent years of stolen paintings serving as collateral in large narcotics deals. That motivation was first suggested in the 1980s, and the benighted Alfred Beit art collection was again at the center of things. In May 1986, Martin Cahill, a legendary Irish crime boss known as "The General," oversaw a virtuoso heist in which his gang stole 18 works of art from Russborough House. Included were a Vermeer, a Goya, and a Rubens. Cahill's gang artfully snookered the local lawmen. On arriving, they cut a pane of glass from a French window and entered the house to set off the alarm. They then retreated outside and hid among some thick bushes until police arrived, poked around, concluded it was a false alarm, and drove off. Cahill's gang entered a second time an hour later and grabbed the paintings. But Cahill was a truly one-of-a-kind crook. (He was portrayed by actor

Brendan Gleeson in the 1998 film *The General,* which features the most true-to-life re-creation of an art heist ever mounted on film.) Big-bodied and balding, Cahill grew up in poverty, loved carrier pigeons and motorcycles, and fathered nine children by two Dublin sisters. Theories abounded about the motive for his art heist. Some thought he wanted to embarrass the Irish government. Others saw the crime as a way for him to leverage the freedom of jailed crime associates. A few speculated that Cahill simply despised the aristocratic and well-to-do and was happy enough sticking it to the country's elite. (Sir Alfred Beit was the heir to a huge diamond fortune, and Cahill's most famous heist was a $2.5 million gold and diamond robbery in Dublin in the 1970s.) At one point, Cahill demanded a $200,000 ransom for the Rossborough paintings. At another, he was supposedly using the art to finance weapons purchases from South Africa for use by pro-British forces in Ulster. Some in his gang who have spoken since the crime say that regardless of motive, Cahill treated the fragile masterworks with ham-handed contempt. Whatever his purposes, enjoying the goods for their beauty and craft was not among them.

The Cahill-narcotics theory was born after pieces of the Russborough haul began turning up during police raids on drug rings. In May 1990, a painting from the Beit collection was seized in Istanbul, a heroin hub. Two years later, a Gainsborough from the collection was discovered in a van by detectives pursuing a drug gang in central London. And ten months after that, yet more paintings were recovered during a drug probe, including the Rubens, *Head of a Man,* which had been placed behind a sofa in a suburban house. In late 1993, investigators had traced four of the costliest items—including the Vermeer, *Lady Writing a Letter with Her Maid* (1670–71), and the Goya—to Antwerp, Belgium. Police theorized that the four paintings were sent there as collateral for a shady loan from a Belgian diamond dealer. The Vermeer was deposited in a bank vault in Luxembourg, and the money it raised was allegedly used by a drug cartel to help buy an offshore bank in Antigua, through which the gangsters hoped to launder money. By 1994, Cahill was dead—shot down by the IRA for helping the pro-English Ulster Volunteers obtain weapons—and his heist motives died with him. If one steps back, it is hard to imagine such a crew of rogues and predators engineering these complex and murky narco-financing schemes. But the drug theory arose anew in 2001, when a criminal protégé of Cahill's named Martin Foley, by now a major narcotics peddler, broke into the Russborough House yet again, stealing two paintings, a Gainsborough and a Bellotto. Both were recovered about a year later with no known drug entanglements.

The art theft–drug smuggling link received a scholarly treatment in 1997, when art writer Martin Bailey published an article in the journal *Trends in Organized Crime*. Bailey charted the movements of the Beit paintings and made a case for those robberies having a secondhand narcotics connection. But few other cases can be found to support the overall thesis. An aborted 1987 heist at Sir John Soane's Museum in London was linked to a possible Venezuelan cocaine transaction. Otherwise, the annals of art crime list very few drug tales. A 2000 Rembrandt theft detailed in Chapter 7, from Sweden, again suggests that the drug explanation is as yet weak. Although the FBI recovered two of the works, including a Rembrandt, from a Bulgarian man involved in drug trafficking in California, the paintings were never used as any form of collateral or currency in the criminal's drug operations.

Even acts of petty art crime motivated by drugs are rare. In New Haven, Connecticut, in March 2009, a small-time criminal named Dennis Maluk was caught using bits of art stolen from Yale University and the New Haven Free Public Library to pay for his weekly heroin fixes. Minor artifacts and antiquities pilfered in petty robberies provide quick dollars for drugs. But associating a museum heist directly with a giant narcotics operation could not be confidently done unless firm proof were to arise. Given the preponderance of Rembrandt thefts in the past century, the fact that not one of his works has popped up as drug collateral highlights the rarity of such a motive.

THE CRIME OF ART-NAPPING

Instances of ransom for art are far more common, even though many cases of extortion are hidden from the public. In Chapter 5, we disclose for the first time that three masterpieces, including a Rembrandt, were lost forever in 1938 when British art thieves burned them as police closed in.

Episodes in which the art was returned for a cash payment by the owner or an insurance company are by far the norm, and can be colorful and controversial. In 1994, two paintings by J. M. W. Turner belonging to the Tate Gallery in London were stolen while on loan to a gallery in Hamburg, Germany. In 1998, the Tate conceived of "Operation Cobalt," a secret buyback of the Turners, *Shade and Darkness* (1843) and *Light and Colour* (1843). The works were recovered in 2000 and 2002 by former Scotland Yard agent Jurek "Rocky" Rokoszynski for about $4 million, all told. The Tate was so sensitive to accusations of "paying ransom" that it insisted the money was used to "obtain information about the whereabouts of the art," and that none of it went directly to the men who stole the works. Today we know that the $4 million went to a Balkan crime ring connected to the actual theft,[6] yet the Tate's director, Sir Nicholas Serota, stated in 2002, "I don't think we have paid the thieves in any sense."[7] In another case, a two-foot-square $9 million masterpiece by Titian, *Rest on the Flight to Egypt*, was recovered in 2002 in a plastic shopping bag at a bus stop in Richmond, in southwest London. It had vanished during a raid on the Marquess of Bath's estate in Longleat, England, in 1995. About $1.5 million was exchanged in that incident, though the owner of the art, Lord Bath, denied the money was ransom, calling it a "finder's fee" for an informant who had provided aid. It must be noted here that the Gardner Museum in Boston has a $5 million reward on the table for anyone providing "information leading directly to the recovery" of its 13 stolen works, including its three Rembrandts, "in good condition." While some have come forward offering such help, none of the leads has led to a recovery.

Cases involving cash handovers have prompted much debate about the propriety of rewards or insurance payouts. Critics naturally question whether they set the stage for further instances of artnapping and extortion. It is not a new controversy, as Chapter 4, detailing a 1973 Cincinnati, Ohio, Rembrandt heist, demonstrates. Two experts—Scottish criminologist Simon MacKenzie and Mark Durney, a specialist on art theft and cultural history and a member of the Association for Research into Crimes against Art (ARCA), a think tank that publishes the scholarly *Journal of Art Crime*—have laid out the issue very well.

According to MacKenzie, scholars and law enforcement officials believe that any type of ransom payment will lead to repeat robberies. They call this phenomenon the "flag effect" and say it was evident in Canada as early as 1959, after the Toronto Art Gallery paid a well-publicized reward for the return of six stolen paintings. At a minimum, experts note, museums in Canada were quickly "flagged" by criminals as soft targets willing to spend to get their items back. While most money-driven criminal predators continued to overlook museums, enough were inspired by the reward/ransom scenario to start casing the institutions and even draw up tentative plans. With such focus and attention came an inevitable increase in robberies in Canada and globally.

Efforts to hush up secret payments made through insurance intermediaries or "lawyers acting on behalf" of those holding stolen art did little to quell the trend, criminologists say, due to something called the "boost effect." This occurs when criminals tell their underworld cohorts that art crime is relatively easy at a specific location. It also arises when word gets out that some museums are willing to spend quietly to recover stolen property. A third phenomenon is called "the known-quantity effect," in which a specific museum becomes a repeat target for a group of thieves after it has been exposed as a sitting duck. In 1975, 28 paintings were stolen from Milan's Gallery of Modern Art and then ransomed back. Three months later, many of the same thieves stole 38 pictures from the same gallery, including half of the ones taken in the first theft.

Such repeat robberies by crews of past bandits show up from time to time. Remarkably, the bedeviled Russborough House mentioned earlier is an example of all three effects. The 1975 theft by Rose Dugdale "flagged" the location as eminently soft. That inspired Martin Cahill's 1986 theft. Cahill acolyte Martin Foley knew the ropes of robbing the Russborough and committed his own "boost" there in 2001. A year later, three men smashed a window at the "known-quantity" Russborough with a battering ram and spirited away five more paintings, including two by Rubens. Bizarrely, the collection was still being watched overnight by a single guard in his seventies. (Beit, who died in 1994, and his successors had tried to make the house less alluring and harder to penetrate. They installed modern alarm systems, and Beit donated 12 of his vulnerable Old Master paintings to the Irish government in 1986.) The five works stolen in 2002 were recovered within a few months. This prompted Irish travel writer Bob Sullivan to declare: "The Russborough has an odd knack for recovering its artworks. Some see skullduggery here—asserting that collection managers may be quietly paying ransom to recover the stolen goods. For the Russborough, recovery efforts have certainly gone better than security procedures. Over $70 million worth of art has been returned since the 1974 robbery. It seems it would take a big ransom budget to accomplish that."[8] While such a legacy of larceny is a grave and unpleasant blemish, it has an indisputable car-wreck-like drawing power. Sullivan included his remarks in a section of his newsletter called "Ireland fun facts" and touted the highbrow crime wave as part of the Russborough's tourism appeal.

Most museums have no such budgets for ransom, and some cannot even afford theft insurance, which would at least make cash available for bargaining. In cases where the art is owned by the state, most nations will simply declare ransom payments a nonstarter. However, it is the rare thief who knows going in whether the art he is stealing is owned privately or by the general public, and whether it is insured or not. This explains why there are so many cases in which thieves mistakenly believed they would be able to barter back their haul for inordinate riches. The characters who steal famous works often have no backup plan other than to sit on their trove and see what develops. Another form of "art theft" is worth noting: robberies engineered by the owners themselves to defraud insurance companies. One 2009 case, according to the Museum Security Network and Dutch newspapers, involves allegations that the late Dutch art dealer Robert Noortman let thieves steal nine paintings from his Maastricht, Holland gallery in 1987, and then lodged an insurance claim exceeding $1.3 million. Noortman made global headlines in December 2000 when he paid $28.6 million for Rembrandt's *Portrait of a Lady, Aged 62* (1632) at Christie's in London, a record for a Rembrandt.

Interest in art crime has widened in recent years. Many excellent nonfiction books have appeared,[9] and colleges are introducing courses on the topic. Tufts University sociologist John E. Conklin, a criminologist and the author of *Art Crime* (Praeger, 1994), has been studying and teaching the phenomenon for 20 years. Since 2009, ARCA has held a masters program in art crime studies in Italy. In 2008, Yale University conducted a semester-long course, and in 2011 Harvard offered a freshman seminar titled "The Culture and Politics of Art Theft, Grave Robbery, and Looting." Museum directors and curators have no choice but to add security and crime prevention to their list of required duties. The floor plans and architectural renderings of museums and galleries—once stashed away in municipal archives or libraries—are readily available online. Tools like Google Earth can be used to examine the roofs, exteriors, and grounds of potential targets. For these and many other reasons outlined in the coming chapters, art crime will no doubt be a growth industry.

The seriousness of art crime in the United States has not always been acknowledged in criminal statutes. It was not until after the 1990 Gardner Museum robbery that federal penalties for crimes against cultural property were toughened and the statute of limitations on art theft was increased from five to 20 years. Perhaps the threat of hard time in a federal prison will keep rogues out of galleries and Rembrandts on the walls. It bears noting that Rembrandt was interested in the criminal classes of his day and produced paintings and drawings showing punishments for thieves and other offenders. He depicted the guilty in stocks and pillories, and an executed woman, Elsje Christiaens, hanging from the public gibbet, a high vertical crossbeam that could accommodate many corpses at once. (Gibbets stood prominently in cities and towns across Holland as macabre monuments to deterrence.) Rembrandt also painted autopsies, which were spectacles attended not just by medical students but also by curious townsfolk. Such dissections usually featured the cadavers of criminals. While the punishment for many crimes often did not extend beyond flogging, branding, and public humiliation, the Dutch were not shy about imposing the death penalty. The man being dissected in *The Anatomy Lesson of Dr. Tulp* (1632), one of Rembrandt's greatest paintings, has been identified as Adriaan Adriaanszoon, an armed bandit and repeat offender nicknamed "Aris Kindt," or Aris the Kid. He was finally hanged, records show, for stealing a man's coat. Another executed felon, Joris Fonteijn, a Flemish tailor known as Black Jack, was the subject of a fairly gory Rembrandt, *The Anatomy Lesson of Dr. Deyman* (1656). Nor were the Dutch averse to using torture to extract confessions or locate stolen goods. Losing a hand or a nose for stealing was possible penalty. There are no known records of art thieves being punished in Rembrandt's time. One can only imagine the penalties such social menaces would have faced.

CHAPTER TWO

Smeared with Blood: The 1972 Worcester Heist

PREFACE

Popular cinematic depictions of daring art thefts often feature a crafty overnight entry into a museum by balaclava-clad acrobats who rappel down walls and use smoke-making devices to maneuver around laser beams while doing the limbo. The stunt is a veritable cliché—few outside a Hollywood studio could pull it off.

It turns out that such intricate feats are hardly necessary. A museum is historically at greatest risk when it is open to the public. This cannot be helped. The goal of a good museum is to present important, inspiring art as accessibly as possible to an enormous audience. Anyone can come in, armed or unarmed (although subtle weapons detection systems are becoming more common). Admonitions to visitors are typically decorous: "Please don't touch" or "Do not get too close" or "No flashbulbs please." In the most glaring cases, the only physical deterrents come in the form of velvet ropes and guards whose long days of boredom can be read in their slumping body language. Service doors and emergency exits might be left unattended. Surveillance-camera sight lines can be blocked by jutting internal architecture. Crowds or gaggles of visitors offer cover and distractions—perhaps even hostage bait.

While the specter of armed interlopers blitzing a cultural institution seems hard to envisage, it has become alarmingly real in recent decades. In Chapter 7, just such a robbery involving a machine gun in Sweden is recounted. Denis Ahern, the director of safety and security at the Tate Galleries in London, put the problem this way: "If criminals are prepared to take lives in order to commit their crimes, there is very little real defense, unless the works are guarded like bullion. This would clearly negate the intent and the ability to display great and iconic works, turning the museum into a sealed vault, and would reduce the number of works that could be shown." He adds, "If you want to give public access to original artworks, there will be risk, and there is no real defense against a thief who is willing to kill in order to steal."[1]

In May 1972 in Worcester, Massachusetts, thieves willing to shoot created a grim precedent—the first known use of a gun to rob a museum—that has been much repeated since then. Their target was Rembrandt.

THE THIEF

It was a mild but overcast Wednesday afternoon in May when two very small-time criminals, handpicked by their boss, Florian "Al" Monday, from his five-person ring, stepped into the Worcester Art Museum. One of them was armed with a .22-caliber revolver bearing a single round. In theory, they were well drilled on what to do to get in and out without expending that round.

Monday was no impulsive villain. He had put a lot of educated thought into the theft. As a boy learning about fine art from his mother in Rhode Island, and as college student in Worcester, he was a regular visitor to the Worcester museum. And, as a budding art thief in his early thirties, he'd cased its long, wide corridors fairly often, gone "inside many times on trial runs, touching and fiddling" and making note of window alarms and panic buttons and security routines. The place was a somber, blocky maze, somewhat forbidding from the outside, but a world-class facility on the inside. Monday mapped out its short cuts and blind spots and the position of its thinly manned guard station. He observed and factored in delivery schedules and the traffic patterns outside the building. The institution's location in an unraveling textile town in central Massachusetts made it a museum off the beaten track, accustomed to inviolability and visitor decorum. An easy score.

The item Monday specifically coveted was hung within a series of interconnected rooms overlooking the museum's central showpiece: an airy, colonnaded Renaissance Court. Although the museum has many riches—silver crafted by Paul Revere, Greek and Egyptian antiquities, paintings by Hogarth and Whistler, and works by Cézanne and Van Gogh—its sole Rembrandt, *St. Bartholomew*, had always been its star attraction. Or, as Monday put it, the "no-brainer" on any theft list.

Now in his seventies, Monday speaks with astuteness and a touch of opinionated snobbishness about great paintings. Although he has spent most of his professional career in "sales," as he puts it, the face of his business card bears a full-color oil portrait of an old woman, an item owned by a friend. He spent years researching the work and has now determined that it is Dutch and dates to Rembrandt's time. Beyond that he is stuck. Although his crusty appearance might suggest otherwise, there is no question Monday loves good paintings. He wears a loose blue tracksuit and ornate golden rings and thickly chained jewelry, dyes his bushy white hair Day-Glo orange, and speaks with a tobacco-scorched rasp. Yet a conversation with him elicits insightful remarks about art history and great or influential painters. "No one touches Van Gogh," he says, "except maybe Renoir." He knows of a lightly guarded Renoir at a small college in New England. "I'm think-ing of banging the place," he said.

Recalling his very brief time as a Rembrandt owner nearly 40 years ago, Monday launched into one of his occasionally stilted monologues: "It's an exhilarating feeling, holding that painting, especially when you have studied it for so long and are now the sole proprietor of said piece. To an art lover, possessing a Rembrandt can be likened to winning the World Series, the Super Bowl, and the Stanley Cup all at once. You feel a real sense of almost being a part of the artist's mind."

Back in 1972, as he plotted his ill-fated heist, it occurred to Monday that taking just one painting, even a Rembrandt, made little sense. Attuned to the accelerating market for early modernists, he scoped out three other Worcester works that might prove lucrative on the black market: Picasso's *Mother and Child,* and two paintings by Gauguin, *The Brooding Woman* and *Head of a Woman.*[2] Beyond their value and portability, the four works were conveniently located just one flight up from the museum's entrance (and exit). They were all easy to yank from the walls, and they all hung in parts of the museum that were sparsely peopled by visitors and guards on weekday afternoons. "You can't take them all," Monday reflected 38 years later. "This was basi-cally a snatch-and-grab deal. Get the Rembrandt, get the others, and get out."

In his youth, Monday was influenced by his mother's passion for antiques, and he majored in art at Assumption College, an Augustinian Catholic institution in Worcester known for its classic liberal arts pro-gram and lacrosse teams. But it wasn't something young Al read in his textbooks that prompted his rendezvous with Rembrandt. Monday points to an article in the Sunday *Boston Globe* in the early 1970s detail-ing the astronomical prices that artworks were continuing to fetch at auction. It dawned on him that most museums were poorly secured warehouses for six- and seven-figure items, and he started thinking hard about an art-theft career. He was artistically and criminally inclined, after all, and with so many juicy targets, he concluded, hold-ing up banks would be "a waste of time."

Monday was on to something—a cultural transformation during which the moneyed and the celebrated commandeered the art world. Art critic Robert Hughes has lamented this "cult of the celebrity masterpiece" and declared: "The book on art became a checkbook." As early as 1966, an article in the *New York Times* by the well-regarded arts writer Milton Esterow, "Rush to Art Turning into a Stampede," outlined the expanding worldwide demand for masterpieces. Hunting the globe on an unsurpassed scale searching for Old Masters, Impressionists, and modernists such as Picasso, Cézanne, and Matisse, Esterow wrote, "are hundreds of Greek shipping nabobs, Canadian mine owners, American magnates and European millionaires."[3] These included American industrialists and English financiers like Andrew Mellon, Edmund Leopold de Rothschild, Henry Ford, J. Paul Getty, J. P. Morgan, and John Hay Whitney. In addition, Esterow wrote, 130 museums had been built in the United States since 1950, and scores more had sprung up across Europe. All were competing for signature pieces. The Metropolitan Museum of Art had stopped buying at auctions after spending a painful $2.3 million for Rembrandt's *Aristotle Contemplating the Bust of Homer* (1653). How could it compete with an Onassis or a Carnegie? Sounding a bit like a tycoon version of Al Monday, wealthy collector David Rockefeller told Esterow, "My interest in art goes back, to a considerable extent, to my parental background. My mother liked beautiful things. I was surrounded by them." Esterow noted that this cavalcade of collectors, museum directors, and speculators was forcing up prices so quickly that agents "have to phone dealers several times a week for current appraisals."

Popular culture absorbed the message. In 1970, Parker Brothers published a board game, "Masterpiece: The Art Auction Game," featuring Rembrandt's *Old Man with a Gold Chain* (1631) on the center of the game board. The game's tagline read: "Your favorite Rembrandt is on the block and you are bidding for it against a dazzling array of eccentric art speculators. Should you go even higher? What if it's a worthless forgery? You'll find out when you play 'Masterpiece,' an exciting, suspenseful trip into the elite world of the international art auction." Bidders included the debonair "V. Elton Whitehall Esq." of London, the crafty Frenchman "Count Francois du Bonnet," and a variety of oil sheiks, heiresses, and banking moguls. (Its original price tag was $4.95. Nowadays a used version fetches $29.99 on eBay.) In such a climate, Monday was among the first to spot an opening for grand theft on an elite scale.

But Monday also was making what would become the fine-art thief's classic mistake: seeing dollar signs inside the frames. He admits he barely considered the trouble he would encounter trying to resell the stolen works. He had no clue whether the Worcester Art Museum was insured, or had the kind of cash reserves needed to ransom back its paintings. And of course he had no buyer lined up. It would not be like stealing fungible cash or meltable gold. It would be like taking a hostage. And hostage scenarios rarely turn out well for criminals.

Monday started out methodically enough, casing museums to strike around New England, using pen and paper to keep a log of his targets. First among them, he says, was Boston's Isabella Stewart Gardner Museum, because its Raphaels were cited in the *Globe* article as having auction value in the $10 million range. He jotted in his notes at the time: "This museum affords us the opportunity of gaining millions in fine paintings. Guards not equipped to cope with armed people. The remuneration outweighs the possible problems. This is an excellent prospect." The notes, reviewed at length by the authors, are eerie, given that the Gardner was famously robbed in 1990. No evidence points to Monday.

He considered other regional art museums, including the Wadsworth Atheneum in Hartford, Connecticut, brimming with works by French Impressionists and Renaissance masters and overseen by "elderly unarmed gentlemen...who would not be in any serious position to hinder a professional thief." His notes include references to "bulk factor" and "location of nearest police." He also scoped out the Museum of Fine Arts in Boston, but decided that the guards "seemed young, alert and observant." Finally, Monday made a shorter trek to the familiar Worcester Art Museum. He knew at once he had his score.

In an unpublished typewritten memoir reeking of cigarette smoke and written long after the theft, Monday called the Worcester Art Museum, or WAM, "an art thief's dream." Although relatively well-protected from nighttime intruders, he wrote, the museum's "daytime security was decidedly non-existent." "The guards were as antique as the relics in the collection. There were no cameras or push-button alarms, which made WAM the prime target for the first armed robbery of a museum in history." Reflecting on his dream to rob museums from Boston to Hartford to New York City, he added: "THIS IS THE PLACE TO START!!!" Say what you want about Monday, but he was completely correct in his assessments of museum security. There was no need for him to acquire high-tech gadgetry, walkie-talkies, wall-scaling devices, and the other must-haves of Hollywood filmdom. All it would take was the wherewithal to pull off a routine home invasion.

Monday concentrated with admirable precision on the logistics of the robbery, something that sets him apart from many subsequent art thieves. He went so far as to get measurements of each of the four paintings on his shopping list and study whether their frames were particularly heavy, wide, or ornate. He was curious at first to know whether the paintings would fit into a specially made overcoat he owned that featured billowing pockets on the inside flaps. The pockets were sewn into the coat specifically for thievery.

When he determined that the framed works were too large for his giant pockets, he gave the measurements to his sister-in-law and had her sew four properly sized cloth bags so that each stolen piece could be hauled off separately. His original plan called for a different-colored sack for each of the paintings, but he scrapped the color-coding idea as unnecessary.

Monday gave much thought to his target's internal security, which back then did not include such basics as video cameras, but he makes plain that doing so was barely necessary. Such was the general state of affairs at museums in the early 1970s. Filching from an art museum of almost any size was likely easier than robbing a drug store or delicatessen. In a small shop, the owner might have his eyes on you the whole time, and a gun under the counter. In a museum, there were many unattended corners and loosely policed exhibits, and never any firearms. Some of the more bare-bones New England museums from that era relied more or less on an honor system. Beneath the glass cases displaying jewels and coins and carvings, curators would often store additional items of equal worth in sliding drawers. If the drawers were locked, which was not always the case, a professional could pick the locks in seconds. The drawers could be slipped open a few inches and their contents palmed with ease.

Massachusetts—much of New England, in fact—is home to hundreds of major and minor museums housing Colonial artifacts, Revolutionary and Civil War swords, rare coins and ornaments, Native-American treasures, early American paintings, and turn-of-the-century works by greats like John Singleton Copley, James McNeill Whistler, and Thomas Cole, acquired long before their fame—and prices—flared. Some of those works would surpass tens of millions at auction today. Through the years, many such places have suffered pilferage at best, grave theft at worst. It was a dirty little secret of New England museums, made worse by the fact that many of the artifacts had never been properly appraised, insured, or catalogued. At the time, that made reselling such objects—even auctioning them publicly—an easy way to convert the loot into cash. In the introduction to his 1982 book *The Art Museums of New England*, Professor S. Lane Faison of Williams College wrote that people would be "surprised to learn what artistic riches exist in out-of-the-way places." He added: "It is fair to say that no region of comparable size anywhere can boast such a concentration of art museums as New England. Even more extraordinary is the concentration in Massachusetts alone."[4] This helps explain why seven Rembrandts were stolen in Massachusetts between 1972 and 1990, helping make the Bay State the nation's art crime mecca. These smaller New England museums have gotten wiser. From 1977 until 1987, when it sold for $53.9 million at Sotheby's, Vincent van Gogh's *Irises* was on display at Westbrook College, a tiny liberal arts school outside Portland, Maine. It hung in a small gallery on campus, which the painting's owner, John Whitney Payson, had built in memory of his mother, Joan. Payson wisely decided that it was no longer safe there and noted that the cost of insurance and security was becoming "overwhelming."[5] *Irises* sold to Alan Bond, an Australian businessman, yachtsman, and America's Cup winner. But he could not cover the cost and *Irises* was sold again in 1990 to the wealthy J. Paul Getty Museum in Los Angeles for an undisclosed price.

Monday was alert to this state of affairs in the early 1970s. He recalls casing the Hartford Superior Courthouse, where rare coins of high value, including gold and silver pieces from 1794 to 1840, sat on display in unalarmed cases easily pried open with a screwdriver. The State House in Boston, as another example, once freely displayed Revolutionary and Civil War weapons and coins, and signed documents from the founding of the Massachusetts Bay Colony along in its corridors. In the 1960s, 1970s, and early 1980s, so many ancestral items were swiped behind the backs of unwary docents and security men that the entire public collection was removed to a secure location by the secretary of state. This regional inclination toward laissez-faire security made the Worcester Art Museum equally vulnerable. Its guards were basically "old-timers," low-paid unarmed retirees dressed in off-the-rack blue blazers, men of fine deportment, trained in courtesy rather than deterrence. In a stern editorial headlined "Art Theft Is Best in Daylight," written the day after Al Monday's armed Rembrandt heist, a *Boston Globe* editorial writer put it archly:

> During the day these treasure troves are protected by nice men— guards, we call them, who are retired military personnel or retired police, gentleman with the best inclinations in the world, trained to be mannerly, living off some other pension, slow in the leg and absolutely, in the country of the .38 revolver, defenseless. . . . This has never been realized before. Or, if it has been, obviously nothing around the world has been done about it.[6]

Some decent security existed at the time, but 1972 was long before museums installed the effective covert alarm systems, electronic-tracking technology, and closed-circuit cameras and recording devices common today. Monday pressed the point in his casing work, stepping as close to the art in the WAM as he could. He saw right off that no buzzers would sound when he drew near and that there were no infrared beams to sidestep. He also noticed that when he approached a painting, ostensibly to gaze from the length of his nose at some curious detail, no one in the museum seemed to remark or care. (More than one museum conservator has noticed a spot develop near the Rembrandt signature on a prized painting, the result of visitors irresistibly pointing toward the famous name and all too often lightly touching it.) Monday became satisfied that a listless or sore-footed watchman, "one old guy in his early 60's," he jotted down, "wasn't going to be an obstacle."

The crucial final step for Monday was to walk his two inside men through the museum. He says he did not want to be on hand himself—a critical error, as it turned out—because he feared being recognized from his frequent forays onto the premises. He calculated that two men could easily haul off the four paintings, which weighed a total of 80 pounds, some 20 pounds apiece, frames included.

From his five-person gang, Monday chose William G. Carlson, 26, and Stephen A. Thoren, 30, to handle the actual theft. Both would later describe themselves to police as "unemployed laborers," a well-worn local shorthand for "career criminal." They were "second-story men"—breaking-and-entering types—and Monday was the "brains" who brought them together.

Monday's plot for his bandits was straightforward: Steal a car, drive to the museum, park legally nearby, walk in, breeze up to the second floor, don ski masks, remove and bag the paintings, exit hurriedly, say nothing, hurt no one, and drive off. He wanted no flourishes or feints. Monday tasked a third member of his gang, a 22-year-old "unemployed laborer" named David M. Aquafresca, or "Ackie," with stealing the car and being the wheelman for the getaway. Despite his youth, Aquafresca was no stranger to major crime, having taken part in a bank robbery, according to police, just one day before the WAM heist itself. Following Monday's orders, Aquafresca boosted a white 1965 Oldsmobile station wagon, a smart choice considering that the paintings, still framed, could then be stacked safely inside the capacious rear of the getaway car.

Monday readily admits today that he left too much to chance. He told Carlson and Thoren to rob the museum while it was open, but said the exact time of day was up to them. And he allowed them a revolver, initially unloaded "so they couldn't hurt anyone." Monday wanted no part of a shooting rap, given that nonviolent art theft (masterpieces included) was treated as a small-time crime in 1972. Sentences were minor and a restitution deal was often enough to let a felon walk away on probation. Today, a similar crime would break federal law and could lead to 25 years in prison. Such has been the pressure on sentencing since the Gardner Museum heist in 1990. But back in Monday's time, an art heist was seen as a bit of a stunt, unworthy of real police and prosecutorial time. Unfortunately, Carlson and Thoren quickly noted the absence of even a single bullet in the gun and balked. Monday knew that a loaded gun was a bad idea. He was confident that just waving the firearm would intimidate anyone in the way. "It would be Barney Fife versus them," he said. But his robbers felt emasculated and complained long and loud, threatening to call off the affair. To placate them, Monday acquiesced by loading the .22 with one round.

For all his inarguable smarts, Monday made blunders typical of those seen in subsequent Rembrandt thefts. He failed to assemble a stable of reliable, professional, and tight-lipped thieves. His team consisted of two small-time career criminals, a drug addict, a woman who drew attention to herself by lighting a cigarette during one preliminary scouting trip in the museum (and who backed out of the plot at the last minute), and a person described by Monday as a "stool pigeon." Nor did Monday command his men properly or scare them adequately about the repercussions of firing their single shot. And, as so often happens, he failed to have a major buyer ready to pay for the art. His was a "gang that couldn't steal straight." But then it is very rare for a Rembrandt thief to gain something valuable from the act. Time and again, robbers, fences, and their associates find that conducting a heist or meddling in its aftermath leads to headaches, betrayals, bad publicity, police surveillance, and, of course, prison time. Better in the long run to steal the money from the museum's donations box than its famous works of art.

THE TARGET

Just two miles from Monday's art history training ground at Assumption College stands the Worcester Art Museum. It is a Classical Revival–style building housing big-name items from across time and around the globe. There are American paintings that depict Revolutionary life, indigenous pre-Columbian carvings, and artifacts from India, Korea, Japan, and the Islamic world. Picture all the top finds from a few seasons of *Antiques Roadshow* and you will get an idea of how varied and valuable its lesser works are. Add to that the many canvases by master painters. And then top it off with a world-class collection of Antioch mosaics, the centerpiece of which is an enormous mosaic on the floor of the Renaissance Court, just a few feet from the museum's main entrance. The composition, titled *the Worcester Hunt*, features hunters and wild beasts in a frenzied tableau.

On the walls of the WAM hang paintings by Gaugin, Picasso, El Greco, Sargent, and Monet, luminaries all. Since its opening in 1898, "for the benefit of all the people of the City of Worcester," the museum has established a demanding tradition: Each of its directors has acquired at least one seventeenth-century Dutch painting. The twelfth director, a highly respected Dutch art specialist, added *Paris and Oenone* (1619) by Pieter Lastman to the European art collection in 1984. It was a great coup. Though Lastman is regarded as one of the finest Dutch masters, particularly for his depictions of religious and mythological subjects, he is better known for his most famous protégé: Rembrandt Harmenszoon van Rijn. The connection between the two is well illustrated at the WAM. Welu chose to place *Paris and Oenone* directly beside the museum's treasured Rembrandt, *St. Bartholomew*.

St. Bartholomew was the Dutch painting acquired by one of Welu's predecessors, Daniel Catton Rich, who bought it from Harvard University on June 22, 1958. He unveiled *St. Bartholomew* that fall, even though the work had for decades been the subject of skeptical scrutiny by Rembrandt scholars. At the heart of the dispute, as is frequently the case with the prolific and oft-copied Rembrandt, was uncontested attribution. Not only had the master painted two other versions of the martyred Bartholomew (such repetitions are not uncommon in Rembrandt's work), but each portrait depicted a drastically different-looking individual as the saint. Could they all truly be by Rembrandt?

Dutch painting expert and author Seymour Slive, of Harvard University and its Fogg Art Museum, wrote in the WAM's catalogue of European paintings that "Rembrandt made two other paintings of S. Bartholomew: one in 1657 and the other…in 1661. The mood of these imposing late works is quite different. The 1657 painting depicts the Saint with his inner conflict resolved; he appears undaunted by the test to which his faith will be put. Rembrandt's last representation of the Saint is even more restrained. The Apostle is seen deep in thought and we participate with him as he seems to think about our destiny as well as his own." The 1657 *Bartholomew*, now at the Timken Museum of Art in San Diego, shows a heavily bearded man in robes with a furrowed brow, holding a long, sharp blade. The 1661 version, at the Getty Museum in Los Angeles, has the saint looking pensive and almost modern-day in his grooming and attire. His knife is shorter and held at the bottom corner of the work. It was created at a time when, to quote one of the many writers on Rembrandt, the painter was "bludgeoned by tragedies that might have crushed a weaker man," mostly as a result of his messy bankruptcy and fall from grace, yet he also found some peace of mind.

Adding confusion to the attribution was the fact that a replica of the *Bartholomew* obtained for the WAM by Catton Rich had floated around for years. Though the copy was often exhibited as a true Rembrandt, and had been "authenticated" by some experts, Rembrandt scholar Jakob Rosenberg found it lacking the artist's nuanced skills. "A comparison of the two heads shows at once how much of the plastic quality is lost [in the copy] by a manipulation of the brush that imitates Rembrandt's strokes but loses control of their modeling function," he wrote. When that copy was bequeathed to Manhattan's Metropolitan Museum of Art, the Met returned it to the donor. Slive dismissed it as "a rather crude copy."

And there was yet further mystery about the Worcester *St. Bartholomew*. The actual subject of the painting was unclear. The canvas, showing a scraggly man with his head turned slightly to his left, grasping a knife in his right hand, was displayed at a 1939 exhibition in San Francisco as *Portrait of an Old Man*. Rembrandt's two other portraits of Bartholomew have also been subject to mistaken identity—they have been described as portraits of an assassin, a surgeon, or a family cook. The blade held by the apostle is likely what led early cataloguers astray. It is now universally accepted that the knife held by Bartholomew in all three authenticated Rembrandts represents his martyrdom: the painting carries on the tradition of depicting saints with symbols of their manner of death.

Bartholomew the Apostle is said to have carried Christianity to Armenia in the first century. He was reputedly flayed alive and crucified upside down for his gumption. Religious works across the centuries show Bartholomew gripping a large blade to emphasize his bloody martyrdom. (He is, a bit ghoulishly, the patron saint of the hide-tanning trade.) In Michelangelo's *Last Judgment*, Bartholomew can be seen resurrected in Heaven with his own skin hanging from his left hand. (He also bears Michelangelo's bearded face, a famous joke by the artist, who considered his years of brutal labor painting the Sistine Chapel as a sort of flaying.) Rembrandt's paintings of imprisoned apostles and prophets such as Saint Peter and Saint Paul also found favor among his early patrons in Leiden and The Hague. When Rembrandt needed money early in his career, and during the period of 1655–1660, he painted saints and martyrs for the brisk northern European trade in household images of suffering and piety. These works were readily marketable all over Christian Europe, even in Catholic Italy, where some of them found their earliest known owners.

Art historians have speculated that Rembrandt's inspiration for the Worcester Art Museum's *Bartholomew* was either a cook in his home or his own father, who died in 1630. The subject has black, sunken eyes and a crevassed face beset by woe. Rembrandt painted it in his twenties or early thirties, according to scholars, and signed it with a flourish along the knife's blade. As art collectors sometimes say of such unhappy images, "Great, yes, but it would be a tough painting to live with."

The current consensus among scholars is that Rembrandt used his father as the painting's stark model. Some will assert the face bears a small resemblance to a 1630 portrait of the elder Rembrandt that hangs at the Ashmolean Museum in Oxford, England. Catton Rich wrote astutely in his WAM acquisition papers: "*St. Bartholomew* was done just before Rembrandt entered into his early success in Amsterdam and began to turn out rather slick social portraits. Its deep, inner power foretells the later, introspective Rembrandts—an interesting link between his youth and old age when he painted some of his greatest works."

While the history behind the *St. Bartholomew* might intrigue a more pensive Al Monday today, in 1972 he didn't much care. He estimated the item to be worth $2 million. That kind of payoff merited the effort to steal it, however hard it was to look at.

THE HEIST

On Wednesday, May 17, 1972, Al Monday's stick-up plan unfolded. William Carlson and Stephen Thoren arrived at the museum in the late afternoon and breezed through the front entrance on Salisbury Street, where the stolen white station wagon sat, parked legally, Aquafresca at the wheel. The museum was very quiet, with just a few dozen visitors roaming its galleries. As the pair made their way to the second-floor target area, Carlson encountered two teenaged girls. Betraying his own amateurishness and displaying an astonishing blend of bravado and boneheadedness, he stopped to talk to them. "He told them, 'I'm gonna rob the place,'" Monday recalls incredulously. Newspaper reports state simply that the young women, high school students both, spotted the duo just before they stole the artwork, and that one of the thieves ordered the girls to sit on chairs, telling them, "this is not a joke." Unbelievably, Carlson had his conversation with the young witnesses before even donning his ski mask.

As they removed the paintings from the walls, Thoren and Carlson were soon noticed by a handful of visitors. But because the duo worked brazenly and in a methodical manner, appearing "to know exactly what paintings they wanted," according to a museum spokesman, the visitors assumed the thieves were museum employees doing their jobs. This claim by witnesses is not outlandish. An art theft in Bennington, Vermont, in the mid-1980s featured thieves wearing matching blue windbreakers, which were assumed by visitors to be some sort of museum uniform. Even the most frequent visitor to a museum has probably never seen how art is in fact shifted about, since the task is almost always done when museums are closed. The sight of men calmly removing paintings from a portrait gallery in full view of the public could easily strike them as a routine activity.

Thoren and Carlson finally remembered to pull down the blue-and-orange ski masks that Monday had expected them to wear from the outset. They placed their respective paintings into their specially made sacks and headed for the exit. They hurried but tried to seem nonchalant despite their clumsy baggage and felonious appearance.

At just about this moment, museum guard Philip J. Evans was speaking to a female visitor near the facility's main entrance. A veteran WAM security man, Evans was known as a courtly representative of the institution. He was well liked by colleagues in a workplace noted for loyalty. He was knowledgeable about the museum's art and was happy to answer questions. Now he stood by his front desk near the doorway, telling the visitor she could check the books and papers she was carrying on a nearby rack.

Just seconds after Evans's conversation with the woman, Thoren and Carlson reached the bottom of the main staircase and made their way toward the exit. What first caught Evans's eye was not their chunky sacks, however, but something every guard watched for as a matter of practice at the WAM. The two "visitors" had bypassed the rails surrounding the large Antioch mosaic in the center of the Renaissance Court, and were walking on the precious tiles. It was another amateurish mistake. Signs clearly marked the tiles as off-limits.

"You're not supposed to walk across," Evans called out. But the words had no sooner left his lips than he realized the trespassers were wearing ski masks and carrying big bags. As the thieves drew closer to the exit, one of them shouted, "Get out of my way! We're going through!" The unarmed Evans moved to block their departure and grabbed at one of the thieves. The man—likely Thoren—struck Evans with his two bags of paintings, knocking him against a wall. Undaunted, the 57-year-old Evans threw his arms around his assailant's neck. It was then that he felt the sting in his hip from a .22-caliber slug, fired by Carlson.

Evans fell to the floor and the two thieves raced toward the Oldsmobile station wagon. As they made their escape, Evans managed to rise and limp after them. Passersby said the thieves put only three of the paintings in the back of the car. Comically, and for reasons unknown, Gauguin's serene *Brooding Woman* was laid on the car's roof rack while the man in the passenger seat stuck his right arm out the window to hold it down. The men peeled off with the four paintings. Witnesses recorded the license plate of the Olds as it sped south on Lancaster Street, then west on Institute Road, toward a rendezvous with a second getaway car parked at Worcester Polytechnic Institute.

Paramedics were called to help Evans. Visitors and staff bunched around him. The woman he'd spoken with before he was shot knelt by his side, applying pressure to his wound. Dazed, he asked why she was holding him so tightly. "I'm a nurse," she replied. The rest of the security staff scattered to summon police, investigate the crime scene, and take an accounting of the galleries. The museum's "red book," used back then to record events of the day, indicates blandly that at

4:30 P.M.: "Missing from Gal. 209 Mother & Child by Pablo Picasso + The Brooding Woman Gaugin [*sic*] 1921.186. Heard a scuffle when in Gallery 200 and came to Gal 209 and found 2 men going out front door past guard + shooting as they went about 4:30 pm . . . also Head of a Woman taken 1921.5 Gaugin also Gal 201—A Rembrandt 1958:35 St. Bartholomew. 5:00 pm Closed Galleries."

Thoren, Carlson, and Aquafresca, meanwhile, arrived at the campus of Worcester Polytechnical, transferred their plunder to the second car, and abandoned the stolen Olds. Next up was a meeting with the mastermind, Al Monday.

*   *   *

Monday was sitting in a bar in Worcester feeling confident and excited when the car with the three men pulled up. As soon as he got into it, Aquafresca spilled the bad news. "They shot the guard."

Monday was apoplectic. "What!?" he recalls shouting. This was the worst news possible, worse than if the thieves had been caught. A robbery arrest could be dealt with. But, as Monday says, the shooting "put blood on the paintings." He lashed out at Thoren and Carlson, demanding, "Who's the genius that shot the guard?" Carlson admitted to pulling the trigger and Thoren came to his defense. "We had to do it. He was in the way," he sniveled. This did nothing to quell Monday's fury. He knew that law enforcement would now triple their efforts to find the robbers. He had not orchestrated a simple theft of paintings that could then be fenced or ransomed. He was now the man behind a violent felony, one that put the lives of genteel art lovers and museum workers at risk. His fate, were he caught, might not compare to that of lonely Saint Bartholomew, but cops and feds had their own way of flaying criminals. Monday knew his skin was on the line.

"The gun had one bullet in it, and the guy fired it—for one old guy at the door, 100 pounds soaking wet," he recalls, still aggravated 39 years later. "They could have knocked him over without stopping."

Shell-shocked, Monday put the four paintings in the trunk of his car. He drove to his home in Bellingham, Massachusetts, and hid the art in a dropped ceiling. While he avoided watching or listening to the news, he was concerned enough about Evans's health to call Saint Vincent's Hospital in Worcester and check on the guard's condition. He recalls breathing easy only after learning that Evans was stable and had not suffered a life-threatening wound. In this regard Monday was luckier than he realized. The bullet had come close to hitting Evans's spine.

"Exceedingly happy," as he put it, that a murder charge was out of the picture, Monday decided to get out of town. The theft was all over the news. "$Million in Art Stolen in Worcester, Guard Shot," read the next morning's *Boston Herald* (no price estimate was yet available). Articles about lax security at the nation's museums hit the regional and national newspapers. More significantly for the Monday gang, experts declared that the paintings would be too recognizable to traffic. "Every one of them is well-known to anyone interested in art," said the WAM's director at the time, Richard S. Teitz. A New York art dealer, Alexander Rosenberg, weighed in that it was "inconceivable" that the thieves could sell the renowned paintings, especially the Rembrandt.[7]

That view wasn't universal. Alan Baer of the International Art Registry in New York speculated that while selling the items in the United States would be difficult, they could be more readily sold abroad. "Someone who wants to buy stolen works will, no matter what the circumstances," he said. Reflecting on what the crime itself revealed about the art world, he added: "Museums act like the problem [of art crime] will disappear if they ignore it."[8]

Speculation about the whereabouts of the art ran rampant. The two Worcester detectives on the case said they believed it remained in the vicinity. In New York, the head of the art recovery unit for the New York Police Department asserted that the works were already en route overseas. But what the Worcester caper truly showed was that similar future art heists would almost always be the work of common crooks, local men whose résumés list bank robberies, armored-car stickups, and far less glamorous heists than those depicted by suave operators like Pierce Brosnan in *The Thomas Crown Affair*. Exhibit A is the crafty and cranky Al Monday, who was stuck with stolen art that was making headlines across the nation and the subject of wires to INTERPOL. He needed to cover his tracks and ease the fears of his now-jittery cohorts. As Monday put it, "I was a local crook. I didn't have international connections to help me out of this." Such can be said of the vast majority of museum thieves who followed Monday's roadmap.

Monday realized right away that he had to stash the art elsewhere. His home was out of the question—he had a wife and children, even a reputation. He reasoned he had best get out of town before one of his confederates turned informant. In fact, Thoren was already bragging about the crime while watching television news reports in a local tavern. While the heist was being likened to the famous Brinks armored-car job and other legendary professional scores, one of its perpetrators was engaging in the kind of indiscreet braggadocio that was apt to get everyone locked up fast.

Monday took the frame off *St. Bartholomew*, reducing the Rembrandt to a simple wooden panel. He grabbed the other three items, packed them all in a steamer trunk, and made tracks 40 miles south to the Picillo Pig Farm in Coventry, Rhode Island, for years a notorious toxic dump site. Along the way he tossed the original seventeenth-century Rembrandt frame into a canal in the town of Millville. It was never recovered.

Once at the pig farm (which blew up due to hazardous waste five years later), Monday hid the works in a hayloft. The trunk, he said, was his nod to the notion that the paintings needed protection from the elements. He stayed away from his home for a few days, hoping the heat would die down and still imagining he might arrange a sale of the works, but in essence he was stuck. The paintings were getting plenty of media attention and even longshot Mafia buyers were backing away.

When he finally returned home he had a rude surprise. There, being served coffee by his wife, were two young FBI agents, one named

Jim Ring. Monday says the FBI agents put pressure on him right away to produce the art. They had not yet tabbed him as the ringleader, but they made clear they knew from informants that he was mixed up in the robbery. The agents left without arresting Monday. They had already tracked down the boastful Thoren and convinced him that Monday would put a hit on him and the others to silence them. The agents felt confident they could turn Thoren into an informant and apply pressure on Monday for the whereabouts of the paintings. Monday decided to lie low and see if he could escape the trap.

Even as the lawmen worked for the art's recovery, a new group of local crime figures began plotting to get their hands on the works. This opportunistic gang, it turned out, had more savvy than Monday's ring. Their scheme was to use the paintings as a chit to win the freedom of a fellow criminal, a man named Anthony Carlo, who was in jail in Massachusetts awaiting trial for armed robbery. They tracked down Aquafresca and had him reach out to Monday for a meeting. Aquafresca called Monday, sounding panicky, and said he needed to get paid fast for his role in the heist to hire a lawyer. When Monday went to see him to settle him down, he recalled, "Four or five guys grabbed me at gunpoint and said: 'We want the paintings. Don't worry, you'll get your cut.'" Monday assumed he was done for. He had no choice but to lead the gang to the pig farm. He turned over the trunk with the art, and to his surprise he was driven back to his car and let go. "I was upset about losing the potential money more than the paintings," he said, "because by then there was so much heat."

While Monday contemplated his best-laid plans gone awry, the new crew in possession of the art contacted a local lawyer named Conrad Fisher, who was involved with the Anthony Carlo case and willing to handle the art swap and the legal work it entailed. Fisher carried one of the four paintings into a meeting with local police and declared that all four items were safe—thanks to a tip from the cooperative jailbird Carlo. The expectation was that Carlo and a codefendant would be granted leniency in their pending case and not have to serve prison time. After the fact, though, both men were sentenced to one to five years for the armed robbery. They were so angered by what they saw as a law enforcement double cross that upon sentencing by their judge they shouted from the dock, "We made a deal!"

Given the number of criminals becoming involved in the rarefied tug-of-war, it is remarkable that the Rembrandt and other paintings reemerged. In the end, their odyssey was brief. After their three weeks at the pig farm, the paintings spent four days in the trunk of Aquafresca's car before they were finally given over to the authorities and returned to the museum with the aid of attorney Fisher. The unfazed Aquafresca even found time to go swimming with his girlfriend on Cape Cod with the treasured Rembrandt in his trunk. As Aquafresca's own lawyer recalled, "Do you believe this? Here is everybody looking for these paintings, and my client went swimming."

All told, the art had spent four weeks in the hands of various felons and hoods, none of whom, except perhaps for Monday, had the slightest idea how to keep it from being damaged. Nonetheless, *St. Bartholomew* suffered only "some moisture damage, and layers of protective varnish were separated lightly," according to a report by the WAM's conservator, Edmond de Beaumont. There were "a few scratches and dents" on Gauguin's *Brooding Woman,* which had ridden atop the Oldsmobile. The Picasso and the other Gauguin were fine. During the time in which the Rembrandt was AWOL, then being repaired, the museum chose not to leave its space empty, temporarily hanging *Joseph's Cup Found in Benjamin's Sack*, by Ferdinand Bol, one of Rembrandt's top students, in its place.

THE AFTERMATH

Even with the paintings out of his hands, Monday knew he needed to get out of town. Shrewder crooks than he had snatched away his score and bartered it back, and there was still a major robbery and a shooting to account for. After a short stint with friends in Abington, Massachusetts, Monday learned of a warrant for his arrest and left the

United States. Joined by his brother and his brother's wife and children, he fled to Canada, where the group rented a chalet in Quebec's Laurentian Mountains.

In a stroke of luck, Monday recalls, he found identity documents in the chalet and soon assumed the name of a French-Canadian, Rock Poulin. He even found legitimate work as a bouncer at a nightclub. But old habits die hard, and Monday again started pilfering antiquities. He claims that he was involved in a museum theft in Montreal in which a Raphael and a Tintoretto were stolen (and later hidden under his brother's bed), and says that when two of his friends, Lewis Mathis and Carl Dixon, famously stole $20 million in Greek and Roman coins from the Fogg Art Museum at Harvard University, they called him and visited him often. Inevitably, Monday took part in yet another robbery: the theft of diamonds in Montreal. When he reached out to a jeweler he knew back in the United States, federal agents were able to trace the call to his Canadian hideaway. On June 24, 1974, more than two years after he masterminded the Worcester art theft, the Royal Canadian Mounted Police approached "Rock Poulin" and told him, "We think you're Florian Monday." They arrested him and deported him to the United States as an "undesirable person."

Monday was arrested by awaiting FBI agents. They hit him with a string of criminal charges in the Worcester case, including being an accessory before and after the fact to armed robbery, and assault and battery with a dangerous weapon. They also charged him with federal stolen-vehicle crimes.

After being found guilty by a federal jury, Monday was sentenced in September 1975, receiving 9 to 20 years in prison for plotting the WAM heist, even though, as his attorney argued, "This man did not pull the trigger. Carlson pulled the trigger." Carlson got 8 to 25 years, and Thoren, reviled by Monday as the informant in the case, received two years' probation. Aquafresca, despite his role in returning the art, received 12 to 30 years in state prison for the heist and two unrelated bank robberies. Finally, Carol Naster, the woman who lit up a cigarette inside the WAM during one of Monday's casing missions, got two years as an accessory. At his sentencing, Monday told Judge Thomas R. Morse Jr. that despite the shooting of the guard, "I am not a violent man. I detest violence. I can stand the penalty but it will be a terrible burden to my family."

Monday never did the nine years he received from Judge Morse. As he tells it, after about a year of incarceration, he went before another judge for a "revise and revoke" hearing and his sentence was cut to 7 to 20 years. This lesser sentence allowed him to serve time in the more relaxed environment of "the country club" prison at Medfield State Hospital, near Worcester, where his brush with Rembrandt was a feather in his criminal cap. He spent years laboriously typing his life story. It ends with Monday taking note from his prison cell of the April 1975 armed theft of a Rembrandt from the Boston Museum of Fine Arts. "Newspapers termed the crime a carbon copy of the robbery perpetrated upon the Worcester museum in 1972," he wrote. "One might conclude that the architect of the first armed robbery of a museum in history had not discarded his mold. One might also deduce that the mold may remain intact."

Almost 40 years later, Monday still crows about the Rembrandt he snatched from the Worcester Art Museum, despite the crime's quick unraveling. He appeared on MSNBC in 2004 and bragged about the affair to host Keith Olbermann. He lays claim to it eagerly, as it lets him assert without contradiction that he is an "innovator" in major museum theft. His innovation: having crooks use a gun.

The heroic guard, Philip Evans, who felt "he was pretty lucky" to have gotten his job at the museum in the first place, returned to work less than six weeks after the shooting. While in the hospital, he was visited by the police and museum officials, including the director. "They thanked me," he recalled. "It was the only time anyone from the museum officially thanked me."[9]

Evans's efforts would not be long remembered by the museum, however. Soon after the paintings were recovered, the museum threw a party for all those who took part in the investigation that led to their return. Evans didn't receive a formal invitation, but the museum director later told him that he and his wife should attend, which they did. Everyone on hand received a small commemorative copy of Rembrandt's *St. Bartholomew*. Everyone, that is, except Philip Evans, the man who nearly gave his life to save the painting. As he remembered, "I did not get one. I had to ask for it."

POSTSCRIPT

Museums are always battling for attention and funding, and falling prey to a heist can be turned into a publicity coup. But in December 2007, the Worcester Art Museum went a step beyond what most museums would contemplate. It allowed movie makers to transform its Renaissance Court and galleries into a set for the $20 million feature film *The Maiden Heist*, and the museum held several benefit screenings of the movie a year later. The publicity releases read in part: "'The Maiden Heist' gives us the most endearing characters ever to commit grand larceny: three museum security guards who live lives of quiet captivation, each enraptured by a particular work of art. Roger (Christopher Walken), Charles (Morgan Freeman) and George (William H. Macy) are each so lost in fascination with the particular *objet d'art* of his affection that although they have been coworkers for decades, they only just meet for the first time when crisis strikes: there's a new curator in town, and his plan is to change the museum's collection entirely, threatening to rob each man of his greatest secret passion in life. However, having found their kindred spirits, the men forge a plan to hold onto the works of art they hold most dear. Though hardly criminal masterminds, their inflamed hearts drive them to plan and execute the most daring art heist ever conceived from the inside—with bumblingly hilarious results!"

No Rembrandts were harmed in the making of the film.

CHAPTER THREE

The Takeaway Rembrandt

Few museum thieves can lay claim to being prolific and successful. Florian "Al" Monday set his sights on a career as an fine-art bandit, only to wind up on the run and in prison after his first try. Myles J. Connor Jr. robbed at least a dozen museums across New England in the 1960s and 1970s, making him one of the busiest art thieves of all time. But Connor (Chapter 6) spent 20 years in jail for his avocation and now lives in humble retirement surrounded by exotic animals rather than priceless paintings. Of the scores of men involved in stealing and ransoming individual Rembrandts, nearly all are of the "one and done" variety—either captured or frustrated into giving back the art by their inability to profit from the exploit. Almost never has a theft brought them riches or happy lives.

Recent history reveals only one art thief who set any kind of standard for prolific success, although his triumph was brief and the thefts were ultimately catastrophic for his spoils. Stéphane Breitwieser, a

French waiter working in Switzerland, stole more than a billion dollars' worth of art from an astonishing 172 museums across Europe between 1995 and late 2001. His motive, he said, was his "love" for the 239 items he filched, most of which he crammed into his bedroom at his mother's house in Mulhouse, France, on the Swiss border. He even kept the lights dim and the shades drawn to protect the paintings from fading. His first crime, stealing a Dutch portrait of a young woman, was motivated by the work's resemblance to a Rembrandt, he writes in his memoirs, *Confessions of an Art Thief.* Early on, he stole pieces by well-recognized masters, including François Boucher, Antoine Watteau, and Pieter Brueghel. By the end, he had become a bit of a pack rat, taking Roman bugles, Greek pottery, and medieval crossbows as well.

Upon his arrest in November 2001, much of his trove met a sickening fate. His mother, Mireille, destroyed dozens of Old Masters by cutting or carving them up, putting the broken frames out with the trash over a number or weeks, and shoving many of the shredded canvases into her garbage disposal. She flung other artifacts, including vases, jewelry, and statuettes, into the nearby Rhône–Rhine Canal. Some were recovered through dredging. When police raided her home, they initially found scant evidence of stolen goods. The mother admitted to her rampage only after some items began washing up on the shores of the Rhine, and then asserted at trial that she was clueless as to the art's value. Alexandra Smith, of the Art Loss Register, the world's largest private database of lost and stolen art, antiques, and collectibles, said at the time: "We've never heard of the destruction of works on this scale. The French police are quoting a value of 1.5 billion euros, and when you are dealing with 60 to 70 museum-quality pieces, that would be about right."[1] Breitwieser, who was in his twenties during his spree, is free and clear after serving two-thirds of a three-year sentence, and tours Western Europe pitching his book.

But save for Connor, Breitwieser, and one or two others, thieves who rob museums more than once are unusual. Rarer still is the painting that is stolen for a second time. Perhaps the most famous of these is Edvard Munch's *The Scream*, although those crimes come with an asterisk. Munch created five versions of his sexless shrieking figure framed by a ghastly, roiling sky. The Munch Museum in Oslo, Norway, holds one of the two versions that he painted on cardboard, and one version he did in pastel. The National Gallery of Norway, also in Oslo, holds the second painted version. A fourth version, done in pastel, is owned by a Norwegian businessman. Munch also created a black-and-white lithograph of the image. The two versions painted on cardboard have each been stolen once. In February 1994, thieves looking to mock the poor security at the National Gallery on the eve of the Winter Olympics in Lillehammer broke in and took that museum's version of the iconic work. Worth perhaps $80 million, it was recovered three months later. Munch's other painted *Scream* was ripped from a wall of the Munch Museum in broad daylight in August 2004 by armed men who made off in a dark hatchback. Recovered two years later, the fragile work suffered irreparable water damage and flaking due to moisture, mishandling, and temperature extremes.

Which brings us back to Rembrandt. For not only does he stand alone as the most prolific portrait painter (and self-portrait painter) among the greats, he owns a far more mortifying distinction. He is the only great master to have had one of his portraits, *Jacob de Gheyn III* (1632), stolen an outlandish four times, all between 1966 and 1983, and always from the same London museum. The ill-starred work is now known to history as "the Takeaway Rembrandt."

*   *   *

The modern adventures of *Jacob de Gheyn* began sometime shortly after midnight, December 31, 1966. A small group of thieves used a drill and a brace to knock out a two-foot-by-one-foot panel from a seldom-used oak door along one side of the Dulwich Picture Gallery in south London. The tight opening provided them with access to the building without setting off the museum's alarm system. It was also just large enough to provide an exit for some of the gallery's smaller pieces of art. Taken during the heist along with *Jacob de Gheyn III* were two other Rembrandts, *A Girl at a Window* and *Portrait of Titus*, the former an engaging painting of an apple-cheeked child, the latter a portrait of Rembrandt's only son, who died of the plague in 1668, at the age of 27, one year before his father's death. The robbery did not end with the Rembrandts. The thieves made off with three works by Flemish great Peter Paul Rubens, *The Three Graces, St. Barbara,* and *Three Nymphs with Cornucopia;* one painting by Rembrandt pupil Gerrit Dou, *A Lady Playing on the Virginals;* and *Susannah and the Elders* by Adam Elsheimer, an influential early-seventeenth-century German artist. Though the police report listed the value of the works at 1.5 million British pounds ($4.2 million at the time), art experts put the value of all eight works at $5 million to $7 million, making the Dulwich burglary the costliest art museum theft of modern times up to that date.[2]

Once the burglary was discovered early that morning, as New Year's Eve was dawning, Scotland Yard detectives, police dogs in tow, arrived in droves and combed the scene. (Amid this uproar, officials reopened the gallery to the public by 10 A.M.) As he personally poked about for clues, Detective-superintendent Charles Hewett, the lead investigator, had his men send descriptions of the stolen works to law enforcement officials throughout Britain. They also contacted INTERPOL to alert worldwide authorities in case the works were moved abroad, and Hewett asked the media to alert the public to the crime. This allowed him to publicize images of the looted art far and wide while signaling to the thieves that enormous resources and heavy heat were being devoted to the case.

Soon enough, Humphrey Brooke, secretary of the London Royal Academy of Arts, which oversaw the collection at the Dulwich Gallery, received a call. A man threatened to burn the paintings if he was not paid £100,000. Though he notified the police, Brooke wasn't alarmed. "Quite frankly I think it was a hoax," he said.[3] In any event, the Dulwich Gallery could not afford such ransom. None of the stolen paintings—indeed, none of the gallery's rich collection—was insured, because the premiums were deemed prohibitive. The museum could offer a reward of only £1,000.[4] Brooke called the crime a "shattering event" and "a major disaster."

Superficial early clues led Scotland Yard to conclude that the infiltration was the handiwork of top professionals. Six of the eight stolen pieces were painted on panels small enough to pass through the hole in the door, suggesting astute premeditation. The two Rembrandts that were painted on canvas were cut from their frames with a sharp razor so they too could be passed through the opening. Given the New Year's Eve timing, there were no eyewitnesses, no videotapes, and seemingly not one hot lead. All this pointed in theory to an act of expertise. But the cigarette-smoking and keen-eyed Superintendent Hewett was not without clues. Much the way art historians gain useful insights into Rembrandt's thinking by analyzing what is present (and omitted) from his paintings, a clever art detective gleans much from studying a seemingly unrevealing crime scene.

Hewett realized that the size of the hole in the oak door provided a rough idea of the intruders' frames—smallish. One of the investigators joked that the culprits "must all have been rubber-boned men to get through that."[5] Left behind at the scene was a two-inch-long, small-diameter drill bit used to bore more than 100 holes around the perimeter of the busted panel. From what investigators saw, the thieves next used a cutting tool to scour the spaces between the holes and complete the door panel's excision. The drill bit, not an everyday piece of equipment, was a rich lead. It would allow police to question local shop owners on the chance that one might have recently sold such an item. Police also found fresh tool marks on the two abandoned Rembrandt frames, made when those pieces were jimmied from the walls. If they could find a matching tool in the possession of a suspect, forensics could tie the item and its owner to the crime.[6]

It had rained the night before, and police spotted a number of footprints in the mud near the break-in point and muddy prints within the confines of the museum. By examining the shoe prints inside the gallery, Hewett surmised that the thieves had made their way through the building in a crouch, perhaps to evade intrusion-detection devices.

Hewett's focus on the footprints, in the grand tradition of Sherlock Holmes, led him to other useful deductions.

As evidenced by the bulletins that were quickly dispatched to air and sea ports, it is clear the authorities worried initially that the art was on its way out of Britain. The reason was imprinted in the mud. Hewett noted that the muck tracked into the museum was drying despite the moist overall weather. He tasked his forensic team to estimate the drying time for such mud in order to determine the approximate hour when the theft—and thus the getaway—took place. The initial finding put the drying time in such December conditions at 12 hours. That suggested that as much as a half-day had elapsed since the break-in, plenty of time for the burglars to flee London or even the United Kingdom. This boded poorly for the investigation and was worse for a recovery because such a long head start is rarely made up. Soon, however, Hewett learned that the museum employed an underground heating system for climate control and dehumidifying in the galleries. The mud's drying time was sliced from 12 hours to 4 hours.[7] Now, instead of being on another continent, the paintings could still be within driving distance of the British coast. As much a cause for renewed investigative vigor as it was a lead, this indication that the paintings had not necessarily jumped the English Channel motivated Hewett and his team to concentrate manpower on local suspects. Hewett was an ideal English bulldog for the crime. He wore the prototypical London detective's uniform—gray fedora and heavy tweed coat—and was known to stay awake on a case for 48-hour stretches. He commanded his subordinates with clarity and brevity, and pursued leads like a hound on a scent.

Three days after the theft, and just a few miles from the museum, Hewett's men located a stolen car with a crowbar in its trunk. The crowbar bore forensic evidence that put it at the scene of the heist: Not only did its edge match up with the gouge marks found where the paintings had hung on the walls, it also showed remnants of gold gilt paint from the abandoned frames. Hewett's alliance with the news media now paid dividends. Newspapers printed pictures of the recovered automobile and radio and television stations broadcast footage and descriptions. The perpetrators panicked. Soon, two men in West Kensington, London, contacted the authorities, telling them they received a wrapped package from a friend and were asked to hold on to it for a while, secreted under a bed. When curiosity got the best of them, they said, they unwrapped it and found the face of *Jacob de Gheyn III* staring back at them, and two of the other missing paintings as well. The men offered up the identity of their "friend," but Hewett waited before moving to arrest the suspect. He felt confident now that the rest of the art would show up and he persuaded the press to keep word of the partial recovery quiet. His patience paid off. Less than a day later an anonymous caller directed police to a gently sloping meadow known as the Rookery, situated on London's Streatham Common. There they found the remaining five paintings wrapped in newspaper and ditched in a thicket of holly bushes.[8]

A fingerprint taken from the newspaper led police to their man: 32-year-old Michael Hall, an unemployed ambulance driver and petty criminal from Norwood, a suburb near the Dulwich district. Hall, a wiry man capable of contorting his body to fit through the opening drilled into the museum door, owned up to the crime, claiming (to a skeptical Hewett) to have acted alone.[9] Hewett and his team recovered all eight missing masterpieces, valued then at up to $7 million, in just four days. The art was returned to the gallery, where it was evaluated and returned to its climate-controlled conditions. Dulwich curator Rex Shaw described the damage to the paintings as "comparatively slight."[10] What was until then one of the great art robberies of modern times was a closed case. Hall, who would be heard from again, pleaded guilty, and the "mastermind" was sentenced to five years in prison. No one else was formally connected to the crime, and *Jacob de Gheyn III* awaited its next rendezvous with criminal destiny.

* * *

The real Jacob de Gheyn III had a brief but significant appearance in the life of Rembrandt arising from de Gheyn's ties to seventeenth-century

Dutch nobility. His portrait had an eventful history long before it became better known as a repeat target for art-nappers. And its existence helps explain a lot about Rembrandt that might otherwise remain mysterious.

The tale begins in 1631, shortly before Rembrandt left his hometown of Leiden for the wealthier precincts of Amsterdam. Just 25 years old, Rembrandt had caught the attention of Constantijn Huygens, an important figure at the Dutch court. The painter had spent his early career proving he could create excellent historical and biblical works, a skill vital to any aspiring artist of that period. He had also done studies of his own face, perfecting his legendary ability to capture dynamic expressions—laughter, anger, shock—as well as subtle shifts of mood in his paintings. Huygens was the secretary to Holland's Prince of Orange and a pivotal facilitator of artistic patronage at The Hague. He summoned Rembrandt for a meeting. The year was 1629, and came after Rembrandt's friend and colleague Jan Lievens had completed a portrait of Huygens himself. Huygens, a 33-year-old poet, composer, diplomat, and polyglot, was struck by Rembrandt's talent. Describing him as "superior to Lievens with regard to judgment and in the power to affect feelings," Huygens took the blossoming prodigy under his wing. In an autobiography penned in Latin, Huygens wrote that Rembrandt "loves to produce an effect in a small painting and to communicate through abbreviation what you would seek in vain even in the largest paintings by others." Huygens went on to compare Rembrandt's *Judas Repentant* (1629), showing the shamed apostle returning his 30 silver pieces, "with all Italy and whatever marvels remain from deepest antiquity... against all the refinement of the ages."[11] *Judas Repentant* is a tightly distilled work on a wood panel that is 2½ feet tall by 3½ feet wide. By contrast, Peter Paul Rubens's *Adoration of the Magi* (1609) is more than 8 feet tall by 10½ feet wide. For Rembrandt, less could be more. Huygens declared rapturously that Rembrandt, although the "son of a commoner," would surpass the greats. "Truly, my friend Rembrandt, all honor to you," he wrote. Rembrandt was aware that he had landed a major patron in the influential and highborn Huygens. He gave the court secretary several works and declared himself Huygens's "obliging and devoted servant."[12]

But in time Huygens would turn on Rembrandt, and the two would have a strained relationship for much of the 1630s. Huygens had mediated the commission to Rembrandt of five paintings for Frederik Hendrik of the Elevation of the Cross, the Descent from the Cross, Christ's Entombment, his Resurrection, and his Ascension. They all found a place in the prince's painting gallery. (Rembrandt's letters to Huygens about the commissions are the only surviving letters from his hand. Huygens's replies are lost.) But it did not take long for Huygens to grow exasperated with Rembrandt, who missed his deadlines and seemed to whip off the paintings only when he most needed money. By 1639, Rembrandt was out of favor and the royal court was granting its commissions to more reliable artists. In the end, though, it was another painting altogether that soured the promising relationship between Holland's top painter and the court's arbiter of taste. Today, that small portrait of their mutual friend Jacob de Gheyn III links Rembrandt (and Huygens) to a unique twentieth-century one-museum crime wave.

Rembrandt moved from Leiden to the far more crowded and lively city of Amsterdam in 1632. That year he was approached by Huygens's older brother, Maurits, and asked to paint "friendship" portraits of Maurits and Jacob. De Gheyn was an engraver and the son of another court painter, Jacques de Gheyn II, and Maurits Huygens was prominent in society as well as secretary to the Council of State. The friends decided that their separate portraits—cut from the same wood panel—would be rejoined after one of them died, to be kept together in memoriam by the surviving friend.

Constantijn Huygens disliked Rembrandt's likeness of de Gheyn. In a peevish poem chiding what he viewed as a failure, he wrote, "Wonder on, then, O reader / Whoever's likeness is this / It's not de Gheyn's." Huygens wrote eight mocking epigrams about the portrait of de Gheyn, and published seven in a collection of his poetry. (The eighth, the only one to name Rembrandt as the painter, was left out.)

In *Rembrandt's Eyes*, the art historian Simon Schama speculates plausibly that Huygens was miffed because his protégé had been "moonlighting" by completing a commission from his little brother rather than from him.[13]

Huygens believed that Rembrandt should spend his career at The Hague, devote himself to historical and biblical works, and compete for global stature on par with Rubens, who brought renown—and large fees—to Holland's rival duchy at Flanders. But Rembrandt knew his business. Portraits sold well during Holland's Golden Age.[14]

Under the canny guidance of Amsterdam art dealer Hendrick van Uylenburgh, cousin to his wife, Saskia, Rembrandt expanded his clientele throughout the 1630s. Demand for polished portraits that could become ancestral heirlooms was sweeping the middle classes. Holland was evolving into a meritocracy in which labor and social contributions were prized above bloodlines and ecclesiastical ties. People wanted to be portrayed as hardworking citizens in good moral standing, and Rembrandt and his circle offered them this novelty. His studio grew into a lively, frenetic place, with models, wild stage settings, and animated conversation at all hours. Rembrandt was not above keeping a trunk filled with props—hats, cloaks, Oriental garb, military armor, feathers, wreaths, and headdresses. He used the outfits to gussy up his friends, his colleagues, and himself and paint "tronies," lively close-ups that depicted exaggerated characteristics and qualities. A foppish man puffing on a pipe, for example, came to symbolize laziness. A cross-eyed fellow with a half-drained beer stein was a lush.[15] Rembrandt took commissions from the humble, the bourgeois, and the blue-blooded. In 1640, he painted a respectable furniture maker named Herman Doomer with such scrupulous accuracy and affectionate insight that the art historian Christopher White says of the work, "The man's honest simplicity could not be more eloquently expressed."[16] (It hangs at the Metropolitan Museum of Art in Manhattan.)

Rembrandt also embraced the virtues of branding and marketing. His many self-portraits and self-etchings had the useful benefit of making him recognizable and famous across a city of 110,000 that was enjoying economic boom times. During the first half of his career, Rembrandt became a wealthy man. Money poured in from paying students and from government commissions as well as family portraiture. He could also rely on selling impressions from his metal etchings for quick income. Great as he was, he was also an early Andy Warhol-like art impresario. "Rembrandt" was a brand name in the painter's own era.

The Portrait of Jacob de Gheyn III (sometimes called *Portrait of Jacques de Gheyn III*) remains notable in Rembrandt studies because of the tart criticism from Huygens and the pledge of loyalty it inspired between the painting's subject and his friend.

In the portrait, the light-haired Jacob III is depicted from the waist up, against a neutral background, with his body turned slightly to the left. He is wearing a black cloak over a black doublet and a wide, pleated lace collar. The work is painted on oak and is about 12 inches by 10 inches. The dimensions make it an exception in Rembrandt's work, since much of his commissioned portraiture was somewhat larger. Today, *Jacob de Gheyn III* offers scholars and students an invaluable piece by which to study Rembrandt. The signature is of interest—it reads "RH van Ryn / 1632" and is placed in the upper left corner. It also bears a Latin inscription on the back that identifies the subject as de Gheyn and refers to it as his "last gift at his death." Such a clear and reliable provenance for any Old Master painting, let alone a Rembrandt, is as informative as it is rare.[17]

De Gheyn died in 1641, at the age of 45, and his portrait was reunited with that of the surviving Maurits Huygens in The Hague. But after Maurits's own death just a year later, no mention of the whereabouts of *Jacob III* can be found for 122 years. In 1764, it is noted as being part of the collection of Allard Rudolph van Waay, a Dutchman in Utrecht—and still in the company of the portrait of Maurits. By 1786, both paintings had made their way to France and, a few years later, to London, although by then they were in separate collections. In 1807, *Jacob III* was bequeathed by an art collector named Noel Joseph Desenfans to his friend and fellow art dealer Sir Francis Bourgeois.

Four years later, when Sir Francis died, he bequeathed it to what would become the Dulwich Picture Gallery, in South London.[18] It was part of a wide-ranging collection of Old Masters intended "for the inspection of the public." In 1817, *Jacob de Gheyn III* was hung in a place of honor at the Dulwich. (Maurits Huygens's likeness wound up in the Kunsthalle Museum in Hamburg, Germany.)

For nearly 150 years, *Jacob de Gheyn III* hung unmolested, available for public viewing in the peaceful London art enclave. From 1966 onward, its historical importance was eclipsed by an unwelcome new infamy: the most frequently purloined masterwork in the world.

*   *   *

In 1973, seven years after its first theft, *Jacob III* was again wrested from its perch on the Dulwich's walls. This time, an unemployed 24-year-old named Norman Rutter visited the Picture Gallery and, on eyeballing the small portrait, was ostensibly so moved that he decided to pluck it down, stuff it in a plastic bag, and carry it from the museum to his awaiting bicycle, all in full daylight. He had possession of the precious work for precious little time, though, as he was arrested within minutes by quick-footed local police. Rutter told officers he took the painting—by now valued in the multimillions—because he "liked the look of it and wanted to sketch it."[19] If true, Rutter voiced a purer motive than most Rembrandt brigands.

A second heist of the same Rembrandt, while rare, is not unique. In Boston, a postage-stamp-sized etching by Rembrandt that was taken from the Isabella Stewart Gardner Museum during its infamous March 1990 heist had in fact been briefly stolen once before. In 1970, a pack of teenagers entered the museum's opulent Dutch Room primed to pull a prank. One of them walked to a corner opposite where the etching was displayed and threw a lightbulb against the tiled floor. The resulting *pop!* drew the attention of the gallery guard. As he approached the culprit, the other teens removed the etching, a self-portrait, from the side of a wooden cabinet where Mrs. Gardner herself had hung it years earlier, and left via the front entrance. With the identity of the light-bulb tosser known, however, it was not long before arrangements were made to have the etching returned.

In 1981, thieves at Dulwich also employed the stratagem of diverting a guard's attention to purloin a Rembrandt. Two men entered the gallery on August 14 during regular hours. As one engaged a guard in conversation, the other set about detaching the targeted painting. Once again the score was the jinxed *Jacob de Gheyn III*, gone now for a third time. The culprits were a "ragtag gang of British and European thieves"[20] who nonetheless managed to secret it successfully and demand a ransom. A nerve-wracking 11 days passed before the thieves made contact with the gallery. Their blackmail request—£100,000 (about $165,000)—was bad news for the brass at Dulwich, which, like many small cultural institutions around the world, could not afford any such payoff. The administrators played it by the book, again calling in Scotland Yard, and the police again showed a knack for recovering *Jacob*. (Charles Hewett was by now retired.) They instructed the gallery to promise a £100,000 reward for the return of the painting. If it had left the United Kingdom, they calculated, the reward would entice the thieves to carry it back onto native soil, a very helpful step in a recovery that might otherwise have border issues. Soon, Dutch police at Schiphol Airport in Amsterdam, acting on a tip, told Scotland Yard that some ripe suspects were on the move. British authorities allowed the men back into the country and put them under surveillance. This is a common recovery ploy. Investigators cannot assume their targets have the art with them when they travel. A premature bust could lead to a failed recovery bid and put any stolen works at greater peril, because those holding them would likely go further underground. Art recovery units always put the art first, and their byword is patience. In this case, they succeeded. On September 2, 1981, in London's Berkeley Square, police arrested four scruffy men in a taxicab. Found with them, in a black briefcase, was the long-suffering Rembrandt. Although removed from its frame, the painting was not damaged. During questioning, police determined that the painting had never left Britain, even though some of the conspirators had. The arrested men included Klaus Echterhoff, a Wallau, West Germany, art dealer, who was charged with receiving the painting "knowing or believing it to be" stolen; Leonardo Smit of Ysselstein, Holland, charged as the fence in the scheme; and a pair of Britons, the two original inside men. Three of them went to jail. Scotland Yard Chief Inspector Collin Evans succinctly told the press, "I think they were just trying to obtain money for it."[21]

* * *

One might think that after three thefts, the Dulwich Picture Gallery's red-faced directors would revise security from top to bottom. This was no longer 1966, when sleepy out-of-the-way museums were rarely bothered by crooks, perhaps out of some residue of civic respect. In the 15 ensuing years, museums large and small had been robbed throughout Europe and the United States. Major institutions like the Museum of Fine Arts in Boston and the Montreal Museum of Fine Arts had lost their Rembrandts. Art-rich but endowment-poor house museums like the Taft in Cincinnati, Ohio, and the Russborough House in Ireland had lost Rembrandts and other Dutch and European works to gun-toting bandits. The value of Rembrandts and works by Old Masters had soared amid frenzied hype, collection building, and aggressive auctioneering. It was open season on fine art, and the museum world knew the dangers.

The gallery did spend close to $20,000 to bolster its security technology. It also bolted the painting to a wall, an acceptable step considering the portrait is painted on a sturdy oak panel. (A bolted canvas, on the other hand, might suffer terrible damage should a thief only partially succeed in tearing it down. Much thought is given to the manner in which paintings are attached to surfaces. Museums nowadays must anticipate scenarios in which criminals might yank or jerk a fragile work.) The Dulwich also rigged its paintings to a central alarm system.[22] But as often happens at museums, extra security approaches such as hiring overnight guards lost out to other priorities—more conservation, better publicity, facility repairs, and keeping the art as accessible as possible. Still, by 1981, Dulwich's old treasures were at last surrounded by a few new layers of protection.

The updated system was soon put to the test. In May 1983, thieves employed yet another strategy to take away "the Takeaway Rembrandt." Using a three-tier ladder under cover of night, they climbed nearly 60 feet to access the Dulwich Gallery's roof. From there, they forced open a skylight above the portrait's gallery and lowered themselves inside. Knowing the painting was now bolted to the wall, the thieves brought along a crowbar. The new security system worked as it was supposed to, signaling to local police that a painting had been tampered with. Law enforcement responded with good speed, arriving within three minutes of the alarm. Too late. *The Portrait of Jacob de Gheyn III* was gone again. The thieves had fled with alacrity, leaving only the ladder behind. The investigating officer informed Giles Waterfield, the director of the gallery, of the loss, laconically telling him, "We've had some bad news, sir. The Rembrandt is gone again."[23] Waterfield, who was also at the helm for theft number 3, said later that "Our chairman said in a jocular manner, 'Well, you've had another publicity coup.'"[24] Stiff upper lips all around. But this time, almost three years would pass before word of the Rembrandt surfaced. And *Jacob de Gheyn III* made the *Guinness Book of World Records* as the most frequently stolen painting in history.

It was not until 1986 that the Dulwich Gallery was notified that a fresh hunt for *Jacob de Gheyn* was under way. Investigators from the No. 5 Regional Crime Squad in Reading, in southeast England, had received a tip and were flying to Dusseldorf, West Germany, in pursuit of the portrait. Within hours, the detectives, accompanied by German police, found the painting at a railway station located within a British army garrison in Munster. There it sat, wrapped in paper and placed inside a series of three boxes, ditched and waiting once again to be recovered, as it had been in 1966. After less than two days in Germany, British investigators returned to London with the painting. They performed forensic tests on the work and the wrapping, found nothing that led them to the thieves, then returned it to the gallery.[25] No arrests have ever been reported.

Burned four times and dubbed "the Dulwich dullards" by Fleet Street wags, the leadership at the Dulwich Picture Gallery was uncertain how to proceed. The museum determined that the painting was in good condition, but its notoriety made it an all-too-tempting trophy, not just to criminals but to glory-seekers and pranksters. Rather than put the hexed work back on display, administrators kept it in hiding, telling the public only that the original seventeenth-century Dutch frame was now missing.[26] Gallery director Waterfield was not enthused about the challenge of securing the painting against yet another potential heist. "The temptation is to lock the wretched thing away and put up a color photograph," he said.[27] The idea did not sit right, though, and within a few weeks, without fanfare, the painting was returned once again to its roost. "I don't think it will boost attendance," Waterfield said. "The people who want to see it already have."[28] And perhaps those who want to steal it already have as well.

Valued today at more than $10 million, *Jacob de Gheyn III* has remained unmolested for a quarter century. But the legend of the Takeaway Rembrandt could yet prompt some new conniver to aim for the record books. It was no doubt a cutting moment for the Dulwich when one notorious criminal boasted in the media, "I could put on a wig and false mustache, walk into the gallery tomorrow and steal the painting...without any problem."[29] That man was Michael Hall, the original purloiner of *Jacob de Gheyn III*. For now, one can still visit Dulwich and see the young, wide-eyed, optimistic Jacob, immortalized friend to Rembrandt, and hope for the best.

CHAPTER FOUR

Snafu in Cincinnati: 1973

PREFACE

While a Rembrandt theft is serious business, sometimes the crime provides as much comedy as tragedy. Time and again, we see break-ins in which thieves initially labeled as "sophisticated professionals" turn out to be bungling amateurs. One little-known heist stands out for its farcical qualities: the overnight armed robbery of two Rembrandts from the Taft Museum in Cincinnati, Ohio, in 1973. Among its slapstick elements: thieves who broke in successfully, only to bypass the museum's two multimillion-dollar Rembrandts and snare a pair of far lesser value; a stolen masterwork handed back to its owners during a live TV news broadcast; and $100,000 in ransom left in an ice machine outside a busy tavern full of Christmas revelers. Our account includes the only interview conducted with the man who planned and executed the heist, Carl E. Horsley.

THE CRIME

In his four years as a night watchman at the modest-sized Taft Museum, 49-year-old Gene Hebel had completed his rounds without incident hundreds of times.[1] The place was beyond sleepy, and guards had never been expected to carry arms. The job was monotonous. After making some rounds on the inside, Hebel was expected to circle the fenced-in area just outside the museum, stopping at various call boxes to insert a heavy-duty key. Doing so left a record indicating that he had made the required patrols at the proper times during his overnight shift. Assigning a guard to check the perimeter of a museum after it is closed may seem like sound security. In fact, it is just the opposite. A guard should never leave his building and become vulnerable to criminals lurking outside. The contents of the building are what matter, not the surrounding shrubs and lawn ornaments. Today, there are two cardinal rules governing museum security guards: Do not go outside if you hear a disturbance, but summon help instead. And under no circumstances let anyone come inside who does not belong in the building.

On the morning of Tuesday, December 18, 1973, Hebel stopped at one of his exterior call boxes at 1:57 A.M. He turned his key, stepped back, and was halted in his tracks by two masked men. One, "the big guy," as Hebel called him, "pointed a gun at my chest, and he appeared to be in charge."

The intruder told Hebel, "Keep quiet and you won't get hurt." The watchman noticed that he sounded young, but he took the threat seriously. "If I'd have made the wrong move at any time, I would have been shot," he told police. "They as much as told me so several times when they warned me that if I didn't make any noise I wouldn't be harmed." Hebel obeyed the robbers as they force-marched him back to the museum's north entrance. Though the thieves appeared to Hebel to be "very nervous and excited," they had a decent plan. They forced the turnkey to let them into the museum and led him directly to the Main Gallery, one flight up in the two-story building. They sat Hebel in a chair, took out a large roll of heavy-duty tape, and bound his arms and legs to his seat. Within two minutes, the Taft's sole guard was out of commission, and the museum and its riches were the dominion of two armed criminals.

Despite all the gold and jewelry for the taking, the thieves went straight to the Taft's Malta Gray Room. There they grabbed two Rembrandts—*Portrait of an Elderly Woman* (1642) and *Man Leaning on a Sill* (c. 1636)—which hung side by side at the intersection of two walls. The paintings were wrenched from their mountings, leaving four ragged, parallel screw holes. By Hebel's estimation, the pair spent 15 minutes in the museum, most of it loosening the Rembrandts. They took nothing else before fleeing the Taft mansion and its grounds, unseen by witnesses on the outside. To the great good fortune of the museum, the thieves had blown their opportunity. They had left behind two Rembrandts of astronomical value, portraits that were regarded among his finest work, and instead stolen one painting appraised at $250,000 (*Man Leaning*) and another at $80,000 (*Elderly Woman*).

Within a half-hour of being subdued, Hebel was able to tear himself free from the tape and contact his supervisor, Morgan Warner, and the Cincinnati police. As night became day, police and FBI agents descended on the scene and combed the museum and its grounds for clues. They canvassed the neighborhood for witnesses and used a vacuum to collect bits of evidence for analysis by technicians at the Ohio Forensic Institute. They formed a task force and asked INTERPOL, which disseminates global information about stolen art, to issue an international alert. The city's afternoon newspapers reported the robbery on their front pages. Wire services issued multiple bulletins. And on the NBC evening news that night, John Chancellor devoted 30 seconds to reporting the crime to a national audience numbering in the millions.

Hebel, who had started his shift Monday evening, was taken in for questioning, which did not end until Tuesday afternoon. All he could offer was that the thieves had "young voices," wore masks and gloves, and seemed "agitated." He described the robbers as white men, one about 6 feet tall and 170 pounds ("the big guy"), the other about 5-foot-8 and 155 pounds ("the little guy"). He added that they were "quick-moving and acted as though they wanted to get out of there as fast as possible."

Hebel agreed to a polygraph exam, which he passed. While the official story to the press was that the 11 hours of questioning were necessary to plumb Hebel's memories, the prospect of his complicity was naturally on the minds of investigators. Today, the FBI estimates that at least 80 percent of art theft is perpetrated with the aid of an insider—a thorough investigation of Hebel was warranted. However, he was soon dismissed as a suspect and allowed to go home. Police could not even say how the thieves had gotten onto the museum's grounds—they speculated that they scaled the wrought-iron perimeter fence, but there was no helpful trail of footprints. Once again, there were no video cameras scanning the exterior. The only small clue police announced was a claim by a witness that a white male wearing a dark overcoat and driving a late-model tan Chevrolet was in the vicinity at the time of the crime.

Despite reasonable conjecture that the paintings had been stolen for ransom—another case of art-napping to extort a reward or insurance money—no ransom calls were immediately forthcoming. While small-time art theft is common enough from private homes, auction houses, and galleries, a theft on the Taft's scale was not something municipal investigators routinely see. The chief of the city's burglary squad called it "a professional job," and in a sense it was. The museum's security was poorly thought-out, allowing two nervous 20-year-olds to outwit it. But they carried out the job without bloodshed or arrest, a sign of skill, and made off with two Rembrandts, a sign of preparation. Museum chairman John W. Warrington offered the most astute remark in the hours after the heist. While acknowledging that the robbery was deftly executed, he said the stolen works were "not salable in the Western world" due to their renown.

The greater Cincinnati area had suffered art theft in prior years, but nothing of such magnitude. Six paintings by Ohio artist Frank Duveneck, a turn-of-the-century American realist, were stolen at the end of 1970 from the Carnegie Library in Covington, Kentucky, a town just over the border. The thieves had entered through a second-floor window during New Year's weekend. By January 3, 1971, according to newspaper accounts, the police had received a tip that "the paintings were stacked next to a garbage can." All were recovered, two of them with slight damage. Another oil painting by Duveneck, *Portrait of Joseph Duveneck* (his father), was stolen from the Mary Ann Mongan Kenton County Public Library in Covington that same year. The small work, 9 inches by 7⅜ inches, was hanging in the children's room of the library and taken from a frame during business hours. It was never recovered.

The chief of the Cincinnati Police Department, Carl Goodin, called the Taft theft "the largest armed robbery, to my knowledge, in Queen City history." He said his task force was weighing three possibilities:

- the thieves would try to extort money from the Taft or its insurer in exchange for the art (this is one of the best outcomes a museum can hope for);
- they would use an international fence to move the goods overseas (a very hard trick to pull off and a scary scenario, because art spirited abroad is notoriously hard to recover);
- the art would be sold to a sinister private collector (a scenario that has never been proven to have come to pass in the past century).

But as bad as the loss was, the Taft Museum was extremely lucky that night. The museum had been heavily promoting the presence of the two major Rembrandts on its walls, one on loan from New York, in an exhibition called "Dutch Couples." The hype had not failed to mention their desirability and eight-figure price tags. Now, just three days into the show, thieves had had their run of the premises yet missed those invaluable targets. The morning of the robbery, the museum was able to open just an hour late to accommodate the lines of visitors eager to see what the criminals had left behind.

THE ARTWORK

The Taft exhibit was designed to celebrate a style of seventeenth-century painting at which Rembrandt excelled. In the Holland of his

day, well-to-do husbands and wives began paying to have their portraits painted and hung near each other above a display cabinet in their
sitting rooms. These "pendants" were kept together by the couples, and
their descendants, as heirlooms. But over time many wound up in the
hands of disparate collectors, seemingly separated forever. Only rarely
were the divided portraits reunited, in part because their owners are
wary of lending them out, but also because experts lacked the technology to confidently match up former pairings. Microanalysis and digital
radiography make pair matching far easier today.

     No one had a problem separating Rembrandt's pair portraits dur-
ing the eighteenth and nineteenth centuries, when his reputation was
somewhat in eclipse. But that has radically changed. Nowadays, much
fanfare greets a "reuniting" of paired Rembrandts. The Rembrandt
House (Rembrandthuis) Museum in Amsterdam strove assiduously to
arrange a pairs reunion to add luster to celebrations in 2006 surrounding the 400th anniversary of Rembrandt's birth. In 1641, the master
had painted individual portraits of his married neighbors Nicolaes van
Bambeeck and Agatha Bas. Those portraits hung together until the
early 1800s, when their divided sale led to a separation that lasted some
187 years. Agatha's portrait was sold in 1819 to the British royal family
and hangs at Buckingham Palace in London. Nicolaes's was acquired
by Belgium's Musées Royaux des Beaux-Arts in 1841 and has hung
in Brussels since then. The two were reunited for the birthday quad-
ricentennial in Amsterdam in 2006 after their owners consented to a
short loan. "It's thrilling to know the couple is together again," Femke
Haijtema, spokeswoman for the Rembrandt House, said at the time.
She noted that the cost of insuring and shipping the traveling treasures
"was quite high but worth it."

     In 1972, the curator of European paintings at the Metropolitan
Museum of Art in Manhattan, John Walsh, visited the Taft Collection,
paying particular attention to its Dutch works. As he studied one of
the museum's finest paintings, Rembrandt's *Portrait of a Man Rising
from His Chair* (1633), he had a thrilling moment of his own. He realized that it was the companion piece to one of his own museum's finer

Rembrandts, *Portrait of a Young Woman with a Fan* (1633). The paintings were a match in size (about 4 feet by 3¼ feet), date, composition, and execution. Subsequent microscopic examination of the thread density and weave of the respective canvases indicated they were cut from the same bolt of linen.

Walsh set about reuniting that Dutch couple in a two-part exhibition, first in New York and then in Cincinnati. The Met already held a good number of seventeenth-century Dutch husband-and-wife "pair paintings" by various artists, so Walsh organized a full-on show of such works. He arranged to borrow the Taft's *Man Rising* portrait and had it shipped from the Queen City to the Big Apple.

Walsh's interest went beyond the sentimental. He wanted to show museum goers how married couples were perceived among the prospering Dutch of the 1600s, a people who venerated marriage yet held to rigid chauvinist notions of male and female comportment. In the case of these separated portraits, the husband is shown rising energetically, a businessman on the go, his left hand gallantly outstretched toward his spouse. She is seen demurely seated, in keeping with the passive household role women were expected to play. Yet with his usual independent flair, Rembrandt sought to tweak the convention. The wife's face glows with good humor and animation, and her body has a slight twist, implying action. She is no household prop. The couple is quite well-to-do, enveloped in black satin and intricate lace, the woman holding an ostrich-feather fan, the man adorned with rosettes and ornamental golden needle pegs. The Dutch were a great European force at the time, purchasers of Manhattan Island, explorers of the Hudson River and the South Pacific, unsurpassed hydraulic engineers, traders with East India and Asia, and bankers to the world. Money was gushing into Holland, filling its seaside warehouses with teas, cheeses, spices, textiles, ceramics, furniture, grains, and wine. About 670,000 people lived in the Netherlands in 1620, compared with 4.5 million in England. Yet Holland was an economic superpower and its biggest city, Amsterdam, a focal point of Western civilization. Sometimes the heady prosperity launched maddening fads and fevers. In the 1630s, the

Dutch unleashed "Tulip Mania" across the European continent, creating an inflated market for the land's signature flowers. It was a speculative bubble that intrigues economists to this day. The couple in the paintings would have paid Rembrandt perhaps 800 florins ($80,000 by today's standards) for the two works. By comparison, the cost of a single top-of-the-line tulip bulb, the Viceroy, could reach 3,000 florins. As with the emu, beanie baby, and dot-com bubbles of recent vintage (but not the Rembrandt bubble), the tulip bubble burst as the market grew saturated and buyers wised up. One might argue that the Wall Street of today, which is built on land first inhabited by the Dutch, is financially rooted in earth fertilized by Tulip Mania.

Experts agree on the craftsmanship and historic value of these two particular Rembrandt pendants. The identities of the couple are lost, and the portrait of the wife is also called *Portrait of a Woman in an Armchair*. Rembrandt's detail work on the painting is close to adoring. The subject's jeweled left hand rests on a table that stands beside her chair. She wears a double-layered lace collar and gigantic scalloped lace cuffs. Her hair is brown, with hints of amber, and decorated with pearls. The Rembrandt Research Project examined the painting in 1969 and found that "there can be no doubt about the attribution of the painting," adding that it matches with "what one finds in portraits from his early Amsterdam years."[2] The only dubious aspect of the painting is the signature. While the date, 1633, is considered accurate, the spelling of the artist's name ("Rembrand") and the "somewhat unsure handwriting" of the signature are considered evidence that it was added later.[3]

Man Rising, also reliably dated 1633, is described as the young woman's "excitable husband."[4] He wears a brash mustache and a broad-brimmed black hat, and his eyes are wide with purpose. Again Rembrandt engrosses himself in the detail work, painting the man's immense collar as if the artist were a lace maker himself. Its signature is considered original, reading, "Rembrandt 1633." While it is unclear when the portraits first parted ways, *Man Rising* came to America via Paris, having been purchased by a French count in the 1850s. In a nineteenth-century monograph, the painting is described as "one of the most important and most attractive portraits painted by Rembrandt at his earlier time in Amsterdam."[5] Both works were completed during the happy year when the artist married his beloved Saskia van Uylenburgh when she was 21 and he was 27. His fame was spreading across Europe, and his circle of colleagues and acolytes was enjoying grand attention and good commissions from many newly wealthy admirers.

When *Man Rising* arrived at the Taft House in 1909, it was met with high praise. In a special cable to the *New York Times* from London, it was announced that "Charles P. Taft, brother of President Taft, will shortly be able to add to the collection of pictures he has in Cincinnati one of the historic Rembrandts of the world."[6] Referring to *Man Rising* as "one of the most famous of all known Rembrandts," the article presciently warns that the president's brother "owes it to his country to put such additions to the artistic wealth of America beyond the danger of loss by fire, and that he should erect a special structure in which to preserve such rare works."[7]

In 1927, Charles Taft bequeathed his 690-item collection and his historic home—in which his half-brother, William Howard Taft, had accepted the 1908 Republican nomination for president—to the people of Cincinnati. In 1932, after extensive remodeling and updating, the house was reopened as the Taft Museum of Art.[8] In 1932, 1973, and still today, the Taft has counted among the finest small art museums in America. A National Historic Landmark, originally built in 1820, it houses European and American masters, Chinese porcelains, European decorative arts, and a renowned Gothic ivory sculpture. Familiar names include Hals, Goya, Gainsborough, Reynolds, Turner, Ingres, Whistler, and Sargent. And, of course, Rembrandt. And not only did the Taft feature the great *Man Rising*, it also displayed two smaller Rembrandts, *Portrait of an Elderly Woman* and *Man Leaning on a Sill*.

Portrait of an Elderly Woman was painted in 1642, the year Rembrandt's beloved and oft-painted wife, Saskia, died. She was 29, and their son, Titus, was only 9 months old. Rembrandt was forced to employ a wet nurse, Geertje Dircx, a woman who would bedevil the artist during his financially miserable later years. No one knows who served as the model for *Elderly Woman*, although some scholars believe Rembrandt often had his own exhausted and withered mother, Neeltgen Willemsdochter van Zuytbrouck, in mind when he painted and sketched old women. She died in 1640, at age 73, having given birth to at least 12 children, nine of whom made it to adulthood.

But Rembrandt was a also great documenter of everyday humanity, and it is just as likely the woman was someone who intrigued him, much as beggars and barrel-makers and slaughterhouse workers caught his artist's eye. The subject is wearing gold earrings that match the two gold clasps on her black, fur-trimmed cloak. The bust-length rendering is nearly life-sized, depicted against a neutral background. The woman wears a dark brown dress and a hood with a white kerchief. Several drawings of the bedridden Saskia from the same period show her wearing a similar headdress.

When exhibited in London in 1903, the painting received good reviews from connoisseurs. Rembrandt expert Cornelis Hofstede de Groot, in his *Catalogue Raisonné* of Rembrandt's works, wrote in 1916 that the "melancholy mood" of *Portrait of an Elderly Woman* reflects the grief the artist felt at the loss of his dear wife. He added, "One cannot help feeling also that this canvas was painted in the seclusion of the home."[9]

The other Rembrandt owned by the Taft was even more enigmatic. *Man Leaning on a Sill* (as it was known at the time of the heist) has also been dubbed *Rembrandt Leaning on a Sill*. But scholars, including those with the Rembrandt Research Project (RRP), have concluded in recent years that the painting is likely not a Rembrandt at all. Walter Liedtke, curator of European paintings at the Metropolitan Museum of Art, said, "The palette alone takes one, so to speak, to the other side of De Gelder (d. 1727) from Rembrandt, while the fluid technique, like this very type of fancy portrait, seems directly of the eighteenth century, and anticipatory of Fragonard's *Portraits de Fantaisie*."[10] (Consider that an emphatic "no.") And in 1986, the RRP made its own painstaking and convincing case against *Man Leaning on a Sill* as being authentic. But in 1973, at the Taft Museum in Cincinnati, it was considered the more significant of these two lesser Rembrandts, which shared space with *Man Rising* in the small institution's great collection.

The "pairs" exhibition organized by John Walsh of the Metropolitan Museum of Art ran there from January to March 1973. *Man Rising,* a temporary guest from Ohio, was centrally featured alongside his bride, *Woman with a Fan.* Walsh expressed worry that his show, titled "Dutch Couples: Pair Portraits by Rembrandt and His Contemporaries," might be a bust. But with the added appeal of the reunified couple, which generated a touch of Valentine's Day media hype, it drew between 60,000 and 80,000 visitors, a good turnout for such a program.

That show was followed by a sister exhibition later that year in Cincinnati. Titled "Dutch Couples: Rembrandt and His Contemporaries," it was set to run from December 15, 1973 through March 3, 1974, allowing Ohioans to view the Met's visiting *Woman with a Fan* and celebrate the romantic reuniting of parted lovers. Quite naturally, word of the exhibition was big cultural news in Cincinnati, and one 29-year-old man took note. Although the historical significance of the Dutch couple was likely lost on him, Donald Lee Johnson was entranced by the multimillion-dollar prices attributed to the works. Johnson, later described by local cops as a "small-time fence," dreamed up a big-time idea. He contacted a young crook he knew by the name of Carl E. Horsley and floated the notion of a heist. Horsley was tepid at first. At 21 he was a veteran armed robber, taking down gas stations and drug stores and sometimes grabbing jewelry from suburban homes. He teamed up with two other young felons, Henry C. Dawn and Raymond E. McDonough, and Johnson handled the hot merchandise. The gang had no experience with art. But the more he thought about it, the more Horsley liked the idea of stepping up in criminal class. "Even though I led the life that I led, I could appreciate art and I certainly knew who Rembrandt was. I decided to case it out," he recalls. "I went to the museum to look over the target paintings."[11]

THE "MASTERMIND"

Carl Earnest Horsley, by his own admission, was a delinquent and a drug addict by the age of 18. He was not shy about pointing a gun in a man's face and demanding money. "Any good pistol would do," he says. But when it came to plotting a museum robbery, he decided he would have to be more methodical. In early December 1973, he started spying on the Taft by night, hiding in the cold along a poorly paved back alley and timing the movements of the museum's lone security guard, Gene Hebel. By December 18, he felt ready. He gathered up Dawn and McDonough and set the robbery in motion.

The three men pulled up outside the Taft in a dark Monte Carlo sedan and parked near a northbound on-ramp to Interstate 75. With McDonough minding the getaway vehicle, Horsley and Dawn donned "your usual burglary get-up, ski masks and gloves," and hopped the fence near the spot where Gene Hebel made his 2:00 A.M. rounds.

"We stepped up just after he hit the clock," Horsley recalls. "We spun him around and I put the gun [a .22 revolver] up beneath his chin to his neck. We told him 'disarm the alarm or you will die.' We walked him back into the museum. We put him in a chair and I told him, 'If you make any sounds you won't see Christmas.' We duct-taped him to the chair.

"We could have taken anything—I mean anything—gold and watches and all sorts of valuable stuff. Henry wanted to grab some, but I said, 'No, we get what we came for. Don't get greedy. Greed always kills.' So we went to get the paintings, went back out the door and over the fence, and tossed them in the trunk. And we drove off." It was not until days later that Horsley realized the two Rembrandts in his trunk were a far lesser target than the two he left up on the museum's walls. "I took the ones I saw," he says.

The men arrived at a safe house an hour later and tuned in to a transistor radio. Sometime after 8 A.M. they heard the first news reports. "I hate to brag," Horsley says, "but when the man said, 'This was obviously done by professionals'—well, you take a certain pride in your work, and that was gratifying, to tell you the truth."

Horsley called his fence, Johnson, and told him to turn on the news. Johnson was flabbergasted, Horsley says. He started hemming and hawing about being able to sell the paintings.

"Turns out he was an idiot," Horsley recalls. "He had no idea what to do with them. He told us to drive here and drive there, up and down the highway, and he'd set up a buyer. It was all bull."

With Horsley and his confederates growing increasingly furious, a desperate Johnson phoned a local real estate agent and self-promoter named James L. Hough. A full day had passed since the heist was discovered.

Hough was 30, owned a Cincinnati bar called the Speak-Easy Nightclub, and was a smooth operator always looking for a fresh business angle. Retired cops and others involved in the Taft case describe him as a "flamboyant" and "obnoxious" con artist who craved public attention.

"He was known for driving around his neighborhood with a pet lion in his convertible," said retired Cincinnati police lieutenant Thomas Oberschmidt, who was deeply involved in the investigation. "He had this know-it-all attitude. He thought he was smarter than he actually was."

Hough immediately told Johnson he'd try to act as an intermediary between the still-anonymous thieves and the museum. Hough went right to the top, choosing to contact the chairman of the Taft's board of trustees, veteran attorney John W. Warrington.

Warrington was a pale and unpretentious man with very little hair and a beaklike nose who favored tweed suits and plaid ties. Unflappable and universally respected, he was home eating supper after two tumultuous and gloomy days at his plundered museum when Hough phoned him around 6 P.M.

"He did not say who he was," Warrington recalled. "He told me he thought he had some leads [on the paintings] and asked me to meet him."[12]

Within an hour, Warrington was at the Tri-County Shopping Center in Cincinnati, trying to look conspicuous enough that Hough could spot him. The three thieves, clueless as to Hough's dealings, were still driving up and down the Ohio-Indiana border with the stolen art banging around in the trunk of their car.[13]

A cautious Hough at last stepped up to Warrington, who had been driven to the location by his 19-year-old son, George. Hough, who towered over the pair, led the elder Warrington to a coffee shop, where they discussed a deal. Hough soon sensed that undercover police were nearby—which was true, because Warrington's worried wife had alerted the authorities to the parley. His son recalled that "the FBI showed up, and I spotted them by their earplugs, so I told them where my dad was meeting." Warrington said Hough asked for a "finder's fee" for playing the go-between role and wanted formal leave to act "as our agent in negotiating the return." Warrington tentatively agreed. Hough would later claim, to no avail, that it was Warrington who first mentioned the fee. "We finished our coffee, which he kindly bought, and I went home to meet with the FBI," Warrington recalled.

By the next morning, Warrington had persuaded museum trustees to authorize a ransom of $100,000. Then Hough phoned to say that he had contacted the thieves and their price would be $200,000. But Warrington held firm—the trustees would not consent to any more money—and insisted on evidence that Hough's associates in fact had the art in hand. Phone calls flew back and forth all morning, until finally Hough told Warrington that one of the paintings, *Elderly Woman*, which Hough mistakenly believed was less valuable, would be returned as proof and a sign of good faith.

Horsley says the decision to return *Elderly Woman* rather than *Man Leaning on Sill* was simple: He figured the larger painting was more valuable than the smaller one, and *Man* was larger in size.

Accompanied by police, Warrington met Hough at a bar near the Indiana border and received directions to the drop point, an abandoned tan Plymouth sedan in a rural part of Ohio. But when Warrington and the officer arrived, there was no painting, just the slight imprint of a frame in some shallow snow. They phoned Hough, who told them the thieves had called to say they'd gotten spooked when they did not see Hough alone in the vehicle and took off with the art.

Warrington rejoined Hough at the bar, but after another hour or so of talking and waiting to hear back from the crooks, Warrington told him, "I've had it, and I'm going home." The lawyer met his wife at a neighbor's house and had a cocktail as night settled across Cincinnati.

Hough wasn't done, however. Shortly after Warrington left, the thieves directed Hough to a barn in Springdale, Ohio, about 25 miles outside Cincinnati. There, he said, he found *Elderly Woman* waiting for him and brought it to the nearby Regis Cocktail Lounge. Word of the Warrington negotiations had yet to leak out to the media, and Hough wanted to lay down a public marker to avert any sting by police. Before calling Warrington, he telephoned a fellow everyone in Cincy knew and trusted—a man named Al Schottelkotte.

THE ANCHORMAN

By 1973, Schottelkotte was a television legend in Cincinnati. A reporter and anchorman with WCPO whose career extended from 1959 to 1986, Schottelkotte had become the dominant news figure across the state, a sort of Ohio version of Walter Cronkite. While he was the anchor, his CBS affiliate led the news ratings morning, noon, and night for 22 straight years. But he wasn't just a pretty face. His exploits included holding down the cough button on his microphone just long enough to punch out a crazed studio intruder while narrating a live video presentation. Now this no-nonsense reporter of Dutch ancestry was called in to handle another bizarre situation: the recovery of a stolen Rembrandt.

With Schottelkotte on the phone, Hough spared no bravado. He urged the newsman to come to the lounge and collect something that all Ohio was on the lookout for: a pilfered masterwork. He also dropped Warrington's name, so the skeptical Schottelkotte called the museum official to ask whether a blustering oddball named Hough could really have the stolen art. "He might," Warrington told the newsman. Schottelkotte and a cameraman drove to the Regis, a roadside bar decked out in Christmas lights. There, leaning against a back wall near where Hough was seated, beneath a white and pink floral quilt, was Rembrandt's 340-year-old portrait.

With cameras filming every moment, Schottelkotte assessed the painting on his knees in the back of the bar while tipsy patrons drawn by the TV lights hovered around, drinks in hand.

The footage shows Schottelkotte and Hough lugging the Rembrandt out of the lounge like a couple of college students trying to move a bookcase. The quilt barely covered the top of the painting, and Hough, who did most of the manhandling, had a lit cigarette in his mouth the entire time. The men shoved the painting into the back seat of Schottelkotte's two-toned Buick coupe and made off for the TV studio.

"I doubt if my car will ever carry a more distinguished bit of freight," Schottelkotte would tell his viewers.

Schottelkotte knew this would be a good story. He raced Hough and the painting back to WCPO and summoned Warrington to its midtown studios. Warrington shot out of his house, instructing his wife to call the police. When the 11 o'clock news came on that night, the scene was unscripted, awkward, and surreal. As a viewership of millions in Ohio, Kentucky, and Indiana looked on from their bedrooms and living rooms, Schottelkotte stood on a blue soundstage before a gray backdrop. Three cameras mounted on dollies recorded his every word and expression, while a fourth camera was deployed behind the first three to document the entire spectacle for posterity. Gazing at the TV audience with his familiar, reassuring face, Schottelkotte began his live broadcast: "I've been in news work for 30 years now, have had some rather strange and unexpected things happen, but possibly the most unexpected of all took place tonight."

Schottelkotte turned, and the camera image shifted. Onstage to his right were two men. One was a short, gaunt, sleep-deprived attorney in a tweed suit, his hands holding on to an antique painting balanced on the floor just in front of him. The other was an extremely tall, bearded nightclub owner wearing a garish disco shirt. Schottelkotte bent low toward the ornately framed painting, which showed an old woman in a hooded cloak, and pointed to a small gold-embossed panel affixed near the frame's bottom.

"You have all heard the story by now of the missing Rembrandt," he said. "As you will see here, one of those paintings has now been recovered. It has been identified by its plaque as *Portrait of an Elderly Woman*, Rembrandt." The camera now closed in on Schottelkotte as he touched the lettering, then stood up. The old woman's wrinkled face momentarily filled the television screen.

"We are doing this to authenticate the fact that the painting is now in the hands of Mr. John Warrington, who is chairman of the Taft Museum," the anchorman said as the camera closed in on the lawyer's earnest face. He then added: "The painting has been turned over to Mr. Warrington by Mr. James Hough, a real estate broker, who recovered the painting in a barn...earlier tonight." The camera now tightened in on Hough, whose sandy-blond hair was matted to his forehead. Hough must have understood that by returning the stolen art, he was casting suspicion on himself as a possible burglar—or even the organizer of the theft. Alert to the tricky position he was in, with policemen eyeballing him from the studio's wings, Hough spoke up: "I would like to say one thing and make it out in the open. I was asked by Mr. Warrington to assist in the possible recovery of this thing. That's why we want to make sure that this is the painting."

Warrington then delivered the lawyerly phrase all had been waiting for, including the viewers responsible for committing the robbery: "To the best of my knowledge, this is the true Rembrandt that was taken from the Taft Museum," he said. Schottelkotte added, "That is all we are going to be able to say at this point. Stay tuned." The program broke off and went to a coffee commercial. For the first time in art-theft history, the news media had been used as an intermediary in the recovery of a stolen masterpiece.

Much would happen in the next two days as the second missing painting, *Man Leaning on a Sill,* was ransomed back. But for now, viewers were left to ponder this strange new use of television as a platform for resolving a case of art-napping.

Warrington took custody of the Rembrandt and police drove it back to the Taft. By now it was not even covered by the quilt. Barely three days had passed since Gene Hebel had been hogtied, and *Portrait of an Elderly Woman* was home. As is the case in many art thefts, the frame, which was painted in gold leaf, was damaged by all the sloppy jostling and deemed irreparable. But despite the rough handling, the painting was unharmed save for some scratches described by conservators as "minor." On closer inspection, the "scratches" turned out to be bird droppings.

Asked to comment on the strange televised transaction, the imperturbable Warrington said, "Well, I was very happy to have one back."

Schottelkotte's fuller report on the retrieval of the painting did not air at the time of the live authentication because he had not had time to edit it. It ran for ten minutes the next evening at 6 P.M. By then, Hough had become a magnet for news reporters. They swarmed his small office throughout the day, peppering him with questions. Hough, smoking heavily, wearing red-checked bell-bottom pants and high-heeled boots, and flicking ashes into a Colt .45 ashtray, did his best to feed them good quotes.

Q. Have the thieves indicated to you what they would do if they do not receive the ransom?
A. They indicated to me that they were going to burn 'em.
Q. Can you shed any more light on how you came across these two people?
A. I beat enough bushes.... Hey, I know that I have got to be suspect No. 1, okay, but I also know I'm clean. I don't think I'm a damned fool. I've got a good business.

CINCINNATI INSANITY

For the cops on the case, watching Hough and Schottelkotte absorb the credit for the recovery of the painting was almost too much to bear. A three-ring circus was in full swing, even as negotiations turned to the second Rembrandt and the ransom demand. Horsley and company were still insisting that they receive $200,000 in unmarked bills for the second painting, and they wanted the money delivered by 2 P.M. the next day. Warrington fielded numerous pressure-packed calls from Hough that day, but stayed glued to his $100,000 payment offer. The thieves balked and began issuing ultimatums. Hough warned Warrington the bandits had threatened to burn *Man Leaning on a Sill* if their $200,000 demand was not met. (According to Horsley, "When the news broke about the burning threat, my dad was with my brother, and my dad looked at him and said, 'I'll bet you your brother has something to do with this.'") Warrington held firm, explaining that the museum's endowment could spare no more. By nightfall, the crooks had lowered their demand to $160,000. Still no deal, said Warrington. Back and forth went the calls, until at last the thieves accepted the $100,000 offer and promised not to burn the painting. Hough again grabbed the limelight, announcing to circling reporters and cameramen: "We have reached an agreement. I am trying to get the money right now." Warrington, who was told the criminals wanted the bills in unserialized tens and twenties, spent part of the next morning pulling together the ungainly ransom. "I had to have it ready," he later said. "I stored it where I could get to it quickly."

The competitive local media took to harrying the police, museum officials, and the smooth-talking Hough. After Schottelkotte's coup, the rest of the press wanted in on the recovery game. Cops had to stay off their radios as much as possible to avoid being overheard. "The press were very aggressive in the reporting of this crime," Lieutenant Oberschmidt recalled. "It was hard to deal with them, but teaming with the FBI, we used their radios, which the press could not monitor. This helped to some degree."

Despite the media stakeout, Warrington and Hough slipped off to a private location and bargained all evening about how to swap the painting for the money. Warrington had not believed Hough when the go-between claimed the thieves were threatening to kill him. But when Warrington got on the phone with them, "my life was threatened as well," he said.

Warrington backed away from his original insistence on a simultaneous exchange. "I started feeling somewhat nervous. I could see how you might get in some sort of gunfire situation with my plan." By evening, the stressed-out thieves again seemed ready to do something drastic, so Warrington decided to allow Hough to see and count the ransom money as a show of good faith.

By now Warrington and Hough had formed a quixotic bond. As Warrington's son George put it, "My father found him sort of fascinating since he was from a segment of society my father never dealt with." When Hough proposed that they drop the money at an appointed site, allow the thieves to collect it and count it, and then await instructions on where to pick up the painting, Warrington took a leap of faith. He knew Hough was on the hook if the plan went awry, so he tucked the cash into a "favorite black briefcase" and told Hough to proceed. The drop-off plan was in keeping with the harebrained nature of the extortion scheme. Hough and Warrington went to the city's Lorelei Tavern and, as instructed, placed the briefcase in an ice machine on the front porch. They were supposed to cover the letter "E" in "ICE" on the machine with masking tape as a signal that the money was there. But they had no tape and the machine was damp with condensation. They did their best to cover the "E" with sticky paper and left, only to get an angry call from the thieves minutes later, from the tavern payphone. They barked that there was no tape on the "E."

Hough told them to look inside the machine, and they finally located the satchel of cash. It was now 11:30 P.M., and the thieves called back seeking 20 minutes to count the take.

"It was a tense waiting period," Warrington recalled. "I went through two packs of cigarettes. By 1 A.M., I came to the conclusion that the whole thing was a fraud, that I'd lost the ransom and the paintings, and I just wanted to go home."

At 1:05 by his watch, the phone rang again. The thieves gave Hough the location of the second painting and Warrington called it in to police. A squad was dispatched, and by 2 A.M. officers had retrieved *Man Leaning* from beneath the steps of a house in Fosters,

Ohio. Hough even boasted about honor among thieves, telling reporters in the aftermath of the recovery, "Just because a guy's a thief, that doesn't mean he doesn't have pride."

With his role now over, Warrington said, "I got a bottle of whiskey and we all had a few drinks." He even clinked glasses with Hough.

The cops took the painting directly to the Taft, where it was quickly authenticated. Just five days had passed, and both paintings were safely home. But the Taft Museum was out $100,000. Or so it would seem. In fact, lawmen had received several underworld tips about Carl Horsley during the week and had him under surveillance when he collected the ransom and left the artwork. By morning, police had him and his two associates, McDonough and Dawn, in custody and had recovered the money. It was all there, Oberschmidt said, "except for $24, which they had spent for food at a fast-food restaurant."

The stickup men wasted little time in pointing the finger of blame at the man who'd had the original bright idea, Donald Johnson. Johnson, in turn, implicated Hough.

At this point the real estate broker turned art negotiator grew nervous. He was aware that Johnson was starting to squawk. Nevertheless, three weeks after the theft, Hough went to Warrington's law office to collect his finder's fee, a check for $15,000.

"He asked my father for legal advice," George Warrington recalled. "He said, 'The police are all over me. If I take this money, does that put me in a worse position?' Dad said yes. Dad then said, 'Tell you what: Sign it over to the [Cincinnati] Fine Arts Fund, so that way you are essentially donating it.'"

Hough immediately did so.

It was too late. The police and prosecutors had it in for Hough, and Johnson told them Hough was the "mastermind" behind the ransom scheme. (He did not implicate Hough in the actual theft.) Johnson and the three thieves all cut deals with prosecutors. They would plead guilty to lesser charges in return for testimony against the glory-seeking intermediary. The gambit worked. While they all wound up behind bars, Hough was convicted of the most serious of the charges: extortion and grand larceny. In October 1974, he was sentenced to 3 to 20 years in prison.

Looking back after 38 years, the younger George Warrington said the whole robbery was "a comedy of errors." Not only were the paintings recovered unharmed in less than one week, but authorities also recovered $99,986 in ransom paid by the Taft Museum. Still, he is proud of how his late father handled the mess. "What my father most lamented was that they had thrown his briefcase in the river. He really liked that briefcase."

POSTSCRIPT

For James L. Hough, life after Rembrandt has had its share of curses. He battled again and again for a mistrial, asserting that the prosecution made him the fall guy for a crime concocted by his codefendants. He was paroled in 1978, having served much of his time in the honor dorm at the London, Ohio, penitentiary and having become president of the prison's Junior Chamber of Commerce chapter. But the legal system had drawn a target on Hough, and by April 1979 the 36-year-old was back in jail, accused of a parole violation. He was found to have played a role in real estate transactions involving historic buildings in Metamora, Indiana, something he had been barred from doing as a condition of his parole. He served another year, during which time he tried again to have his original sentence overturned and pronounced at one point that his case "was getting ready to blow sky high."

During this time, Hough had one stalwart fan: George Warrington. "I cannot understand how he got involved in this," Warrington wrote in a 1978 recollection of the episode penned for the Literary Club of Cincinnati. "He seemed far too intelligent to risk what he had at stake here in Cincinnati for an escapade such as this. Jim had made it! If I, having stolen the paintings, needed a negotiator, I could not think of a better person to choose."

After a few mildly successful years as the owner of a small business in Indiana, a roadside restaurant named Trappers Rendevous Hog Roast, Hough ran for sheriff of Franklin County, Indiana, in 1986. His campaign flyers were done up as wanted posters, featuring Hough in a brimmed hat and beard touting "Justice, Not Just-Us" and "Non-Harassment for Local Gentry." On the back of the flyer he "hung out all his dirty laundry," including being "a former convicted felon, 3 counts organized crime and 1 count parole violation" and having "a thorough understanding of the law from all sides!"

Norma Hooper, vice chairwoman of the Franklin County Republican Party at the time, was not a backer of her potential candidate. "It's making a farce of the political system," she said. "If he were elected, some legal procedure would need to be taken for his removal from office, especially impeachment."

Hough was not elected. But he did share one final similarity with Rembrandt: He filed for bankruptcy in the late 1980s.

In the years since the robbery, the Taft Museum has become a far different place. According to Lynne D. Ambrosini, its chief curator, The Taft Museum of Art went through a major renovation in 2001–2004 that included the installation of a state-of-the-art security system. "It would no longer be possible to carry out such a theft without immediate detection and police response," she said.

Carl Horsley's post-heist trajectory has also featured ups and downs, and today at age 59 he said he is happy to have turned his life around in time to start a real estate business and pay attention to his grandchildren and two cats.

Horsley said his three years in jail were not especially hard because he enjoyed a bit of status for pulling off the museum heist. "When I got there, I knew a lot of people already, and the stigma of being involved in that, well, they would call you 'Rembrandt' and things like that. It was a form of criminal prestige, I suppose—I didn't go around bragging about it. Hell, in prison I got a college education, and when I went legitimate, I was even asked to sit on arts committees."

The former Rembrandt bandit also had some moments to live down. He was out celebrating his prison release in Kentucky, he said, when he was arrested for shoplifting some toothpaste and candy bars. "They got wind of that bust back in Cincy and the press had a field day—'Rembrandt thief picked up for petty theft.' I was embarrassed by that—that's for sure."

He has even returned to the Taft Museum. "I went back to the museum, one time, and they had so much security up there it was kind of crazy. They had security everywhere—it was nothing like before we hit it. I guess we made a difference that way."

CHAPTER FIVE

Wolves at the Door: Heists from Homes

PREFACE

In the fall of 1638, the Dutch master Rembrandt van Rijn and his wife, Saskia van Uylenburgh, spotted a good-sized four-story house made of brick, stone, wood, and leaded glass at No. 4 Breestraat in a fashionable quarter of Amsterdam. Both the house and Rembrandt were about 32 years old; Saskia was 6 years younger. The couple liked what they saw and in early 1639 signed on to buy it for 13,000 guilders (about the cost of a town house today in an expensive neighborhood in a fashionable city), to be paid in installments.

Rembrandt was already well established—he had just been awarded a prestigious commission to paint *The Night Watch*—and he wanted a home grand and important enough to suit his reputation. He set up a studio on the top floor, where high windows let in the most daylight, and embarked on a two-decade spree of masterpieces. Assistants made his chalk-based paint and prepared his canvases. Housekeepers and servants handled the meals and the guests. Artists' paraphernalia lay scattered about, while strange weapons and giant seashells and stuffed animals sat on shelves around the walls, there to be used by Rembrandt and his pupils as models and props. A cabinet off to one side of the studio held the artist's large, expensive collection of costumes and curios from around the world.

Rembrandt carried on his art-dealing business in an elegant ground-floor salon with a marbled fireplace featuring Holland's classic blue-and-white Delft tiles. He received his clients with a glass of chilled wine from a well-stocked cooler. The walls were covered with dozens of paintings for sale, since Rembrandt sold his own works and those of his pupils and also dealt in paintings by other masters. Rembrandt had Flemish and Italian works in stock, but most of the sales items were by Dutchmen. Given that "Golden Age" Dutch families sought to cover their walls high and low with paintings, and might own 30 or 40 at a time, the art business was a solid avocation.

Rembrandt also used the house to print and vend his incredibly varied etchings, which featured biblical tales, scenes from daily life, and people, portraits, landscapes, nudes, foreigners, and workmen. His ground floor included a large etching and printing apparatus and his bedroom featured a sitting area and a heavy boxed-in oaken bed.

Although he earned good money, enjoyed great prestige, and owned fine belongings during his time on Breestraat, Rembrandt was unable or unwilling to pay down his large mortgage. By 1656, he was tumbling toward bankruptcy, and the house and its contents, including Roman busts, Japanese armor, furniture, and pots and kettles, were inventoried for his creditors. His personal effects and his collections of art and curiosities were sold off (Dutch newspaper ads announcing the cut-rate sales have been preserved), and the house was auctioned in 1658 for 11,000 guilders. Shamed and shunned, Rembrandt moved to a small rented house, where he lived until his death in 1669.

The Breestraat house was nearly demolished several times through the centuries. In 1906, the City of Amsterdam bought the dilapidated building and gave it to a foundation that did its best to conserve its older features while making the location a modern setting for a collection of prints and etchings by its most famous occupant. Today the *Rembrandthuis*, or Rembrandt House Museum, can also be rented out for weddings and banquets (which are held in an adjacent wing). Given the allure of Rembrandt and the imagination of thieves, it comes as little surprise that the Rembrandt House itself has been robbed through the years, making it a fitting symbol for the homes, apartments, sales galleries, modest museums, and other small properties so often struck by Rembrandt thieves.

On October 10, 1994, a burglar with a sledgehammer smashed a window at the house and stole a single painting, *Man With a Beard* (1647). The work had once been considered a Rembrandt, but is now attributed to an unidentified student of his. Its theft occasioned this inevitable headline in the *International Herald Tribune*: "Rembrandt Needed a Night Watchman."[1] *Beard* made its way back four years later after being seized from an Amsterdam lawyer who was reputed to be a shady intermediary for art recovery, having been involved in a van Gogh case as well. The lawyer was privately reprimanded, a fairly light penalty for such transgressions by Dutch historical standards. In Rembrandt's century, the judiciary was more ruthless when dealing with theft, housebreaking, and serving as a known fence. The penalties included amputation of a hand, nose, or ear, branding and scarring of the cheek, and even the gallows for repeat offenders.[2]

Sadly, many house and museum thefts that net burglars a Rembrandt composition fail to end with the gratifying recovery of the immortal work. In researching this book, we have come across a grim bit of previously unreported history. In 1938, the grand home of an English noble family in Kent was robbed of five masterpieces. As you will see, three of them, including a Rembrandt, met a terrible fate. Just as owning an expensive house proved a boon and a curse for Rembrandt, having one of his paintings in one's home or small museum can lead to both joy and tragedy for the collector.

THE FBI EXPANDS ITS ROLE

In 2004, prompted by the astonishing growth and complexity of art theft, the Federal Bureau of Investigation established its Art Crime Team. The squad, part of the Bureau's major theft unit, consists of 13 special agents nationwide who provide guidance and rapid deployment for field colleagues coping with complicated art thefts. Though theirs are not full-time assignments, members of the team do not wait long to become enmeshed in an art investigation in the United States. The Art Crime Team handles thefts of antiquities and collectibles as well as paintings, and has been front and center in newsy cases like the recoveries of Pearl Buck's original manuscript for *The Good Earth*, a copy of the Bill of Rights commissioned by George Washington in 1789, and an antique pistol that belonged to President Theodore Roosevelt. Members of the team have, of course, been instrumental in the recovery of numerous priceless paintings, by artists as varied as Rembrandt, Mark Rothko, and Norman Rockwell.

Robert K. Wittman, one of the heroes in the recovery of the Rembrandt *Self-Portrait* stolen in Stockholm in 2000 (see Chapter 7), was a driving force behind the creation of the unit. Geoffrey Kelly, the FBI's lead agent in the investigation into the world's biggest art heist, the 1990 theft from the Isabella Stewart Gardner Museum, is a key member of the team. Kelly has recovered seven stolen paintings missing for 28 years, including works by the Expressionist Chaim Soutine and the French modernist Maurice de Vlaminck. What might come as a surprise is that the Art Crime Team's national program is not run by a typical FBI agent, but managed from its headquarters by a non-agent employee.

Instead of practicing arrest skills along Hogan's Alley at Quantico, the FBI's legendary agent training ground, Dr. Bonnie Magness-Gardiner earned a doctorate in Near Eastern archeology at the University of Arizona, and worked for the Library of Congress and the State Department. Those experiences led directly to her role as program manager for the Art Crime Team. Her background as an academic and an expert in archeology and antiquities, as opposed to law enforcement, suits her role. The FBI traditionally relies on its cadre of experienced field agents to oversee so-called specialty programs, and when it comes to art crime, those agents generally do not need guidance handling criminal aspects of the investigation. But they do need someone to help them navigate the complexities of the art world.

Dr. Magness-Gardiner has helped bring basic information about art theft to the public's attention. In a 2010 interview, she spoke of the places most often eyed by art thieves: "Residences tend to be the target," she stated. "When art is stolen it is often someone who has access to the house, like a service person or contractor."[3] Such was the case in the theft of Rembrandt's *The Raising of Lazarus* in 2006. A 49-year-old handyman named James Otis Denham stole the etching from a home in Broken Arrow, Oklahoma, where he had been hired to do work. Denham did not set any standards for craftiness. After lifting the $6,000 item, he tried to sell it for $1,500 out of the trunk of his car—to a woman he met at a nearby Torchy's Legends Bar. She noticed that the actual owner's name was still on a document authenticating the work. She copied this provenance and learned that the etching was stolen after calling its owner, Barbara Dorney, to double-check its authenticity. Police arrested Denham when he was invited to exchange the etching for the cash. "At least he was stupid, and I got it back," says Dorney.

Access to a home is just a start. Also important is the information an insider collects within the residence. A person with only occasional access to a premises will quickly recognize that he or she is in the home of an art collector. If the home is in a well-to-do neighborhood, a thief can surmise that he is looking at something of value, rather than a print or copy, even if he has little knowledge of art. Collectors buy art for display, and it is natural for great pieces to be positioned where guests can see them. Few people will spend tens of thousands of dollars on a work only to put it in a dark hallway or a safe, and collectors also like to brag about their finer acquisitions. An opportunistic serviceperson or contractor is in an ideal position to determine whether the home is alarmed and whether the residents actually engage their systems (many people with elaborate security systems grow complacent and fail to set them or even turn them on). He will observe how the owner hangs a painting or secures an object to the floor or a raised surface. Many times he will be free to do all this casing while alone on the premises.

Such opportunities make art theft from a home or private gallery far less daunting than from a large museum, and works by Rembrandt have been a prime target of insider thieves dating back to the early decades of the twentieth century. On November 13, 1933, the home of a Stockholm art collector, M. Herman Rasch, was broken into by thieves who robbed him of a number of his works, chief among them Rasch's prized Rembrandt, *Jeremiah Mourning for the Destruction of Jerusalem* (1630). The painting is legendary. It depicts the aged prophet Jeremiah seated with his weary head resting in his left hand. At the time of the theft, *Jeremiah* was considered among Rembrandt's 25 greatest works, and that was at a time when an inordinately large number of works were attributed to the artist, many wrongly.[4] Famed German art historian Wilhelm von Bode described the painting as a jewel among the masterpieces from Rembrandt's younger years, comparing it favorably with most of his later works.[5] As one of Rembrandt's early religious works, it had been kept from public view for years while in the possession of Russian count S. A. Stroganoff in St. Petersburg before the First World War. Fears that the Rasch theft might mean *Jeremiah* was now lost to the ages happily dissipated when the work was located just a day later. A German workman who was restoring the Rasch premises confessed to the crime and implicated a Polish coworker. He led investigators to the masterpiece, then valued at $100,000, which he had stashed in the woods near Stockholm.[6] Today it resides safely in the Rijksmuseum in Amsterdam and is valued at $100 million.

Five years later, on September 9, 1938, Rembrandt's *Old Man with a Fur Cap*, another work completed in 1630, was taken from the Bayside Hills, Queens, home of art critic George R. Cobham. Cobham was the manager of the noted Duveen Brothers art firm on Fifth Avenue in Manhattan and had a rich pedigree in the art world.[7] The brothers

Duveen rank among the most important art dealers not only of their time, but of all time. Born in Holland, they branched out to Britain, France, and then the United States, exporting innumerable treasures from Europe. They set up shop on Fifth Avenue and at Place de la Concorde in Paris, displaying fine art for the first time with dazzling retail stagecraft and convincing turn-of-the-century millionaires to spend lavishly for paintings and antiques. Their influence shaped many of America's most famous private and public collections. These include works that today sit in the National Gallery of Art in Washington and the Henry Clay Frick Collection in Manhattan.

Dr. Magness-Gardiner's warning about service people and contractors being likely suspects in Rembrandt thefts resounds when examining the theft at Cobham's home. The crime took place while Cobham and his wife were abroad, and it is likely the thieves knew they were away. The Cobhams learned of the burglary when they found the door to the house ajar on their return. Startled and fearful for their safety, the couple contacted police and stood by. When New York City detective John McDermott arrived, Cobham re-entered his premises, only to discover the extent of the damage. In addition to stealing two paintings from a lower floor, the trespassers ventured into the renovated attic, where they lifted four others. The thieves' M.O. with all the paintings was similar: They turned the frames to the wall and took the art out from behind. It's safe to assume a thief has intimate familiarity with a home when he can locate high-value art hanging in a remodeled attic and take the time to separate canvases from frames. Investigators said the scene indicated the thieves knew the Cobhams' floor plans well and may have used a passkey to enter, since the front-door lock showed no signs of damage. The thieves also knew Cobham's collection, taking what police described as six of his most valuable pieces, including works by Renoir and Hals. In all, the stolen objects were valued at $26,500, *Old Man with a Fur Cap* making up the bulk of the estimate at $20,000.[8] That painting, which has also been known as *Rembrandt's Father* (despite no evidence that the sitter was in fact his father, Harmen), depicts a man wearing a tall fur cap and a cloak with a fur collar. His lined, bearded face is turned slightly to the left, and his eyes are cast to his right. In tone, it is not dissimilar to *Jeremiah*. Fortunately, *Old Man* was recovered and today is in the Tiroler Landesmuseum Ferdinandeum in Innsbruck, Austria. As with many Rembrandt cases from this time period, most details of the crime and recovery are unavailable to researchers. Those secrets either died with the people involved or were neither recorded nor permanently archived by law enforcement.

Even setting aside the World War II years, when the Nazis set their vile standards for state-sponsored art looting, the 1920s, 1930s, and 1940s were active times for Rembrandt-coveting house breakers like those who hit Rasch and Cobham. In 1930, three paintings, said at the time to be by Rembrandt, *An Old Beggar*, *Leonardo Da Vinci*, and *The Reformer*, were part of an 18-painting haul from the Carleton House Galleries on Lower Regent Street in London. All had been put on exhibition by private owners. Some were sliced from their frames, others removed from the frames while still attached to their wooden stretchers. Scotland Yard said the burglars had duplicate keys to the gallery, took only the most expensive items, and left no fingerprints. They were never rounded up, and the works remain unaccounted for to this day. On April 10, 1936, an etching by Rembrandt of *Christ's Descent from the Cross* was stolen from a home in Segovia, Spain. It was Good Friday. In 1942, when the Netherlands was occupied by the Germans, a lone thief stole a Rembrandt painting featuring a man cutting a goose-quill pen from an Amsterdam home. The Dutch police were allowed to probe the matter as a local crime and recovered the painting, which fortunately never left Holland. In January 1937, two ink drawings by Rembrandt, *Woman Carrying a Child* and *Children Playing Rummel-Pot* (a noisy Christmas game in which Dutch children used reeds and animal membranes to generate loud rumbling sounds from ceramic pots), were snatched from the walls of the Fogg Art Museum at Harvard University. The items were recovered, and what remains from the episode is a vague presumption that it was a student prank.

As noted previously, there is nothing surprising about Rembrandt thefts with Massachusetts connections. In 1920, long before the Fogg, the Museum of Fine Arts in Boston, and the Isabella Stewart Gardner Museum were robbed, a dozen privately owned stolen artworks, including Rembrandt's *Christ Healing the Sick*, were recovered from a stash house in Boston. That robbery is among the earliest newspaper and wire service accounts of stolen Rembrandts, but little is known about the theft. Heists from the era in Europe include Rembrandt's *Man Wearing a Skull Cap* (1643), which was stolen in 1921 from a home in Hamburg, Germany, and hunted from Poland to England. One of four paintings cut from their frames, it was never recovered. A year afterward, *St. Paul in Prison*, a beloved Rembrandt oil panel that thankfully was recovered, was stolen from a small family gallery in Stuttgart, Germany. In Moscow in 1927, religious works by Rembrandt, Titian, and Correggio that had once belonged to Russia's imperial Orloff-Davidoff family were ham-handedly purloined from their home. The Associated Press account reported that the thieves gained "easy access" by breaking a small pane of glass and opening a ventilator into the residence. "They treated all the paintings with such vandalism that unless entirely ignorant of their value they must have been according to the authorities seeking some mysterious revenge," the news account read. "More probably they were some sort of religious maniacs, as all the paintings were portraits of religious subjects. From the middle of the Rembrandt a jagged lopsided oval containing the figures was cut out and the rest of the canvas was slashed and scarred. Even if the center is recovered, restoration would almost be impossible. The Titian was cut even more disastrously, completely destroying Christ's hand, while four smaller pictures were torn clumsily from the stretchers. Although their total estimated pre-war [World War I] value is $330,000, they are now clearly worth many times that sum." Happily, the criminals were not complete vulgarians. The Rembrandt and the other works were recovered four years later, buried in tin boxes at two separate locations in Moscow. "The tins were found sealed and the pictures were covered with a special composition to protect them from damage," the AP reported in 1931, adding that experts saw hope in restoring them despite their brutal treatment.[9] The Rembrandt, *Christ with Folded Arms*, is now in the Hyde Collection in Glens Falls, New York.

While the 1920s ushered in the great age of Rembrandt thievery, major art theft itself had gained steam at the turn of the twentieth century, when Italian masters from before and during the Renaissance were most at risk. The 1911 theft from the Louvre of the *Mona Lisa* is seen by many as the historical turning point, but between 1904 and 1920, thefts of works by Titian, Caravaggio, and Fra Angelico kept English detectives hopping. One hundred years before the founding of the FBI's Art Crime Team, British police needed to assign specialists to assist Scotland Yard with art crime. A 1923 headline from the *New York Times*, above a 2,000-word article on the problem, reads much like stories written today. The tone is a bit quaint: "Art Thieves Ply Trade Defiantly: 'Industry Is Growing'—Hopeless Task to Trace Man with Priceless Bit of Canvas" (*The New York Times*, November 4, 1923, p. 4). But it is comparable to these reports: "Art-Work Thefts Seen Pointing to Cross-Country Gangs" (*The New York Times*, January 8, 1979, p. A14), "Art Theft Is Booming, Bringing an Effort to Respond" (*The New York Times*, November 20, 1995, p. A11) and "Art Theft Underworld Frustrates France with Its Mystery" (*The New York Times*, August 26, 2010, p. A1). The 1920s closed out with an early-December 1929 Rembrandt theft from Massimo Palace, an ancestral home in Rome. Although *The Head of an Old Man* was recovered just before the new year, today several dozen long-stolen Rembrandts still remain missing, many taken from private homes.

A TALE OF CRIMINAL DESTRUCTION

While the thefts from the homes of Rasch and Cobham involved important Rembrandt works, neither of those crimes compares with the residential heist that took place at the home of British financier Sir Edmund Davis in 1938. Of the five items removed, two were efficiently recovered just six days later. As for the other three, headlines from the era say only that they "remain missing." In reporting this book, we learned that all three, among them a Rembrandt, were destroyed by the criminals, who were never arrested or identified. Newspaper accounts and police reports from that time state that the lost Rembrandt was a work titled *Saskia at Her Toilet* (1641). Rembrandt expert Gary Schwartz informed the authors that the portrait stolen from Kent appears in Kurt Bauch's 1965 catalogue of Rembrandt paintings as "*Bathsheba* (?)," with the location: "London, Coll. Sir E. Davis (destroyed in 1938)."

To refer to Sir Edmund's dwelling as a "home" does it little credit, for his residence was Chilham Castle in Kent, England. The imposing estate, built in 1616, has roots as far back as 709 c.e., when the king of Kent built a wooden fort at Chilham. The medieval castle grew to cover eight acres, and was owned by some of Britain's most prosperous families. In 1892, Sir Edmund purchased the castle from the Hardy family, who had made a number of changes to the estate, not all of them well received. It was no surprise then that Sir Edmund spared little expense trying to rebeautify the property, since the Australian-born British aristocrat and his wife (and first cousin), Mary, were preservationists and connoisseurs. Sir Edmund was an accomplished artist and amassed a significant collection for the castle, including a Rembrandt and a Gainsborough.[10] He also acquired works by Velazquez, Hogarth, and Rossetti, among other fine pieces, and surrounded his swimming pool with sculptures by Rodin.

On April 23, 1938, as 20 guests (and five dogs) slept amid these splendors, thieves infiltrated the premises through a mullioned window from which they had quietly removed a pane of glass. One can only imagine the horror Sir Edmund felt when he made his way downstairs the next morning to find five empty frames laid atop pillow cushions on his great-room floor. *Time* magazine called the thieves "knaves with knives" after it was reported that the paintings had been "neatly" cut from their frames.[11] In all, an estimated $500,000 in art had been taken, leaving the nobles financially wounded and emotionally bereft. Missing were two Gainsboroughs (*Lady Clarges* and *Pitt*), Van Dyck's *Man with Dog*, and *The Earl of Suffolk* by Sir Joshua Reynolds. The greatest loss, however, was the Rembrandt, which Sir Edmund had acquired in 1900 for approximately £50,000 (the equivalent of $5.9 million today).[12] Coincidentally, government officials in the Netherlands had only recently requested that Sir Edmund lend them the painting for an exhibition in Amsterdam to celebrate the birth of Princess Juliana's first child, the future Queen Beatrix. Because the painting was so valuable, he declined the request. Had he said yes, it stands to reason the painting would not have been in the castle for the thieves to steal.[13]

The heist sent shock waves across Britain, and journalists likened it to the *Mona Lisa* crime of 1911 and to the theft of the *Duchess of Devonshire* from a London gallery in 1876. (The latter was similarly slashed from its frame—by the infamous art thief Adam Worth, the so-called Napoleon of Crime, who ransomed it back 25 years later for $25,000). Authorities on both sides of the Atlantic went on notice. British officials began searching parcels destined for the United States, and air and seaport authorities kept a close eye on passenger and freight departures, hoping to prevent the masterworks from leaving the United Kingdom.

Spirited theories abounded about the motive and destination of the paintings. John Duveen, a sibling of the aforementioned Duveen Brothers, said it would be "next to impossible" for the thieves to sell the highly recognizable paintings. The *New York Times* posited that the theft had been planned months in advance, with the intent of making fraudulent copies of the works. Sir Edmund also weighed in with an opinion on the perpetrators. "The men obviously were members of an experienced gang of art thieves," he said. Immediately contradicting that assessment, he added, "they ransacked a number of rooms and took away other things of comparatively little value."[14] While the pieces the thieves chose were clearly valuable and worth the effort, the men did leave behind high-priced works. In their forays throughout the castle, they bypassed a 12-inch golden idol and left another Velazquez on a wall near where they lifted the rest of their loot.[15] While not efficient at cashing in fully on their opportunity, the thieves were nonetheless careful not to leave a forensic trail behind. Sir Edmund told the press that signs of gloved hands were found about the scene, and Scotland Yard could locate no fingerprints.

Fortunately for investigators, they would not need prints to resolve the matter. Less than a week after the heist came a major break. A local insurance agency that had posted a reward was approached by a worka-day Londoner, George Owens. The police were notified and the crime was solved with Owens' arrest. He proved to be a rather unremarkable mastermind whose clumsy effort to monetize his loot cost him his free-dom. Here again, a dramatic theft from an august castle with an aura of villainy associated with Dr. Moriarty from *Sherlock Holmes* ended with seeming banality. But in this case there is a grim postscript, papered over at the time. While both Gainsboroughs were indeed recovered, the authors are reliably informed by Michael H. Peters, a longtime vol-unteer at the Chilham Castle, that the Rembrandt "and the two others were burnt, lost forever."

Although the Chilham Castle crime demonstrated well before mid-century that art robbers were unlikely to get away or grow rich, such thefts hardly let up in the United States and Europe. Chilham is far from the only castle to be struck. In 1959, Germany's Marienburg Castle, which served as the seat of the last king of Hanover, lost an unnamed painting that was described as "possibly by Rembrandt" (it wasn't) as well as a work by Lucas Cranach.[16] That same year, the Dahlem Museum in West Berlin was robbed of a 10-inch-by-12-inch Rembrandt study of Christ's head, an oil on wood. It turned up two years later in a locker at the city's Brunswick railway station, after a tele-phone tip. In July 1962, thieves again set upon the home of an art col-lector, this time in Holland, stealing a Rembrandt valued at $110,000 from Jonkheer John H. Loudon, the head of Royal Dutch Petroleum.[17] The painting was recovered a month later.

Not coincidentally, those three crimes took place at the dawn of an era when the market value of big-name art began to skyrocket. The triggering event was Sotheby's famous Goldschmidt sale of 1958, in London. The Goldschmidt collection consisted of seven of the most alluring Impressionist and modern paintings yet to go before the gavel. As a later account put it, "An evening auction was decided upon—the first at Sotheby's since the 18th century—and those attending were to wear evening dress. Some 1,400 did attend, including Somerset Maugham, Anthony Quinn, Kirk Douglas and Lady Churchill, as well as hundreds of art dealers from around the world. The seven pictures were all sold in just 21 minutes. They fetched £781,000, or $2.2 million, the highest total ever reached at that time at a fine art sale. Cézanne's *Garçon au Gilet Rouge* was sold to financier Paul Mellon for £220,000, more than five times the previous record for a painting at auction."[18] The event was seen as "the social highlight of the year" and possibly "the most exciting art auction of the century." Every detail made its way into breathless transatlantic dispatches. The Associated Press reported: "Arrangements are being made by the New York art dealer Georges Keller for the removal to that city—probably by air—of the paintings. The clients want complete secrecy about how and when they are going. A spokesman for Sotheby's said, 'We shall be glad to see them away.' "[19]

By 1961, Rembrandt had topped all seven in one gavel blow, fetching $2.3 million at auction for *Aristotle Contemplating the Bust of Homer,* purchased by the Metropolitan Museum of Art. And in 1963, First Lady Jacqueline Kennedy, a devoted art lover, stage-managed exhibitions of the *Mona Lisa* in New York and Washington, D.C., adding even more cachet—and cash—to the world of art masterpieces.

Clearly aware of these stunning new valuations, criminals worldwide embarked between 1959 and 1979 on a Rembrandt theft spree that netted at least 25 of his works. No place seemed safe, not even peaceable Canada. In Toronto, in mid-September 1959, the city's Art Gallery of Ontario was looted of two Rembrandts, two Halses, a Renoir, and a Rubens, all cut from their frames in what was then labeled the largest art haul in that nation's history. The thieves also slashed several more paintings but left those behind. The burglars hid in the gallery until after closing time, tore away the art, then escaped by breaking an unalarmed window on the gallery's second floor and dropping to the empty, rain-drenched street below. Only the first floor of the gallery was had alarms at the time.

"The thieves were very clever about casing the job," gallery curator Martin Baldwin told reporters, according to news accounts. "They took our best paintings. But they obviously did not know how to handle the pictures. They bit off more than they could chew."[20] Three weeks later, all six items were recovered, wrapped in heavy paper inside a residential garage in Toronto, marred but "not irreparable." The police had received an anonymous tip and staked out the garage, but determined that its owner was not in on the heist. The thieves were never captured. Baldwin said the paintings, including *Portrait of a Lady with a Lap Dog* (1662) and *Portrait of a Woman with a Handkerchief* (1644) by Rembrandt, had suffered "scratches and abrasions, but just how serious the cost of the damage will be is a matter of arbitration with the insurers."[21]

In Montreal in October 1964, *The Death of Jacob* (1641), a Rembrandt drawing, was stolen from the city's Museum of Fine Arts. Valued at $30,000, the 10-inch-by-14½-inch Old Testament depiction was pilfered from its perch between two other Rembrandts in a second-floor gallery. Police speculated that the robber had hovered near the drawing with a screwdriver and loosened its screws from its wall bit by bit, stepping back and palming his tool whenever a guard or visitor passed by. A witness said later he had seen a six-foot, 200-pound man leave the museum with what appeared to be the drawing under his arm. The museum offered no reward and the drawing seemed lost to the ages. Five years later, a break came when three men in Bar Harbor Island, Florida, Max Cohen, Seymour Jacobsen, and Harvey Cohen, were indicted for "conspiring to receive, conceal, sell and dispose of stolen property having a value in excess of $5,000." The property was the recovered Montreal Rembrandt.

Those relatively happy Canadian outcomes were overshadowed in 1972, after the Montreal Museum of Fine Arts was targeted yet again in a crime that, like the Isabella Stewart Gardner Museum robbery of 1990, remains unsolved. Eighteen paintings, including Rembrandt's

Landscape with Cottages (1664), an oil on wood panel, and 39 other art objects were taken. It is the largest heist in Canadian history, with the items now valued at some $50 million. (The tragic unsolved Montreal and Gardner cases are discussed in this book's epilogue.)

TARGET-RICH ENVIRONMENT

The litany of Rembrandt thefts from the 1960s and 1970s makes it clear that thieves were taking advantage of immense gaps in security at private homes, small museums and galleries, and other locales featuring anywhere from one to a dozen Rembrandts. But it is fair to say that there was also a widespread failure of imagination among owners and caretakers. Art collection then was largely a genteel avocation. Trying to shoehorn together the tasks of security and curatorship is difficult even today, when technology makes safeguarding works a far less clunky and intrusive problem. In that era, security was not just more lax but hostage to the traditions of the locations in question. In her will, Isabella Stewart Gardner wrote that "the guards shall be young men whose business is ushering. The night watch shall attend the furnace."[22] Few museums, homes, and colleges thought in terms of security professionals. In many cases, then and again today, college students and minimum-wage workers were entrusted with these pivotal duties.

Consider this maddening list of Rembrandt heists attributable to absent, ill-conceived, or quaint security at smaller institutions:

- April 30, 1965: Rembrandt's *Death of a Virgin* is stolen from the Falvey Memorial Library at Villanova University in Philadelphia.
- January 11, 1966: An unidentified Rembrandt is among 54 drawings stolen around midnight from the provincial Museum of Fine Arts in Besançon, France. In May, Camille Gahier, 39, a Frenchman who had been sending ransom notes to the Ministry of Culture, is arrested near the theft site. He leads police to a Swiss accomplice, Jean-Marie Boury, 19, living just over the border with his parents.

All the items are found wrapped neatly in mattress ticking in the Bourys' attic.

- November 23, 1968: A small Rembrandt oil portrait on wood, valued at $100,000, is reported stolen from the Museum of Art and History in Geneva, Switzerland. The work features the artist's long-suffering mother, Cornelia, who lived to the age of 72.
- February 18, 1969: A Rembrandt painting valued at $200,000 is stolen from the Cumberland House art exhibition in Portsmouth, England.
- September 19, 1971: A Rembrandt is reportedly among seven paintings stolen from an art gallery in Zagreb, Yugoslavia, in what is described as the biggest art theft in the communist nation's history.
- December 21, 1971: *Flight of the Holy Family to Egypt* by Rembrandt is stolen from the Museum of Fine Arts in Tours, France, by a 23-year-old Czechoslovakian art student. It is recovered in West Berlin in November 1972 after an intermediary tries to sell it for $35,000 to a local police agent masquerading as a shady art buyer. The sting was set up by INTERPOL after a tip.
- November 6, 1976: Thieves chip through the rear wall of a private gallery on the north side of Chicago and steal works by Rembrandt, Renoir, and Da Vinci. They are recovered after the men fail to find a willing buyer.

A few of the cases from this fertile period for thefts highlight the role loose lips often play in the robbery and recovery of a Rembrandt. Gabbing too freely about being the legitimate possessor of a Rembrandt can prick up the ears of criminals on the listen for easy break-ins. Similarly, unchecked chattering by the robbers once they have landed their prize will give informants an easy chit to hand to law enforcement when they need to trade their way out of a prosecution or prison term.

In 1968, thieves entered the Eastman House in Rochester, New York, and stole Rembrandt's *Portrait of a Young Man* (1660). The Eastman House was an interesting choice for a Rembrandt theft. While it is considered a museum, photography rather than painting is the focus of its collection. In fact, the stolen 30-inch-by-40-inch oil portrait, purchased by George Eastman, the founder of Eastman Kodak, was actually the property of the University of Rochester, to which Eastman, a New York native, had willed the piece upon his death in 1932. It was loaned by the university back to the Eastman House when the Eastman opened as a museum of photography in the 1940s.

Around 7 A.M. on January 31, 1968, guards making their rounds in the Eastman House noticed the Rembrandt missing. One of them, Charles Rampick, inspected the building entrance and found the front door unlatched. Police were summoned but found no clues indentifying the thieves. They did make one fresh discovery, though. It turned out that another painting, a work by Arthur Davies titled *Cabin Interior—Rainy Day*, was also missing. Officials put the value of that painting at $400, a far cry from the $250,000 price tag attributed to the Rembrandt.

Portrait of a Young Man was quite heavy. Just months before, it had been removed from the museum's walls to be photographed. Three men were needed to assist in the operation, as the work weighed close to 200 pounds, including its frame. This is likely why investigators discovered the frame discarded by the thieves and hanging on a nearby fence.[23] Other than this, little was left behind for investigators to pounce upon.

Some ten months afterward, a nondescript panel truck carrying 18 law enforcement officers rolled into the airport in Plattsburgh, New York, just east of Interstate 87, as dusk settled on the Lake Champlain town. Another half dozen cops waited on the perimeter of the airport. Prompted by information from a Canadian source, the police were there to conduct surveillance on three men seated in a station wagon awaiting the arrival of a small chartered aircraft. At about 6:30 P.M., the plane arrived, and the police watched for an exchange between the three men and the passenger on the aircraft. One of the three men, 39-year-old Thomas F. Gordon, a self-described "import-export consultant," approached the plane and accepted a briefcase said to hold

$50,000 from a pilot. That's all the police needed to see to launch an arrest. As Gordon made his way back to the car, investigators seized him and his cohorts, charging them with criminal possession of stolen property. The pilots of the aircraft, however, were not arrested. Investigators determined they had no knowledge of the crime and were merely being used as unwitting couriers. Police found *Portrait of a Young Man* secreted in the station wagon, wrapped in tissue paper within a plywood box. The entire operation turned on the fact that an informant was willing to tip off the law to the Gordon outfit's illicit transaction.

Gordon's associates, Russell DeCicco and Carmen Bonnano, both of Rochester, were career criminals with a history of burglary and robbery. While their criminal expertise suited them well for the heist, the New York state police were suspicious of a wider conspiracy, perhaps because the trio intended to send the painting to what sources described as an "unidentified Montreal man." *Portrait of a Young Man* was returned to the Eastman House relatively unscathed, suffering just two small, repairable scratches on the painting's background.[24]

Within days, the state police hunch about a wider conspiracy proved accurate. On October 24, 1968, DeCicco's wife, Renée, and three others were charged with conspiracy in connection with the theft and the attempted interstate transportation of $1.5 million in art. The Eastman House Rembrandt was not the only target of the crooks, who had broken into other locations featuring artworks, including the home of Seymour H. Knox, a Buffalo banker. At the time of the arrests, Knox's art was not recovered.[25]

The criminal grapevine played an active role in a Rembrandt house theft a decade later in Cohasset, Massachusetts, an upscale suburb located on the road from Boston to Cape Cod. The town is so quintessentially upper-crust New England that it served as the backdrop for the film *The Witches of Eastwick*, and some of Boston's more affluent figures have called it home. But Cohasset is also located in Norfolk County, a playing field for some of Boston's more notorious criminal figures. One such individual was Myles J. Connor Jr., the mastermind behind some of the most storied art crimes of the twentieth century, including thefts at Boston's Museum of Fine Arts (which involved a Rembrandt portrait), Salem's Peabody Museum (now the Peabody Essex Museum), the Woolworth Estate in Maine, the Boston's Children's Museum, and untold other places. Connor is famous today for claiming to have inspired the 1990 Isabella Stewart Gardner Museum heist, an assertion that has not been substantiated but cannot be easily dismissed. However, his reputation in the world of Rembrandt theft is due largely to his role in stealing, and then returning, Rembrandt's *Portrait of a Young Woman* from the Museum of Fine Arts in Boston in 1975 in order to curry favor with prosecutors and ease a pending prison sentence (for, what else, art theft). The precedent that Connor set by stealing a painting to gain leverage with the justice system (see next chapter) established an ominous new motive for art theft. But 1975 was not the only time Connor was involved in the return of a Rembrandt.

In 1978, a young woman attending a summer pool party in Cohasset told friends about a particularly lavish home where she worked as a babysitter. The nearby home of Arthur Herrington, a wealthy doctor, was brimming with valuable paintings, the starstruck woman said. The gossip she shared at the party was not meant to cause the family harm or inspire a crime. Herrington's collection was simply awe inspiring, she said. It did not take long for the babysitter's tale to plant a seed in the mind of a budding thief eager to pocket some serious cash. Just a few nights after the pool party, on August 17, 1978, David Thomas, a former philosophy student at Suffolk University in Boston, crept into the Herrington home as the family slept upstairs. In short order, Thomas (and an accomplice who has never been publicly identified) took six paintings and two Chinese Ming vases worth at least $2 million all told from the Herrington home. Among the paintings were works by El Greco and Pieter Brueghel. Also stolen: Rembrandt's *Portrait of a Lady*.

One year later, Boston's police commissioner held a news conference to announce that the art had been recovered. Commissioner Joseph M. Jordan told the press that the "priceless" works were discovered in a safe house in the Dorchester neighborhood of Boston. While the police were tight-lipped about what led them to the location, the name Myles Connor was synonymous with safe houses in the neighborhood. (It would not be the only time valuable museum pieces were found in a Dorchester stash house frequented by Connor. In 1984 lawmen discovered a Colonial-era state document that had been stolen in a robbery linked to Connor.) So it came as no surprise when Weld Henshaw, a prominent Boston attorney with experience in art law and counsel to the Herrington family, declared that Connor had arranged for the return of the Rembrandt. Connor was never charged with a crime in the Herrington matter, but admitted to being in on it during several interviews for this book. David Thomas, however, did not fare as well. On Christmas Eve, 1979, he pleaded guilty to charges of breaking and entering as well as larceny in connection with the Cohasset heist. Judge Edith W. Fine presented Thomas with a gift far worse than a coal lump when she sentenced him to 13 years in a state penitentiary.[26]

POSTSCRIPT

If history has taught us anything about the thefts of Rembrandts, it is that no place—neither home nor gallery nor rich estate nor great museum—is safe from the designs of thieves as long as works by the Dutch master hang on the walls. In 1962, the set of the play *Lord Pengo* (a character based loosely on the life of fine-art impresario Lord Duveen) lost a Rembrandt to thieves. Fortunately, the work was merely a copy of the great *Aristotle Contemplating the Bust of Homer*.[27] It is not known whether it was taken by someone who imagined it to be authentic, or by a fan seeking a keepsake from the production, but taken it was. In one almost amusing case in 1976, a thief stole a Rembrandt self-portrait from the Granet Museum in Aix-en-Provence, France, after entering the building via a scaffolding put up by workers installing—of all things—a new burglar alarm system.[28] But the ultimate irony, if not insult, is that art has been stolen more than once from Rembrandt's former house in Amsterdam.

The stolen pieces have not exclusively been Rembrandts. Witness the October 10, 1994 sledgehammer crime. That theft was so brazen that Dutch police wondered whether the interloper was the same man who had broken open the museum's front door with a blowtorch in July of that year and stolen two paintings by one of Rembrandt's teachers, Pieter Lastman. Those paintings, *The Crucifixion* (1628) and *The Lamentation of Abel* (1623), were eventually recovered. "The first of the two break-ins was peculiar because they attacked the front door at a time when there were many passers-by," says Martin Kok, the museum's insurance adjuster.[29] "They just kept working and nobody took any notice. The alarm system worked perfectly, because the police were there within a couple of minutes. In this last case, though, the thief didn't attack the door because it has been reinforced. So he broke open the window with heavy tools, and kept working even though this enormous alarm went off just above his head. The museum is very worried. Psychologically it is unprecedented. You can't imagine a real criminal would do something like this. It's rather sick."

In 1989, the world learned that a uniquely important drawing by Rembrandt himself had been stolen from his former home. On June 16 of that year, an art dealer from Italy walked into Christie's auction house in New York City with a small, double-sided drawing measuring 3 by 4 inches with the hope of identifying the work and its creator on behalf of a friend. On one side was a drawing of a woman, her eyes half-closed, appearing to be nodding to sleep. On the other was a sketch of a toddler, half-length and looking forward. Christie's Old Masters drawings expert, Beverly Schreiber Jacoby, inspected the work and was struck by its quality. "When I saw it," she said, "I realized it was fabulous—a fine Rembrandtesque work." She immediately consulted Otto Benesch's *The Drawings of Rembrandt*, an important catalogue of those works, which are numerous and varied and revered as much as drawings and sketches by Da Vinci and Michelangelo. She quickly located the drawing, and its owner, which the book identified as "the

Museum het Rembrandthuis, Amsterdam." The woman in the drawing by Rembrandt was his beloved Saskia, depicted during a period of illness. The work is known as *Saskia and Rombartus*.

Christie's estimated the value of the drawing, which had been sandwiched between two pieces of glass and featured a gold border added in the seventeenth or eighteenth century, at more than $100,000. After identifying the work, Jacoby investigated how it had gotten from the Rembrandt house into the hands of the Italian art dealer. She contacted its director, Eva Ornstein-van Slooten, to see if the drawing had been deaccessioned, or voluntarily sold off. The curator, elated, told Jacoby the work had in fact been pilfered ten years earlier, in 1979. An attorney from Christie's initiated the return of the piece, informing the Italian dealer that Christie's was convinced it was a stolen Rembrandt. The dealer and the owner cooperated and were reportedly happy to return the piece, but asked to remain unidentified.[30] As with so many transactions in the Rembrandt netherworld, how it fell into their hands remains a mystery.

CHAPTER SIX

Devil's Bargain: The MFA Heist

Myles J. Connor Jr. asserts pride of authorship for his catalogue of art crimes with the same flourish that a portraitist might use to sign a fine work of art. He looks back on his life of crime as an oeuvre of sorts—a compilation of good and sometimes masterly efforts to bypass security, slip in and out of museums and estates and private collections, and get away with paintings and other objects of beauty. He put it this way during one of our interviews, some conducted verbally and some in which he wrote down his answers:

> My life includes many museum thefts and robberies of the utmost interest that are deeply fascinating to the lay reader—mostly unsolved. They include thefts of Rembrandts and other masterpieces that have a combined value in the hundreds of millions of dollars. Little known but also included in this category are the instances when I masqueraded

as a doctor of letters in order to facilitate my entry into the hallowed depths of the storage vaults of some of the biggest and most major museums in the country. I was even offered the title of 'Curator of the Asiatic Arts Department' at one museum, an offer I unfortunately had to turn down for fear of being recognized.

Startling as it seems, for months at a time, primarily in the 1970s and early 1980s, Myles Connor, a well-known Massachusetts art thief, had the keys and unfettered access to the cellars of important museums around New England. It is just one aspect of his tumultuous and oddly public life as that rare criminal creature: the connoisseur outlaw.

Given that Myles (he is known by his first name even among the police and prosecutors who abhor him) views much of his life in a cinematic vein, the following account of how he executed the robbery of a Rembrandt from the Boston Museum of Fine Arts in 1975 illustrates his M.O.[1] It shows that some heists can be crisper and more masterful than others, even though the acts are by their nature coarse and destructive.

* * *

On a sun-gilt fall Monday morning in 1975, shortly after 10 A.M., an ordinary-looking group of six male and female tourists stepped into the cool, marbled interior of the Museum of Fine Arts, a vast stone and granite landmark in the center of Boston that had, minutes earlier, opened to the public for the day.

As tourists often do, most of the little gaggle headed upstairs to the museum's Dutch Room, featuring major paintings by Rembrandt— some part of the collection and others on temporary loan from the Dutch government or private individuals. They shuffled about the vast corridors in what appeared to be a random way. A few stood near the top of the main stairs; others ambled over to spots where the museum's gray-haired security guards were posted—not too close but not too far. All of them wore watches set to the same time—to the same minute.

At 10:15 A.M. two things happened. First, a nondescript white Volkswagen van pulled into the large semicircular drive outside the museum and idled by the curb. Inside were a driver and two black-clad men armed with machine guns. Second, a natty little man in a tweed suit and fedora, with a curly black beard and thick-rimmed glasses, stepped up to a Rembrandt painting titled *Portrait of Elizabeth Van Rijn*. Slightly awed, and whispering "Easy now" to himself, he plucked the "surprisingly insubstantial" work from its hook, put it nonchalantly under his right arm, and headed down the main steps toward the museum's front entrance.

"Hey!" shouted a nonplussed security guard standing in the gallery where the painting had just hung. "What are you trying to do with that painting?" As he moved after the little gent, the guard felt his feet go out from under him. A tall, professorial-looking man who had been studying a large landscape painting—a man the guard barely felt the need to observe—had quite expertly thrown him onto the hard floor. The man pointed a gun at the prone guard, Vito Magaletta, 53, and said, "Shut up or I'll kill you." A pointy-toed shoe then struck the guard in the solar plexus, winding him instantly and painfully for a good three minutes. By then, the professorial assailant was long gone.

The guard's "Hey!" had, however, echoed across the gallery, and been taken up, chorus like, by some of the other security personnel. Their calls traveled down the museum's main staircase, drawing attention to the elfin man. He was descending briskly toward the ground floor and its giant steel exit doors, which were thrown open to the crisp sunny morning, when several more guards stepped forward to intercept him.

To their surprise, they found themselves stumbling into a few matronly female tourists who, seemingly oblivious to the unfolding pursuit, were meandering up the stairs. Yet the man in the tweed suit holding the painting was trotting down the same stairway unimpeded, and heading all the more briskly now toward the doorway. His female accomplices had done their job well, obstructing any headlong pursuit from behind.

The sole armed guard on the museum's premises that day, a powerful 65-year-old retired cop named John J. Monkouski, was stationed on the ground floor near the ticketing booth. He also heard the "Hey's!" echoing down the stairs and, sizing up the matter quickly, tried to intercept the bearded thief as he hurried through the main lobby carrying what looked to be an oval portrait under his right arm.

Monkouski did not think apprehending the little man with the big painting would pose much of a challenge, and moved to collar him. But when the elfin fellow put out his left arm stiffly to fend him off, Monkouski felt as if a steel rod had been rammed into him. Stunned by the small man's strength, he was pushed aside before he could gain a grip on his quarry.

"Stop!" Monkouski shouted, but there were too many tourists around the entryway, older men and women among them, and even a lady with a pram, and the thief was now tearing toward the front door. The guard hustled on foot after the mysterious little man.

It was almost 10:16 A.M. now and the thief had broken into a dead sprint. He burst through the turnstiles where, only minutes earlier, he had paid his $2.25 entry fee, and headed for a white van idling in the driveway about 15 yards away. As he approached the van, its back doors swung open wide, and a big man in black clothing hopped out, a machine gun against his hip.

Monkouski, panting, exited the museum and continued his hot pursuit. Just then a gust of wind kicked up, catching the oval portrait like a sail and slowing the thief's progress as he charged for the back of the van. Monkouski ran harder, sensing he might catch up to the robber, perhaps grab him before he stepped into the van with the art.

The man with the machine gun held his position, ignoring the guard trailing his confederate and staring at the museum entrance. In a few seconds, as he expected, he saw other pursuing security guards spill from the tall front doors. As a half-dozen of them hit the top of the outside stairway, the gunman in black laid down a burst of machine gun fire along the bottom of the steps. The bullets pinged and puffed smoke and threw up pellets of stone as they smacked against the granite stairs. Yelps of dismay were heard above the *rat-tat-tat* of the gunfire. The half-dozen blue-jacketed security guards performed almost cartoonish about-faces, retreating with impressive foot speed behind the towering steel doors of the main entry.

The man with the machine gun stepped back into the van, sat down, and trained his weapon through the passenger-side window. But only some tops of heads and sets of widened eyes could be seen poking around the museum's doors. By now, the man with the painting was at the rear of the van, ready to climb in. His escape was being covered by the second black-suited accomplice, who had his machine gun pointed toward the van's opening. As the gent climbed in, he placed the oval painting on a quilted mat covering the van's hard flooring. This brief action gave Monkouski, now on the man's heels, a final chance to lunge for the van and snatch hold of the painting's golden frame. The little thief grabbed the painting, too, and amid the loud chaos of the robbery a fierce tug-of-war silently ensued.

The second accomplice, eager to give the "Go!" sign to the tensed getaway driver, stepped forward with his machine gun, looking as if he intended to dispatch the obstinate security guard.

"No!" shouted the bearded gent in a commanding voice. The man with the machine gun took his finger from the trigger, then lifted the weapon like a bludgeon and brought the barrel down on the stubborn guard's head with a merciless *thump*. Monkouski dropped woozily to his knees in the street, letting go of the frame at last, and the thief hauled the painting back into the van. "Go!" the man with the machine gun ordered as the gent grabbed two ropes tied to the van's back-door handles and swung the doors shut with a rowing motion. The van careened into the traffic along Huntington Avenue, where cars and trolleys competed for road space. Soon enough it was abandoned in favor of a dark Monte Carlo sedan stashed on the grounds of a nearby housing project.

"Tough old bird, that guard," Myles J. Connor Jr. told his black-clad accomplice as he removed his tweed jacket, false glasses, and fedora and stored the Rembrandt in a wooden crate. "Damned good thing you didn't shoot him, or we'd really be in trouble."

* * *

The headline-grabbing armed robbery of a Rembrandt from the Boston Museum of Fine Arts had its genesis two years earlier, as a result of another art crime in New England.

In 1973, the Woolworth mansion in Winthrop, Maine, was looted of art and antiques. The FBI set up a sting to catch the thieves, pretending to be in the market for the stolen works. The agency soon found itself negotiating with an ex-jailbird named Myles J. Connor. Wearing a disguise, he led the agents to a U-Haul truck on Cape Cod. There they found one painting by Andrew Wyeth and three by N. C. Wyeth—all items missing from the Woolworth estate. Connor was arrested on federal charges of interstate transport of stolen art and faced Massachusetts state charges, too. Through clever lawyering and other delaying tactics, his trial was not scheduled to take place for almost two years, and Connor, the son of a Milton, Massachusetts police officer, was able to remain free on bail. He spent his time collecting antique Japanese swords and playing guitar with his rock 'n' roll band, Myles and the Wild Ones, at the Beachcomber nightclub in nearby Revere. He was billed on the marquee as "the President of Rock 'n' Roll," a name he assumed as a wry nod to Elvis Presley, the "King." He played frequently with Sha Na Na.

As the day of courtroom reckoning approached, Connor decided that imprisonment would interfere far too much with his music career. But what to do? As he talked over the predicament with his father, a bold idea popped into his head. Why not solve an open crime and gain some leniency? It could work, his father said. It was not uncommon. But what crime to solve? And equally important, how to avoid being tarnished as a "rat"?

Connor realized that he had "access," as he puts it, to some items that were still being sought by law enforcement. There seemed to have been a lot of museum robberies and other notable property thefts over the previous five years. One college museum had lost some Dutch paintings, and another important Boston institution had been stripped of a large assortment of Asian antiquities, including rare fourteenth-century Samurai swords. "I knew of quite a collection of Japanese weapons and Chinese bronzes that were missing from smaller New England museums," Connor says. So he approached an old friend of his father's, a Massachusetts State Police official, Major John Regan, and offered to "broker the return" of some missing objects he had heard about. The way the silver-tongued Myles presented it, Regan and the state police would look good for solving an important case or two. In return, prosecutors would agree to cut back Myles's prison time.

At first, Regan said such a mid-level swap was not enough to tempt federal officials. Connor recalls the fateful conversation this way:

"I said, 'For Chrissakes, John, what will it take to get me off? A Rembrandt?' And Regan told me, 'That just might do it.'"

The die was cast. Connor proceeded to arrange what remains his boldest and most daring theft: the daylight removal of a Rembrandt on loan to the MFA. He pulled it off on the very morning his lawyer and prosecutors were picking jurors for his trial. "I remember thinking it was like performing at Carnegie Hall to plan to rob the MFA," he said. "I had some jitters the night before. I always loved that heist. It was just like Hollywood."

*   *   *

Portrait of a Girl Wearing a Gold-Trimmed Cloak (1632), occasionally misidentified as *Elizabeth van Rijn*, is an important work for art historians studying the development of the young Rembrandt, who had only recently left his hometown of Leiden for the opportunities in the Netherlands' bustling commercial hub, Amsterdam. From his signature on the painting, we can see that his move away from Leiden meant a shift from his use of mainly the monogram "RHL" (Rembrandt Harmenszoon of Leiden) to the addition of "van Rijn" after the initials. It was during 1632 that he changed his signature again to simply

"Rembrant" (sans the "d," which he added a year later). The painting is considered an excellent example of Rembrandt's early social portraits, displaying his remarkable technical skill. The work also has been described as having an "outer distinction"—a certain aura that sets it apart from other works and plays on the emotions of its admirers. Moreover, it is in excellent condition, making it useful to scholars as an example of his skills at age 26.

In the oval portrait, painted on a single thin plank of mahogany, a young woman is depicted from the breast up. Her head faces the viewer directly, while her body is turned slightly to the left. The sitter is wearing a black cloak atop a white pleated shirt that covers her neck. On the shirt, Rembrandt famously scratched the wet paint to display the pleating. The cloak is closed at the top center and features a broad band of gold embroidery along the collar. Through her hair, which is a mix of ochre with sandy and dark brown shades to accentuate her blond curls, runs a row of pearls that matches her earrings.

Legendary Boston art dealer Robert C. Vose held a spot in his heart for *Portrait of a Girl*. And that's no small claim: He spent 67 years in the fine-art trade, and a painting from Vose is now displayed in practically every major museum in the United States. Of the many stories he accumulated during his lengthy career, he said the one about Rembrandt's *Portrait of a Girl* pleased him most. While visiting a client in Los Angeles in 1929, Vose was asked to appraise a collection of paintings at a monastery in the nearby Hollywood Hills. Vose's experience told him that he would likely find only copies of great works. As he made his way through the art, his doubts about their authenticity were confirmed. Until, that is, he reached the final part of his visit. In a small room, Vose came across an important Rembrandt portrait of a young woman. He soon learned that the *Portrait of a Girl Wearing a Gold-Trimmed Cloak* had been sent to the monastery ten years before by a bishop in Switzerland in the hopes of finding a wealthy Hollywood art lover to purchase it. Unfortunately for the art community of Hollywood, Vose's keen eye would land the painting in Boston.

When the bishop learned of Vose's interest, he and his entourage made their way from Chur, Switzerland, to the United States for a meeting. After about a week of negotiations, the parties agreed to a price of $100,000. Vose turned a quick profit by selling the Rembrandt to Boston aristocrat and art collector Robert Treat Paine II for $125,000. Paine, descendant of a signer of the Declaration of Independence, loaned the painting to the Museum of Fine Arts, where it hung until the theft in 1975.

The provenance of *Portrait of a Girl* can be traced back nearly 250 years, when it was listed for sale in Paris in 1767. The painting was sold at least seven times in France in the next 122 years, then found a home in Vienna in the collection of Prince Johannes II of Liechtenstein. By 1908, it was in the hands of Georg Schmid von Grüneck, the Bishop of Chur, where it rested until being sent to California in search of a buyer and its rendezvous with Robert Vose.

The painting was examined by the Rembrandt Research Project in October 1970 and judged to be a definitive work by the master. In fact, the only feature of the painting not thought to be original to Rembrandt is the shape: Researchers doubt that the 23½-inch-by-17-inch painting was oval to begin with. Beveling of the wood on the back of the painting casts doubt on oval as the original shape, they said. The research team speculated that the original shape of the work was rectangular, citing the painting's "highly effective execution, familiar from other works, that produces a vivid suggestion of space and depth, and [its] reliable signature" as key indicators in judging it an authentic Rembrandt.[2]

The identity of the sitter is less certain. Perhaps this is why the painting has no shortage of names attributed to it. Though it is known as *Portrait of a Girl Wearing a Gold-Trimmed Cloak*, the painting has commonly been referred to as *Rembrandt's Sister* and *Elizabeth Gerritsz Van Rijn*. The last two names, are the result of the early belief that the sitter was Rembrandt's sister, Elizabeth. However, later scholars have concluded that the identity of the young woman is unknown. What is known is that her likeness can be found in other noteworthy works by the master. His *Young Woman in Profile*, also from 1632, depicts the same woman from the side, wearing clothes closely resembling those in *Portrait of a Girl Wearing a Gold-Trimmed Cloak*, but with pearls around her neck and red in her outfit. Interestingly, *Young Woman in Profile* hangs at Stockholm's National Museum of Fine Arts, the site of the infamous December 2000 theft of a Rembrandt *Self-Portrait*. Clearly, the significance of *Young Woman in Profile* was lost on the Stockholm thieves.

Features from the same sitter appear in other Rembrandts. She has inspired the looks of many of Rembrandt's heroines painted in the early 1630s. *The Abduction of Europa* (1632) stands as perhaps the most notable of these. *Portrait of a Girl Wearing a Gold-Trimmed Cloak* later hung next to *Abduction* at the Getty Museum. The Rembrandt Research Project team also considers *Portrait of a Girl* to be a "proto- type" for a number of paintings produced by Rembrandt's workshop, including three versions of *Bust of a Young Woman* that hang in Milan; Allentown, Pennsylvania; and at the University of North Carolina (the last painting is believed to have been completed by Isaac Joudreville).

* * *

Myles Connor stands apart from most art thieves. He has an educated, debonair facade and can take a joke at his expense. Had he not asso- ciated so long with hardened criminals, and stolen so much private property, he could be a charmingly roguish literary character. He is a member of Mensa, the international high IQ society, and spent his years in prison learning Japanese and sketching details of his sword collection from memory. He has traced his mother's roots back to the Mayflower, knows as much as any man alive about antique swords and cutting weapons from around the globe, and dabbles in herpetology, with a special interest in snakes. (He kept a cobra with him for many years in a box that read, "Careful! Hot inside!" He was worried, he said, that it might bite a police officer during a raid on his safe house and lead to a murder charge.) Today, Connor lives in semi-retirement on a small farm in Massachusetts. His home shelters exotic birds, stray dogs, various snakes, and other amphibians, and an alligator lives in the bathtub. In very cold weather, he and his girlfriend let a pet horse step into their living room to warm up.

The character Connor most resembles is Arthur J. Raffles, a literary figure created in the 1890s by E. W. Hornung, a brother-in-law to Arthur Conan Doyle, the originator of Sherlock Holmes. Raffles is a "gentleman thief" living at the Albany, a prestigious address in London. He plays cricket for the Gentlemen of England and supports himself by carrying out ingenious burglaries. He is referred to as the "Amateur Cracksman" and stands aloof from what he refers to as the "professors"—professional criminals from the lower classes. Raffles is one of the earliest fictional characters who secretly surrounds himself with fine art obtained under mysterious circumstances in the manner of "Dr. No." Another is Captain Nemo of the submarine *Nautilus*, from *Twenty Thousand Leagues Under the Sea*, who was invented in 1870 by Jules Verne. Here is how Nemo is described in the novel: "He had very fine taste in art, possessing several masterpieces of both painting and sculpture, from ancient and modern European masters, all of which were housed in the Grand Salon of the *Nautilus*, along with his inestimably valuable collection of pearls, corals and such other marine products, which he had gathered with his own hands. In the opinion of Professor Arronax, the collection of the Grand Salon far outstripped that of the Louvre. However, Nemo regarded them as little more than the remainder of a past life, a life he chose to forget, but yet retain some memories of, for according to him, these were but a part of his original collection."

The best way to understand Connor is to read and hear his own words. His tone is usually mischievous, and only occasionally malevolent. He speaks with a noticeable Massachusetts accent, but the high-brow kind one hears in Manchester-by-the-Sea or Hyannis Port, not on the streets of South Boston. He can also affect an excellent Irish brogue and a convincing working-class accent—useful skills for mixing with criminals in the Boston area. Here is a partial transcript from many hours spent with him discussing his Rembrandt heists, museums, crime, art, the penal system, and the vagaries of a life as a notorious thief. These interviews were conducted in 1998, both in person and in writing, before Connor suffered a memory-impairing stroke in prison. Fit and healthy today, he now can recall many details from his past. These transcripts have the benefit of reflecting Connor's thoughts, voice, and tenor from his very robust pre-stroke period.

MYLES J. CONNOR JR.: The state might be interested to learn that I owe them many of my insights into the inner workings of museums. You see, it was really the State of Massachusetts that placed me inside a museum, back in the 1960s. Back then, and up into the early 1970s, you see, they had many programs at the various state prisons for reintegrating criminals into society. And one of the programs involved taking hold of inner-city kids with impoverished backgrounds and trying to guide them down the straight and narrow. So, what did they do? They took these virginal young thugs and they put them on work-release programs in the bowels of museums and in other places, where they were needed for heavy lifting and other such tasks. But in fact they were often self-supervised, living in halfway houses and whatnot, and expected as a condition of probation to report to work each day. Well, they reported all right. They reported because they soon realized that they could steal to their hearts' content and no one would notice. You see, I was among them, put in a supervisory role of sorts, owing to my interest in art and antiques. And I was well aware of the immense value that many of the items stored away in museum basements could hold.

TOM MASHBERG: Wait, are you saying that you and other thieves were actually assigned to work in the basements of art museums and the like?

CONNOR: Indeed. And it was possible at times to gain access to the areas where great works were kept while they were being cycled through the public exhibition spaces. Minor Impressionists and the like. But removing anything so noticeable would arouse too many suspicions.

The real mother lode was the property the museum simply had no way of dealing with and left in quasi-storage in its basements. You see, many people who die without heirs, and even some of those who have heirs, they will bequeath some of their better antiques to the Museum of Fine Arts or the Smithsonian, for example. Older people in particular—the Brahmin dowagers of Boston, who live into their nineties and are surrounded with heirlooms and cats in their tidy Beacon Hill parlors. Often these items have considerable merit—artistic or intrinsic or monetary—but there is simply no way for the museums that receive them to put them on display or to devote the manpower needed to put them up for auction. So they store them in these cavernous subbasements, hoping that perhaps someday one of their curators might find the time to catalog them and select out the better stuff that they might want to keep for their Early American department from the stuff they might as well sell off....

Now most people would have a tough time discerning the value of many of these things. They look like ugly old furniture, and in the sixties and seventies, there was this movement toward all that cold, hideous modernistic furniture—everyone wanted an Eames chair or some bastardization thereof, and they were just chucking away anything that looked old and fusty. I mean, you could pick up authentic Victorian highboys and Shaker benches for five or ten bucks in antique stores back then, because there was such little demand. And now the Shaker items command tens of thousands from these Wall Street or Hollywood airheads who want to fill their Montana ranches with the stuff. But if you're like me, and you've taken a long view of art, then you could get a sense of the value of those items by looking them up in books and important auction catalogues, especially if you are a student of the decorative arts, as I was and always have been.

I remember quite vividly one day coming across a gorgeous ebony armchair designed by John Pollard Seddon in the mid-1860s. Now Seddon was the scion of a family of royal Windsor furniture designers, and his items blended Gothic imagery with the simpler forms emerging in the Edwardian period. They are very, very important pieces, as anyone in the field of antique furniture can tell you, and at auction would easily bring tens of thousands of dollars. And here it was, sitting amidst a batch of old pine cabinets and other odd-lot items that had just been deposited in storage. Well, that chair did not last very long in cold storage, and of course no one ever noticed its departure. But these were the kinds of things one could come across. The first place I'd dig for treasure if I was an alien archeologist arriving on Earth in a few million years would be under the site of an old museum. But that's another story.

MASHBERG: What were these storage areas like, exactly?

CONNOR: Well, let's start with the Boston Museum of Fine Arts. Their cellars are very much like catacombs—they go on and on into the darkness, twisting and turning. They are as vast as the museum's grounds themselves, yet the tunnel systems connect up with tunnels running under the whole of the Fenway district of Boston. A lot of this area was filled in, and they basically tunneled out acres and acres of space and then buttressed it all with stone or wooden pillars and then coated the insides of the tunnels with concrete. Many of the tunnels are closed off by steel doors or even old wooden doors sporting padlocks.

If you get into these rooms, you essentially have large storage crates or even old display cases, often with nice items still displayed inside them. There were many lovely Japanese items stored this way—right in their original display cases.

I'd say that the MFA displays roughly in the vicinity of five percent of what they actually have on hand, and that includes not just fabulous exemplars of Empire furniture or Hepplewhite chairs, but also quite a few of the paintings and sculptures that a visitor might see. I mean, for every 2,000-year-old marble Hercules up in the museum's Early Roman section, there are more in storage, some of them quite great.

Now, one would not find a Rembrandt, necessarily, in those boxes. Rembrandts and such would of course be on display in the museum itself. But you would get many, many other types of fine art—Asiatic arts, including samurai swords and ivory-inlaid screens and lovely jade figurines; and Colonial decorative arts, like a mahogany pier table or a card table from the Philadelphia school; and silverware and porcelains, like a 1790s Paul Revere silver teapot, say, or a Wedgwood & Bentley creamware tureen; and landscape artists! There were literally dozens of works by [John] Constable or Thomas Cole and other members of the Hudson Valley School—maybe fifty or sixty of them just lying in storage. And if you're talking about rare prints, well, there were hundreds or thousands of them from every era—drawings and sketches and engravings by Watteau and Pillement and Nast.

* * *

In his six years as an on-and-off probationer, curator, and consultant at the MFA and other institutions in Massachusetts, Myles built up a collection worth hundreds of thousands of dollars. During that time, wearing a fake beard and moustache and employing a vaguely Teutonic accent and a pseudonym ("Dr. Joseph"), Connor roved the cellars of the museum, finding among its uncatalogued treasures the early makings of his own collection, and even the glass-topped display cases in which to display them. Part of his motivation was revenge upon one of the institutions, he says, because it had accepted some items of his that had been confiscated by the police, who assumed everything he had belonged to someone else.

"Those were legitimate family heirlooms, and to make matters worse they had placed these objects on open display," he said.

When Connor needed cash, he would sell off some of his ill-gotten museum antiques though legitimate auction houses and galleries. The items he brought in often had paperwork attached explaining their provenance and origins, because that material was usually stored beside them in the museum. The legitimizing documents kept him from arousing the sellers' suspicion. Myles had found an ideal system for turning purloined antiques and collectibles into clean hard cash. He was a one-man antiques roadshow.

Connor is also a bit of a walking encyclopedia on museum robberies. Here is a discourse on the subject from the criminal perspective that should prove useful to museum managers and security officials.

Connor could easily serve as a consultant. The problem is, even at age 70, he is fit and nimble-minded and notorious. While he has sworn off crime after losing too many years to prison, inviting him in to assess the security of a museum filled with tempting Rembrandts would probably not go over well.

CONNOR: To most museums, I suppose, my name is like Darth Vader. I'm quite capable of breaking into any museum, and I have been in places, such as the Smithsonian Institution's storage warehouses, where they would not be happy to know I have been.

Most museums are highly vulnerable. You know, you cannot make a museum into an armed camp, even with today's so-called "laser" technology, infrared beams in the baseboards and moldings, and so on. These systems all must be supplied with mundane electrical power to work, and it is rarely complicated to bypass or cut off the power. There are all kinds of ways, just as there are all kinds of ways to deal with an alarm system. It's the rare museum that has a backup generator running its electrical systems, for instance. I can't tell you how many museums rely on that little 100-amp wire that runs off the electric lines out in the street for their electric power. Out there in the criminal underworld, I am told, there are people of great sophistication, people who are familiar with all sorts of wiring techniques and alarms and alarm backup systems. People who themselves might be quite good at developing such systems, were that their calling, instead of disabling or overriding such systems and infiltrating the target by night.

And then there is the process of robbing a museum in broad daylight. You probably read from time to time in the newspapers about banks and such still being robbed by dudes with guns? Well, banks have armed guards and the money is in a vault and the tellers are behind all sorts of Plexiglas and still they are robbed. Well, museums generally have unarmed guards and the good stuff is just sitting out on tables or hanging on walls. So they are really far better targets than banks, simply for the fact that they have fewer impediments in place against theft.

Museums are often full of people, too, and they simply cannot risk having a major armed confrontation—a shoot-out, if you will—with nice ladies named Rockefeller and Cabot and Lowell or their equivalents suddenly running around on the third floor, getting in the line of fire and tearing their nylons and so forth. Some museums do have armed guards, certainly, but those places are usually in higher-crime areas. And those guards are usually there to contend with outside crimes: someone who might be lying in wait outside the museum at closing, ready to snatch a gold necklace or a clutch purse, as opposed to someone who is running out the front door holding a Rembrandt.

But even if the armed guards were there for that sort of theft—well, museums are really not hard targets. It's unfortunate for them, because they could think of many things to do to make it truly difficult for people like me to get away with a caper. But I guess I'll have to give up those secrets to perfect security when I get out and retire into a position as a high-priced security consultant!

MASHBERG: Give me a generic account of an average museum robbery from your heyday. It's clear you operated in a time when security measures were "old world."

CONNOR: Yes, well let's take Museum X. Back then there were very rarely any security cameras mounted anywhere on the outside. One could spend a long day and night casing a place—even up in a tree outside the museum—making mental notes of the comings and goings of the guards. They were rarely a crackerjack team. Just the usual motley crew of college kids and older fellows in blue blazers shuffling about, looking bored and staring at their shoes.

The reason you have a security camera on the outside is that you can record the license plates of any cars that might have been parked outside in the days leading up to a theft, and of course just after the time of a theft itself. That's standard practice at well-secured museums. You'd be surprised how many criminals make the idiotic mistake of parking near the target they intend to case or rob. I've called off jobs because one of my scouts came back with a parking ticket on his windshield. That's a great way to get identified as having been in the area in the days leading up to the caper.

By the way, any such cameras should be self-contained units, so that the film they record cannot be accessed or destroyed by the thieves themselves. This probably sounds obvious today, in an era of handheld camcorders. But in the 1980s, it took a small leap of imagination and a willingness to incur great expense to arrange for this level of security.

Now, a second key flaw is the very bad training of the night watch. The idea that you would let in anyone at off-hours, even someone dressed up as, say, a police officer, is just ludicrous. Do you have any idea how easy it is to obtain a policeman's uniform? You can order the damn things via catalogue or buy them at an Army-Navy or costume surplus store. You can snatch a bag full of them from the back of any precinct house on laundry day. And you can get badges and nightsticks and belts and all that chest adornment in a novelty shop. Yet I suppose we are all such trusting souls in so many ways. We are brought up to believe that the nice policeman is a symbol of upstanding behavior and purity and truth. All you need to get the drop on someone is to prey on that naïve mindset for a second or two and *whop!* I doubt there are too many people who would not succumb at least for a moment to their childlike faith in the policeman.

Now as for the job itself, you can get away with most any museum robbery with four people when the job is done at night. You'd have two men who go in, and the getaway-car driver, who'd be parked carefully keeping the engine warm. And then the lookout, who would be in touch with the getaway car by walkie-talkie or cell phone and positioned on a main street to watch out for police.

Now, in the daytime, you definitely need a fifth man driving a "crash car," because the likelihood of pursuit is higher, and the crash car can really wreak havoc by basically clogging up an intersection to the point where the police simply cannot get after you. And you might want a sixth man who rides shotgun in the getaway car to scare off any pain-in-the-neck would-be heroic bystanders.

That fellow will generally keep a sawed-off shotgun under a rain-coat and just flash the barrel at any good-Samaritan types who want to intervene. Believe me, that's enough of a hint. Seeing those twin barrels leveled at your face gives you serious pause. So the shotgun rider is not there to shoot—just to intimidate. If he has to shoot, it's always low, at the tires. There's never any point in ratcheting up the level of excitement over a museum robbery by wounding some inno-cent party. The media get quite agitated, and the police suddenly seem to get far more intent about solving the matter. Also, one doesn't want to be thought of as a "killer bandit" by the public when the term "gentleman bandit" sounds so much more dignified.

Now, at night, when it comes to a stealth burglary scenario, the "lookout" might also serve as the crash-car driver, since the likelihood of needing a crash car for a night job is remote. The crash-car ruse really only works when there is a lot of normal traffic, and the driver who "accidentally" rams into the pursuing police cruisers can in fact make a case that he or she bumbled innocently into the path of the on-rushing police cars, which are always running red lights. Clearly, though, that "innocent person" can't also be in possession of a shot-gun. Now they will be questioned, because police know about the whole crash-car ploy, so they must have a clean record and be a cred-ible citizen and also a stand-up person who will not just rat everyone out.

Conversely, late at night, with no traffic about, a crash car would look pretty dubious to law enforcement. As I say, they're well aware that crash cars are used, and they usually arrest any driver involved in a hot-pursuit crash—even the truly innocent little old lady—and drag them in for interrogation.

Suspicious bastards! Anyway, late at night, you're better off with an armed man in a backup car who watches your back while you make your getaway. Trust me on this. It's just the dynamics of the night getaway versus the day getaway.

By the way, given the fact that they are always arrested for questioning if they take action, the best crash-car drivers come from Charlestown.

You find a teenager with a clean record and there is really nothing the cops can do to get anything out of him, because first of all he has no record, and second of all, those young boys grow up with the "code of silence" imperative imbedded in their genes. They just won't talk. It's a wonderful quality, one sadly lost nowadays among the convicts one runs across in the prison system. These days, if someone liberates even an apple from the commissary, you will see two dozen of these newer convicts falling all over themselves to rat out the thief to the warden or the line boss for nothing more than a roll of toilet paper as inducement. It's revolting, really, this newer class of prison convict.

There are essentially two types of museum robberies. One is the lightning sortie in broad daylight, as was the case with the Rembrandt from the MFA, while the other is more of a cat burglary scenario, really. [Connor employed the cat burglary approach when he stole his first Rembrandt.] One thing that I might help teach owners and directors of museums is to be aware that people like them who spend their lives isolated in museums are easy prey in the end for professional thieves, because they maintain a rather charming degree of confidence in their fellow man. An authentic, ingrained belief in civil society and in law and order and all those fine things. It speaks to a divine trust in "The Uniform"—whether it be a policeman's jacket or a fine-fitting Brooks Brothers suit that says "banker" and "legitimate citizen." Clearly, if you want to fit in at the yacht club, you will have your blue blazer and white pants and Docksiders on. Let me just say that I have nothing against civil society or honest Americans. But this outlook helps explain how "Dr. Joseph" could be invited into museums left and right, when that man was me.

MASHBERG: What do you make of this "Dr. No" notion, the idea that super-rich and greedy people order up the thefts of Rembrandts and other great works?

CONNOR: Would the Sultan of Brunei or Bill Gates or H. Ross Perot or the Emperor of Japan want to purchase it on the black market? Just in order to own it for selfish reasons? To show to close friends and concubines in privacy? I've never believed in that scenario, tempting as it is. It's far too risky when the item is internationally notorious. Ultimately, word would leak out, and then the guilty party would be embarrassed, especially if he is a man with an international reputation. These people are rich enough to buy art legitimately, anyway. Why risk a sting or some other plot that might catch them up in a criminal nightmare?

No one has ever approached me or anyone I know for such a thing. Imagine how many people would have to remain quiet if such a crime was to succeed? Not just the ringleader and his crew, but any person the sultan might be tempted to show the art to. Even if you were hired through an intermediary, a lawyer or agent of some kind, that would still be a link. So then they would have to trust that we were never arrested in the years to come and tempted to spill the beans. Not that I would do that, but there are many types who could not be expected to stay quiet in the face of prison. And as people get older, they might change their minds about keeping quiet. They might have an attack of conscience! So you are really relying too much on the character of the criminal.

And even if you bought it on the black market after the crime, people are just not that discreet. They would show the art to someone—a wife or associate or house guest—who could eventually betray them. Especially with a reward out there as incentive.

No, it seems to me the likely buyers are either the museum itself, through a broker or a front man or an insurance company detective, with the price being what can be negotiated secretly among the parties; or a third party, one that wants to barter the art for some larger political or personal purpose, such as gaining freedom for some jailed associate of theirs, and does not want to hold on to it forever. As you know, I was involved in doing just this sort of thing on my own behalf back in the days of the MFA heist. It was a fine scam that worked well for me from time to time, although not without the rather obvious potential of arrest and prosecution. So one can only go to that well so often in life.

MASHBERG: Please provide as many details as you can about the MFA heist.

CONNOR: The surveillance into the operation and of all aspects of the MFA's security was intense, including fly-overs and around-the-clock observation. A burglary via underground passageways was not ruled out. But as the time closed in, the most direct method of a lightning-strike sortie utilizing disguises that were impenetrable was finally decided on. There was no chance of failure no matter who might accidentally show up. There were two back-up plans and fail-safe contingencies. Everyone would leave with the painting.

It was done with extreme precision. The time was chosen because it was just after rush hour.

*   *   *

Connor says two moments from the robbery are ingrained in his memory.

The first was when his confederate laid down a spritz of machine-gun fire at the feet of the trailing guards. He almost lost it laughing out loud, he says, when "the whole pack of them turned tail in unison, like the Keystone Kops in a Buster Keaton movie, and galloped back up the steps and into the building, their knees almost touching their chins as they pumped their legs. They even peeked back around the museum's huge metal front doors, their eyes bulging."

The other was his tug-of-war with the relentless cop Monkouski. "My pal with the machine gun just stepped up and whacked him with the barrel of the gun, at which point the cop let go of the painting and crumpled onto the sidewalk. What stands out is that he made a loud 'Nguuhh!' sound, almost like a cartoon. I must say I respected him—a typical Polish cop," Connor says. "But our goal was no injuries, especially to civilians, and we met that goal."

Connor secreted the painting under the bed of his friend and music manager, Al Dotoli, in Quincy. "Everyone loves the thought of owning a Rembrandt, if only for a little while," he says. "My friend was thrilled at the concept, and there it remained."

Some three months went by, but police investigators could shake loose few clues. Powerful friends of the MFA were urging a resolution.

There was embarrassing international attention, and the Dutch were worried about other Rembrandts on loan to the museum. The federal government was ready to deal if only the painting was returned.

Connor sought out Major Regan to help "broker" the work's return and called on his masterful criminal attorney, Martin K. Leppo, to get a deal in writing. Once law enforcement agreed to his demand for a shorter jail term, Connor wasted little time arranging the return of the MFA's Rembrandt. With Regan and an assistant U.S. attorney, David P. Twomey, overseeing state and federal criminal matters and the promise of leniency, Connor summoned Al Dotoli to handle the hand-over. Dotoli engineered a careful transaction in which he was able to put the Rembrandt, wrapped in a quilt, into Twomey's wife's car in the parking lot of a restaurant and hotel complex along the Southeast Expressway in Massachusetts. Dotoli wore a ski mask the whole time—it was January—and his identity was never made public until 35 years later. Connor notes with pleasure that all 17 people involved in the MFA heist—among them the decoys on the inside, the lookouts on the sidewalks, and the crash-car drivers—remained anonymous and never said a word.

Most significantly, Connor had consummated a peculiar trade-off—fine art for freedom—that became a fresh motivation for museum thieves. And it took nothing less than a Rembrandt to make it happen.

POSTSCRIPT

While the theft, recovery, and backstory of *Portrait of a Girl Wearing a Gold-Trimmed Cloak* are remarkable enough, the Rembrandt has another intriguing story tied to it. In 1943, Robert Treat Paine II, who had originally loaned the painting to the MFA, died, leaving the work to his son, Richard Cushing Paine, who agreed to continue the loan. The Paine family was happy to see the painting back at the MFA after its brief disappearance, until a sweeping 1987 tax bill altered their thinking. Heirs to the father and son Paine decided to beat an 8 percent increase in capital-gains taxes written into the bill by selling the masterpiece at auction. "It is being sold now for tax reasons—we wanted to have a 1986 transaction," said a family spokesman. On December 10, 1986, at Sotheby's in London, *Portrait of a Girl* was offered for sale. Expectations were high. Old Masters specialist Nicholas Hall of the esteemed London art dealership Colnaghi said of the portrait: "I was struck by the condition, which is absolutely beautiful.... The general surface of the painting is superb and the modeling of the features is incredibly haunting. To have something as fine—an accepted portrait in good condition—is a remarkable event at a time when everyone is talking about the unavailability of first-rank works."

The sale price proved Hall—and the Paine family's financial advisors—prescient. *Portrait of a Girl Wearing a Gold-Trimmed Cloak* sold at auction to an anonymous bidder for $9,372,000, a record at the time for Old Master prices. Almost 25 years later, the purchase still ranks among the top ten ever paid for an Old Master at an auction.

It wasn't until 2009 that the painting made a public reappearance. Its unidentified owner loaned it to the J. Paul Getty Museum in Los Angeles for an international exhibition titled "Drawings by Rembrandt and His Pupils: Telling the Difference."

*   *   *

Myles Connor's worst deeds caught up with him in the late 1980s, and he spent a dozen years in federal prison for trafficking in art, antiques, and allegedly cocaine. By now his name as an art criminal was legendary, and one might argue that his punishment was light. By the standards of seventeenth-century Amsterdam, it certainly was. Rembrandt's two famed paintings of anatomical demonstrations feature repeat offenders being dissected after their executions. In *The Anatomy Lesson of Dr. Tulp*, the criminal is identified as Adriaan Adriaanszoon, alias Aris Kindt, who was hanged in 1632 after a long career in thievery and his body made available to the surgeons' guild. Rembrandt's other famed dissection depiction, *The Anatomy Lesson of Dr. Joan Deyman*, features a criminal named Joris Fonteijn of the town of Diest. A thief and highwayman, he was known far and wide as Black Jack, and was hanged in 1656. Before he was put to death, he was condemned by the judge for his crimes with harsh words: "Such a thing is intolerable in a civilized state." The paperwork says Fonteijn was then "by the worshipful lords of the Law Court granted to [the surgeons' guild] as an anatomical specimen."[3] His intestines, stomach, and skull were removed, and his brain matter examined.

Myles Connor, a career criminal, might reflect on how easy he got off compared with Black Jan. As he stood before Federal Judge Richard Mills in Chicago in 1989 for sentencing, Mills told him: "Each time in the past you've been nailed with something...you'll come in and plead and you'll barter off this and you'll barter off that. And all of a sudden another piece of antiquary will surface. You've done nothing but hurt, and take, steal, barter, deal in stolen property, weapons involved, attempted escape. Unfortunately, you're rotten to the core. We simply don't need you, Mr. Connor."

Connor was sentenced to 20 years, served 10, and, unlike his Dutch criminal predecessor, has gone on to live a quiet, retired life, raising exotic animals and admiring the few things he still owns from a long life of crime. It turns out that while Connor was in jail all those years, a petty criminal associate who was supposedly guarding his antiques was in fact selling them off, piece by piece, to feed a heroin habit. (An echo of how Rembrandt himself was plunged into penury when his own beloved art collection was sold at auction in the 1650s to pay off his enormous debts.) Connor the master had been undone by a minion. He seethed for a long time, but has finally grown philosophical.

"Listen, I must confess that this is kind of a karmic boot in the ass that I had coming for a while, in the sense that someone like me, someone who has been involved in a professional way with taking advantage of museums, how can I then complain if property is taken from me, especially if it's stolen property that I did not even own?"

Rembrandt's St. Bartholomew *(oil on panel), stolen from the Worcester Art Museum in 1972 by a gang led by mastermind Florian "Al" Monday. (Worcester Art Museum, Worcester, Massachusetts, Charlotte W.W. Buffington Fund)*

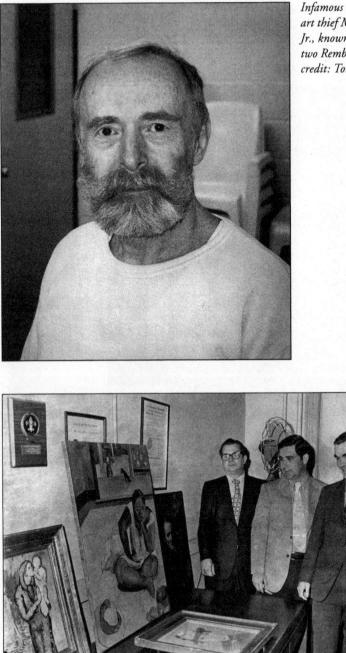

Infamous New England art thief Myles J. Connor Jr., known to have stolen two Rembrandts. (Photo credit: Tom Mashberg)

Worcester Police and FBI investigators pose by the priceless Worcester Art Museum paintings they worked tirelessly to recover. (Worcester Telegram)

Stolen from the Taft Museum in 1973. Scholars, including the Rembrandt Research Project, have since concluded that the painting is not by the master, nor does it depict him. (Rembrandt Leaning on a Windowsill c. 1650 (oil on canvas) by (follower of) Rembrandt Harmensz. van Rijn (1606-69) Taft Museum of Art, Cincinnati, Ohio, USA/Bequest of Louise Taft Semple/ The Bridgeman Art Library)

Sir Edmund Davis surveys the damage to his collection after the 1938 theft of five masterpieces from his home at Chilham Castle in Kent, England. Among the five was the only Rembrandt painting known to have been destroyed by thieves. (Photo courtesy of the Wheeler Family)

Wires that once held paintings including Rembrandt's Portrait of Jacob de Gheyn III *hang empty at the Dulwich Picture Gallery as E. C. Snow, Keeper of the Gallery, stands nearby. (PA Archive/Press Association Images)*

A panel from the doors to the Dulwich Picture Gallery is found to be missing after a thief—or thieves—removed it to gain entry to the museum. Eight paintings, including three Rembrandts, were stolen during the 1966 heist. (PA Archive/ Press Association Images)

Rembrandt's A Girl at a Window *was one of the eight paintings stolen during the 1966 theft at the Dulwich College Picture Gallery in London. Also stolen were three works by Rubens. (PA Archive/Press Association Images)*

Jacob de Gheyn III, *commonly referred to as "The Takeaway Rembrandt." The portrait has been stolen four times. (PA Archive/Press Association Images)*

Even Rembrandt's home in Amsterdam, which is preserved as a small museum, has been broken into by thieves. (The Rembrandt House Museum, Amsterdam. www.rembrandthuis.nl)

Rembrandt's Girl with a Fur-Trimmed Cloak, *formerly thought to be a portrait of (his sister) Elisabeth van Rijn, which was stolen from the Museum of Fine Arts in Boston in 1975 in a theft involving art thief Myles J. Connor, Jr.* (Boston Herald)

The Fall of Man, *also called* Adam and Eve, *is among Rembrandt's largest and most significant etchings. Valued at $60,000, it was stolen while on display at the Hilligoss Gallery in Chicago in May 2007. (Rembrandt van Rijn,* The Fall of Man *(1638), collection of The Rembrandt House Museum, Amsterdam)*

Rembrandt's The Print-Dealer Clement de Jonghe. *This work, created in 1651, was stolen multiple times in its different states from a number of separate owners. (Clement de Jonghe, 1651 (etching) (b/w photo) by Rembrandt Harmensz. van Rijn (1606–69), Musée de la Ville de Paris, Musée du Petit-Palais, France/Giraudon/The Bridgeman Art Library)*

Rembrandt's 1630 self-portrait, one of a handful of his works painted on copper. It was stolen from the National Museum of Stockholm in 2000. Five years later, it was recovered by the FBI and European police. (Self-Portrait, 1630 (oil on copper) by Rembrandt Harmensz. van Rijn (1606-69) © Nationalmuseum, Stockholm, Sweden/The Bridgeman Art Library)

CHAPTER SEVEN

2000: The Stockholm Blitz

PREFACE

The undercover sting operation—it is hard to imagine a more satisfying finale to an act of art-napping. Overconfident criminals anticipating a fat payday. A law enforcement mole seducing and betraying those who deserve it most. Armed cops observing and videotaping the transaction for trial. The irreplaceable object safely recovered and the embarrassed thieves brought to justice.

Sting-style recoveries of great art are rare, particularly for Rembrandts, which for the most part have been handed back by intermediaries or deposited in some shabby location—a shed, a saloon, a thicket of shrubs—for officials to collect. Still, there are a few good examples of undercover ruses leading to Rembrandt recoveries. One of the more famous of these took place in 1994, when a former British police agent, Charlie Hill, went underground to buy back *Rembrandt's*

Mother Reading (1630), attributed by some to Rembrandt and by others to Rembrandt's circle (and thus valued anywhere between $500,000 and $10 million). The painting was acquired by Britain's Earl of Pembroke under the reign of King Henry VIII and had hung uneventfully for 309 years in the Great Ante Room at Wilton House, an estate in Salisbury, Wiltshire, that is open for public visits. It was stolen on November 5, 1994, under the covering noise of England's annual Guy Fawkes Day fireworks, which drowned out a burglar alarm on the lightly policed estate premises.

Three years later, as Hill hunted the men trying to fence the Rembrandt for the equivalent of $250,000, he heard them refer to it as "The Granny" and "The Old Lady." One criminal even observed that "it was so ugly only her son would have painted it."[1] Not much respect for such a trophy. Newcastle native David Duddin, 51 at the time, was the black-market operator who finally stepped into Hill's snare. He was a bit of a pleasant rogue, but much like Rembrandt's careworn mother, no great looker, weighing in at 300 unkempt pounds. As is often the case in art-for-ransom exchanges, the law enforcement mole (Hill) convinced the black marketeer (Duddin) that he had to "authenticate" the work before paying him for it. The men met in London, and after a satisfactory inspection Hill "agreed" to buy the canvas for resale "on the American market." Arrangements were made for the Rembrandt and the cash to be exchanged in a railway station park lot in western London. Within minutes of the swap, Duddin was arrested carrying £105,000 in identifiable bills. The painting went back to its peaceful wall in Wiltshire, and Duddin went to prison.[2]

The Duddin double cross is a lively but fairly straightforward story of a law enforcement setup. Duddin's own tendency to lip off about his art holdings and underworld access helped do him in. Far more challenging and internationally complex was the recovery of a Rembrandt self-portrait stolen from the National Museum in Stockholm in 2000 and retrieved in Denmark five years later. That case featured a rare armed daylight blitz on a museum, springing from an unfortunate tradition of lackadaisical security. It culminated in an elegant transnational sting operation that serves as a solid lesson in recovering stolen paintings and arresting those who conceal them.

*   *   *

Bob Clay, a crooked middle-aged art expert with trim gray eyebrows and a borrowed Rolex on his wrist, was sitting in a Copenhagen hotel room, murmuring into his cell phone, when he finally heard the knock.

The date was September 15, 2005, and Baha Kadhum, a 27-year-old Iraqi in a pink polo shirt and shiny shoes, stood at Clay's door with a delivery for the ages. A fair-skinned man with broad shoulders and a round, good-natured face, Clay was to all appearances a self-assured American art connoisseur traveling Denmark on behalf of the mob to buy Kahdhum's uniquely hot item. Apprehensive but ever ready to appear nonchalant, Clay shut his phone and reached for the handle. He was relieved to find Kadhum alone outside the door, and even more pleased to see him holding a velvet bag. He welcomed the slender Iraqi into his small room, which featured a double bed and tiny bathroom, two flights up from the lobby of the spare and antiseptic Scandic Hotel.

The room was unusually bright to be the focal point of such a shady transaction—one in which $245,000 and a Rembrandt self-portrait were to change hands. Yet Kadhum walked in unworried. He felt at ease because a Bulgarian gangster named Boris Kostov was already seated in the room on a little wooden desk chair, offering him a big smile. Kadhum knew Kostov, knew he'd played a central role in locating Clay as buyer for Kadhum's piece of stolen art. Kostov was also the father of Kadhum's close partner in the crime, Alexander "Sasha" Lindgren. There was little to sweat. It felt just like family.

The Iraqi handed the velvet bag to Clay, who at once tried to free up the angular, two-to-three-pound item inside. He felt confident that it would be a real Rembrandt, in this case a self-portrait on copper exactly 375 years old, solidly framed in black mahogany and worth

$40 million at auction. Clay knew how to handle such items with impeccable care. He did not want even a minuscule paint chip to flake away. He was well aware that the painting had a hardened varnish on its surface, the kind prone to craquelure—the tiny jigsaw pattern of hairline cracks that often form on old paintings. Those cracks could lead to ugly chinks, the kind that would take art conservators and restoration experts weeks to repair.

But Clay hit a glitch. He couldn't seem to untie the string securing the bag. He tugged at it. He twisted it around the corner of the item. He even turned to Kadhum to ask if the young hoodlum might give it a try, but Kadhum begged off, fearful himself of marring the work. After a good four minutes, some of it involving his teeth, Clay at last won the battle against the string. As he slowly loosed the contents from the red velvet sack, he saw emerge before him that familiar probing face with its bulging nose gazing back at him, a face so iconic in the world history of great portraiture. The face of Rembrandt van Rijn.

Clay grasped the item by the sides of its frame and stared at the handsome 24-year-old painter. Rembrandt wore the dashing beret, dark cloak, and white linen collar typical of his mid-twenties dressing style, a period when the artistic prodigy's career was blossoming. The face was confident, well groomed, well fed. The lips were a brash shade of red, the eyes calm and probing. Casually, Clay posed Kadhum a question.

"You an art lover?" he asked.

"No," the Iraqi replied. "I just want the money."

* * *

Money. It is the rare art thief (and perhaps even the rare museumgoer) who doesn't eye a fine or famous painting and hear a cash register ring in his head. With fantasies born of popular mythology and imaginative media, criminals see art, and paintings in particular, as a simple and lucrative score. On the surface, they are being sensible. Of all the objects in the world valued in the multimillions, the items easiest to see, to touch, to potentially grab, are great paintings. Egyptian gold, royal jewels, jade and porcelain from the Far East—rarely does such bounty sit out in the open in a museum or palace. But paintings—there they hang, secured by little more than ceiling wires or a few screws. Portable, enticing riches.

That is the cross museum administrators, curators, and security professionals must bear. They are engaged in an endless struggle to make art approachable without making it vulnerable. It leads to hard choices between security and accessibility, decisions that carry risks. Museum officials are not managing banks or armories. Most abhor the idea of whistling alarms and jutting barriers that limit a viewer's proximity to a signature piece. These would disrupt the reflective comings and goings museums wish to foster. Everything from lucite barriers to modern tracking devices presents a double bind. Security measures must never endanger the art or detract from one's appreciation of the work. Even advanced technology like GPS systems or radio frequency identification devices (known as RFID tags), which emit signals that can be tracked by satellite, raise concerns. They can be unsightly. Most use battery-operated transmitters that pose a risk of leakage. And some thieves might be tempted to tear them away, prompting damage. Security tactics that seem simple or obvious often risk unintended consequences.

There are many examples of masterpieces around the world shielded by nearly impregnable cases and attended nonstop by sentries. That strategy generally applies to works of unrivaled fame and value, or to previously stolen items that seem to have acquired a bull's-eye. Da Vinci's *Mona Lisa*, long behind obscuring layers of protection at the Louvre, stands as an extreme example. It was infamously stolen in 1911 by Vincenzo Peruggia, an Italian laborer at the museum who wanted to repatriate the masterpiece to Leonardo's homeland. It is simply too famous to leave to chance. In a more mundane example, there is a fine portrait by Anthony van Dyck, a noted Flemish contemporary of Rembrandt, wisely displayed behind thick glass at a private retirement home in Riverdale, New York. It is difficult to make out its details through the resulting glare, and the work is hung too high to be appreciated. But it is no sitting duck.

When major thefts occur, as happened during the Stockholm Museum blitz in 2000, administrators often shrug and cite their built-in dilemma. Torsten Gunnarsson, head of collections at Sweden's National Museum at the time of the blitz, highlighted his institution's predicament hours after the Rembrandt was whisked from its wall a few days before Christmas.

"What would be the purpose of having this art if we did not display it for all to see?" he said.[3] "We took the normal measures. We've never had a similar robbery with weapons in Sweden, as far as I know." It is hard not to sympathize with Gunnarsson and other administrators in his position. But the "normal measures" were clearly insufficient to protect *Self-Portrait* (and two works by Pierre-Auguste Renoir, *Young Parisian* and *The Conversation*) from three well-rehearsed men who pulled off the most dauntless of all museum thefts: the lightning-fast armed invasion. As a result, it took almost five years of fruitless searching and an intricate transatlantic flimflam to bring the Rembrandt home.

*   *   *

The afternoon was crisp and idyllic in the Swedish capital on Friday, December 22, 2000. A light snow fell on Christmas shoppers as the hectic workweek at last came to an end. Motorists were making their way home for the annual holiday weekend, with herring and smoked reindeer, aquavit and lingonberry pastries, their cars filled with gift-wrapped parcels, liquor bottles, and fresh delicacies. Then, quite inexplicably, many found themselves thrust into a suffocating gridlock. Traffic had come to a standstill, the drivers would soon be told, due to an odd pair of occurrences. On both the Södra Blasieholmshamnen and the Nybrokajen, two vital thoroughfares leading into the capital's toniest peninsula, sizable car fires had broken out. The first report to the fire department came in around 4 P.M., and responders rushing to the scene found a Ford fully ablaze on the Södra Blasieholmshamnen. The firefighters were forced to block the boulevard with their trucks to gain rapid access to the flaming car, halting traffic in and out of a teeming section of the port city. Stockholm is a tough-to-navigate archipelago of larger and smaller islands bound by rivers, bays, and inlets, and one burning sedan was bad enough. But soon, and by no means coincidentally, officials learned of another car fire. This time a Mazda was engulfed on the nearby Nybrokajen roadway. Speeding, bleating fire trucks and police cars made their way to the second scene, and the pre-holiday snarl-up swelled miserably.

While firefighters battled the auto blazes, guards at Stockholm's National Museum, a stately copper-roofed bastion less than 200 yards from both car fires, started to close it up for the evening. The Renaissance-style museum would appear quite well protected to the average eye. Its three front doorways face the choppy, fast-running Norrström River. Its sides and back are built of essentially unscalable marble and stone. Visitors experience a no-nonsense Nordic air among the staff and guards, and a confident punctuality during business hours. On the inside, the museum is capacious and airy but hardly insecure looking. It is dominated by an enormous, beckoning flight of stairs that vaults the public toward galleries resplendent with drawings and paintings from the Middle Ages to the Impressionist era. There are 100 or so seventeenth-century Dutch masterworks, several by Rembrandt, as well as ancient marble sculptures, Roman antiquities, rare and delicate porcelains, and goblets of crystal and gold. Inside, the museum is a congenial smorgasbord of artistic treasures that draws several thousand people a day. On the outside, the building is a fortress, a stern stone vault built along a river that might as well serve as a moat. It was opened to the public in 1866, and in 134 years no one had ever tried to besiege it.

Minutes before the museum's 5 P.M. closing time, as visitors streamed toward the main exit and out into the frosty late-afternoon air, three masked men, two of them armed with pistols and one with a submachine gun, surged into the building through its tall glass entrance doors. Shouting threats and waving their weapons, they ordered everyone within range to hit the floor. One gunman held his handgun to the head of a guard outfitted with a radio, freezing the employee in his tracks. "I could see his eyes through the slits in his mask," the guard told police. "He meant business."

Other than a few yelps, those who saw and heard the gunmen complied with the directive to lie still and silent. Almost redundantly, one of the thieves, speaking in Swedish, called out, "Stay calm!... Stay quiet and you won't be hurt!"[4] The man with the submachine gun left no doubt that any sudden move or foolhardy act of heroism would be unwise.[5]

The outburst of violence was "a shock for many people," said Hans-Henrik Brummer, acting director of the museum's fine-arts gallery, and one of many employees who were in their offices during the heist and had no idea it was taking place. "Things like that just don't happen," he added, in a peaceful and law-abiding country like Sweden. Police Inspector Dan Boija, one of the first detectives at the scene, described it this way: "It's just before closing time, so the grand foyer is full of people who are going to leave, and there was this man standing there with this automatic gun. There were some screams from women and teenagers. A girl, three or four, was crying. It was a very scary time for them."

The three thieves had no time for tears. With the machine gunner holding his position and the crowd cowed, the other two ran up the museum's broad marble stairs to the second-floor picture gallery. One veered into the French Room and went directly to *Young Parisian* and *The Conversation*, by Pierre-Auguste Renoir. He had evidently made walkthroughs and knew his exact destination. The other man made for the Dutch Room, repository of Rembrandt's shimmering *Self-Portrait*. Working quickly with cutting tools, the men snipped the skinny suspension wires holding all three works in place and grabbed them by their frames. The two gunmen then retraced their steps and made for the front doors, carrying the paintings under their left arms and their guns in their right hands. As they bolted for the entrance, they were covered by the machine gunner, who followed immediately behind. In two and a half minutes, art valued at $50 million to $60 million had vanished.

As soon as it seemed safe to move, museum officials alerted Stockholm police to the theft. But due to the twin car fires it took them 45 minutes to make it to the crime scene. Investigators soon realized the fires were no accident. Near the burning cars they discovered road spikes known as "hedgehogs," used to puncture tires and disable pursuit cars. They soon deduced that the museum thieves had set the blazes, using a dousing of lighter fluid as fuel, then laid out the spikes to further impede response to any emergency call. The fires hadn't just spoiled the pre-Christmas commute. They'd ensured a clean getaway for three men with a better means of transportation at hand.

On exiting the museum, the thieves headed around its corner to a darkening jetty and boarded the well-chosen conveyance they had used to get there—a 15-foot reddish-orange speedboat with an off-board motor. The engine fired up immediately and the boat surged into the river. The three raiders were getting away without so much as a foot chase. As they sped through Stockholm's spiderweb of waterways and canals, a pall settled over the palatial museum, and soon enough over the capital. The thieves had not only manufactured a traffic jam, they had also set off a national crisis that would sting Sweden's Viking pride.

* * *

Görel Cavalli-Björkman, director of research at the Swedish National Museum, was "home baking for Christmas when a journalist phoned me and said, 'What can you say about the Rembrandt that has been stolen?'

"I didn't even know, so I got a shock," she said.

She hurried to the crime scene, filling now with police, news media, gawkers, and museum staffers. Breathless, surrounded by demanding reporters, she gave blunt and direct answers: "Nobody has any idea who these people are.... It was done the way you rob a bank.... It seems a bit overdone to use machine guns when you go to a museum.... We think somebody hired them.... Of course they took the small paintings because it was easiest. With a gun in one hand, it is not easy to take large paintings.... They can't be art lovers.... They knew exactly what they were coming for. They had planned it very carefully. They must have made studies before of the rooms to be able to just choose the smallest paintings on the wall.... You could say they made a good choice because they took some important paintings."

Along with the rapid-fire questions, there was some rapid second-guessing and finger-pointing in the hours and days to come. No one accepted blame for what was considered a huge national security fiasco, Sweden's biggest since the assassination of Prime Minister Olof Palme in 1986, a crime that remains unsolved.

"I was a bit disappointed about the museum's security," declared Inspector Boija, who took over the case. "I thought that valuable paintings were alarmed. They just hang on thin wires. And we found out that they were not covered with video surveillance. At the beginning we hadn't a clue who these guys were."

Agneta Karlström, speaking for the museum, retorted that administrators had been asking the state for better protection for years, including cameras, only to be rejected by Stockholm county authorities. It wasn't that Sweden lacked the latest surveillance technology. Government officials and most Swedes simply considered videotaping in public facilities a privacy intrusion.

"I never understood it—they have cameras at McDonald's, but we weren't allowed to install them," Karlström said. "Only after the robbery did we get permission, and there are still discussions going on about what we can and cannot do."

*   *   *

Security cameras and other fail-safes would seem natural for such a top-flight cultural institution. Built between 1850 and 1866, the Swedish

National Museum ranks among the world's greatest art showplaces. It sits across the Norrström River from the Swedish Royal Palace and rivals that ancient home to kings and princes in its prominence and grandeur. The museum features dozens of complex bas-reliefs and glistening marble statues along its façade. When lighted at night it gives off a soothing rosy glow. The National Museum's picture gallery alone holds more than 1,000 works. The museum in its entirety has half a million items on display or in storage.[6]

The museum is also notable for its excellent collection of Rembrandts, and features works from all stages of the master's career. Among its most famous holdings is *The Conspiracy of Claudius Civilis*, painted in 1661, five years into Rembrandt's bankruptcy. A number of his unsatisfied creditors were still waiting for their money and the artist was not his own man. It was to be hung in the Town Hall of Amsterdam and earn the artist a decent fee, but he was never paid for it. Either it turned out to be too large—about 65 square feet—or Rembrandt failed to produce the triumphal image Dutch town fathers had envisioned.[7] The painting was returned to Rembrandt, with a compensation of 18 guilders for the canvas. It was probably the artist himself who then cut out the central narrative scene and put the masterpiece on the market. By the end of the seventeenth century it was in Sweden. Today it is universally admired, and its value has reached $120 million. It holds an important spot in Rembrandt's oeuvre as his last immense canvas, and Sweden treats it as a national treasure.

There are other important Rembrandts at the National Museum— *St. Anastasius* (1631); *St. Peter* (1632); a portrait of Rembrandt's wife, Saskia, in the prime of her beauty; and *Portrait of a Young Girl* (1631), traditionally identified as one of the artist's sisters. None of those Rembrandts was molested by the men who knocked over the National Museum in 2000. They chose instead the very portable *Self-Portrait,* yet it was by no means a second-rate choice. The portrait features the artist as a youthful sensation, brimming with vigor, his body turned slightly to the left and his head facing a bit to the right. Just 24 years old, he was by now a well-paid artist and tutor in his hometown of Leiden, and had been noticed by the court at The Hague. Atop his wild chestnut hair rests a plush black velvet cap, and he wears a thin white collar under a dark mantle and a red doublet. In the top left corner are the remains of the signature that Rembrandt used in that period: "RHL 1630" (indicating "Rembrandt Harmensz of Leiden" and the date).

Rembrandt was born in Leiden in 1606. After Amsterdam, it was the second-largest city in Holland, with about 45,000 residents, and home to an emerging textile industry and expanding bourgeoisie. Rembrandt was well educated at its Latin school, and was registered to study at Leiden University when he was just 14. His father was a well-regarded miller and his mother, conveniently for business, came from a family of bakers. These were respectable but workaday trades, and his parents had higher aspirations for their gifted ninth child. But a university diploma was not Rembrandt's wish. He left school at 15 to serve an apprenticeship in art, and this two-and-a-half-year period in Leiden (from 1621 to mid-1624), under the tutelage of painter Jacob van Swanenburgh (1571–1638), was very formative.[8]

But Rembrandt's next six months of study, in Amsterdam under the tutelage of artist Pieter Lastman (1583–1633), are viewed as his most influential training. Lastman specialized in dramatic historical and biblical paintings—scenes depicting Christ's crucifixion or the tale of Balaam and the ass. He had lived for years in Italy and absorbed the techniques of the Italian masters, which included the intricate play of light and shadow known as *chiaroscuro* (literally, "light and dark"). Rembrandt was to learn that specialty from Lastman and take it to its undisputed pinnacle.

After his time with Lastman, Rembrandt, just 18, returned to Leiden, set up a studio in his parents' house, and began associating with the painter Jan Lievens, who was 17. The pair rapidly grew famous portraying saints and soldiers and scenes from mythology and the Bible, as well as the local citizens. By 1628, Rembrandt had taken on a well-paying apprentice of his own, Gerrit Dou, and by 1630 Rembrandt and Lievens were established as master artists. (It was this year that Rembrandt lost his father, Harmen Gerritsz van Rijn.[9]) By age 24,

Rembrandt had completed some of his most expressive youthful self-portraits, among them the work on copper and gold leaf stolen in broad daylight from the Stockholm Museum almost four centuries later.

It was during this period that Rembrandt perfected his talent. Ongoing research into such details as the length and width and thickness of his brush strokes has given scholars fresh data about Rembrandt's early techniques. He was exploring novel uses for materials and painting processes, and some of them are evident in the Stockholm self-portrait. Rather than painting directly onto a typical layer of chalk and glue "ground," Rembrandt applied a thin layer of gold leaf to the surface as well. Art historian Christopher White calls this "extremely unusual, and so far it has not been discovered in the work of any other artist." White adds: "Undoubtedly, Rembrandt intended to create a glow beneath the surface of the painting."[10]

There is naturally some controversy about this. The use of costly gold leaf led the Rembrandt Research Project, in its exhaustive four-volume *A Corpus of Rembrandt Paintings*, to attribute the Stockholm work to "the circle" of Rembrandt—his peers and acolytes—rather than to Rembrandt himself. "No definite conclusion can be reached as to an attribution to Rembrandt," they declare.[11] But Harvard Rembrandt scholar Seymour Slive is among many who dispute that finding. He believes the stolen self-portrait is authentic.[12] The difference—which boils down to whether Rembrandt applied most of the brush strokes, held the student painter's hand, or simply touched up the work of colleague—could alter the value of the painting by tens of millions of dollars.

The portrait is historically important because it is one of very few Rembrandts painted onto copper (others include *Old Woman,* in Salzburg, Austria, and *Man Laughing,* at The Hague), and it was completed at a major juncture in the great master's career.

Rembrandt painted more than 50 known self-portraits on canvas, wood, and metal during his lifetime, a remarkable tally that has provided historians with a multimedium chronology of his life and career. (He also drew and etched himself numerous times.) Art historian Kenneth

Clark says "with the possible exception of van Gogh, [Rembrandt is] the only artist who has made the self-portrait a major means of artistic expression; and he is absolutely the only one who has turned self-portraiture into an autobiography." Clark also observed: "To follow his exploration of his own face [through the decades] is an experience like reading the works of the great Russian novelists."[13]

Given the dearth of Rembrandt's personal writings, which amount to seven or so formal business letters, it is fair to say the self-portraits are his intimate diaries, a singular record of a great man's rise and decline. There are so many that they are usually distinguished by slightly clumsy add-on phrases—self-portrait "frowning," self-portrait "in work clothes," self-portrait "in a plumed hat and gold chain."[14] His self-portraits on paper and metal plates are also adventurous, showing him grinning, glowering, laughing, even as a street beggar. Scholars try to learn about the inner Rembrandt from these and other works. His self-portraits depict him looking magisterial and slovenly, rich and poor, unyielding and crushed. He almost never surrounds himself with symbols of great learning—globes and books and scientific implements. But he is relentless when it comes to capturing the blemishes and creases on his cheeks and chin, the blobby asymmetry of his nose, "the ugly and plebeian face by which he was ill-favored,"[15] as seventeenth-century Florentine art historian Filippo Baldinucci declared. To stare at a Rembrandt self-portrait is to feel his penetrating gaze and sense his introspective nature. White says of the portraits: "He is watching as much as he is being watched. He does not yield up his secrets easily."[16]

The self-portraits can tell us much about Rembrandt's mind-set, but hardly everything. For example, although Holland was going through its 80-year war of independence when Rembrandt painted, and the Dutch Republic was heavily garrisoned, Rembrandt rarely portrayed himself in arms. He was never in the militia, although a few early artworks show him donning a gorget, a hinged metal collar piece that barely covers the shoulder tops. It was probably more of a fashion statement than a bid to appear martial. Through the decades,

Rembrandt depicted himself as a brash rising star, a middle-aged Italian Renaissance master, a debauched tavern rascal, and even as St. Paul the Apostle—neither pious nor beatific, but full of the hapless humility Rembrandt felt beginning in 1661, when he was out of money, out of favor, and personally abased. His panoply of self-portraits offers a Dorian Gray–like journey through Rembrandt's life of highs and lows, glories and degradations. They make up as keen an autobiography as any writer's set of notebooks and letters. As such, each one is deemed a historical treasure. Losing one to thieves would be akin to losing one of Shakespeare's folios or Leonardo's journals.

*   *   *

The Stockholm self-portrait's whereabouts during its first 150 years are obscure. The earliest known owner was one Elias van der Hoeven of Holland, but the date he acquired it, and from whom, remains a mystery. The painting was sold from the Dutchman's collection in 1768 and listed as a "fine little head by Rembrandt van Ryn, being his own portrait."[17] While the Amsterdam-based Rembrandt Research Project once questioned its attribution (they accept it now), there had been no hesitation on the part of one J. van der Marck, who, after reading the sales description, handed over 35 guilders for the painting. Five years later, he sold it for 50 guilders (about $2,500 in today's money), describing it as follows: "Rembrand van Rhyn. This hero of Art has portrayed himself in this work, wearing a cloak and a velvet cap. Very vigorously painted on copper."[18] The painting next made its way to Paris aristocrats and then back to Holland before landing in a private collection in Vienna. In 1956, the self-portrait was permanently acquired by the Swedish National Museum after it was included in a Rembrandt exhibition in Stockholm. It hung there unbothered for 44 years before three men stormed in and took it on a wintry December day.[19]

Where the three thieves who stole the Rembrandt and two Renoirs took their haul just after the theft is a mystery. Museum Director of

Research Cavalli-Björkman recalls initially fearing the worst: "We were afraid it was lost. We had all kinds of thoughts. Maybe they lost it in the water and we would never see it again."[20] Her panic was understandable given that investigators had no leads. The lack of surveillance video, the roadway delays and diversions, the ski masks, and the overall speed and efficiency had granted the thieves a sprinting head start. It seemed they had committed a perfect crime. But art crime is rarely perfect.

As the thieves made their way out of the museum and onto their orange-red outboarder, they made the type of blunder that would set investigators hard on their trail. Overcome with excitement and adrenaline, the men were not careful to slow down and board their getaway boat in silence. Darting past a small shelter along the jetty near their vessel, they turned boisterous and gleeful, crowing over the successful caper. The uproar drew the attention of a man working inside the shelter, and he watched as the threesome clambered onto their launch. Curious about the odd commotion, the man stepped into his own motorized canal boat and decided to follow the spirited fugitives from a cautious distance. The thieves sped through the labyrinthlike canals of Stockholm, past Skeppsholmen Island, under Danvikstull Bridge, and across a bay before tying up at a small fishing harbor on the banks of Mälaren Lake. There they ditched their vessel and slipped into the forested countryside. When their silent pursuer caught up to the boat at its drop-off point, its engine was still warm. Realizing that this was where the noisy men had gone ashore, and still dubious about their behavior, he phoned the police.

It was an amazing coup. Investigators moved quickly to publicize the boat and gave photos to the news media. The picture made the cover of the full-color *Aftonbladet* tabloid, Sweden's largest daily, and was shown repeatedly on television. It did not take long for someone to recognize it. A local man named Pär Lundmark came forward and told police it was a boat he had recently sold for the equivalent of $300 in cash to a Dutchman whose main concern was whether it would start reliably in cold weather.

"I had already bought a new boat and I put the old one out for sale, and this man called and was very eager to buy it," Lundmark said.[21] The buyer, satisfied after a test run, made the purchase. He asked Lundmark if he could borrow his trailer to transport the vessel, and the seller agreed—on one condition: that the buyer provide a cell phone number for surety. The buyer agreed.

Police were delighted to find that Lundmark had kept the receipt, on which the man's number was still scribbled. They had gone from no clues to the likely phone number of one of the pirates in barely 24 hours. "That was probably the biggest mistake they made," Inspector Boija said. "That phone number gave us a lot of leads to go for, so that was the key."

Investigators set about researching the history of calls to and from the cell phone and found that the number was connected to a gang of crooks and car thieves operating in southern Stockholm. "These guys, they were not big criminals," Boija said. "They had done petty crimes like car thefts, drug peddling, and so on. Not masterminds." One number harvested from the phone records belonged to a known criminal who specialized in stealing makes of cars "just like the cars that were put on fire outside the museum," Boija said.

The car thief had links to two men who were serving prison sentences in a minimum-security jail ten miles from Stockholm—a Swedish national named Stefan Nordström and a Russian named Alexander Petrov. And while being behind bars during the commission of a crime seems like a perfect alibi, Nordström and Petrov happened to be inmates at a facility that allowed "low-risk prisoners" to take weekend furloughs. Unlike Petrov, Nordström had not returned from his last furlough, shortly before the robbery. He remained unaccounted for.

A search of Nordström's cell led to news clippings about past art heists. Some told of a Stockholm heist from 1993, one of the very few in which the robbers did in fact employ a hint of Hollywood-style derring-do. The thieves in that case bored a man-sized hole in the roof of the lightly protected Swedish Museum of Modern Art, lowered themselves by rope into its galleries, and looted the place of six Picassos and two works by Georges Braque. Insurers valued that haul at $52 million. The burglars exited the way they had entered, even leaving footprints on the walls.[22]

Police also discovered that Nordström had been visiting auction houses in Stockholm.[23] With the Rembrandt valued at $40 million and the Renoirs together at perhaps $15 million, Nordström and Petrov became the obvious suspects in the biggest robbery in Swedish history. That they planned the crime in a jail cell, and committed it during a furlough, was not lost on Swedish officials. "It's embarrassing," admitted Justice Minister Thomas Bodström.

On December 28, a week after the heist, Petrov's lawyer contacted the police and offered to serve as intermediary in the return of the paintings. Investigators met with the attorney, who provided hostage-style photos of the Renoirs next to recent newspapers. The lawyer said his professional oath required that he keep the names of the thieves confidential.

But with plenty of leads, no one involved in the recovery was in the mood to pay ransom. "It is not our task to deal with stolen art, and our attitude is that we do not negotiate with criminals," Police Superintendent Leif Jennekvist announced. "We will not pay a single penny. As long as there are those who are willing to pay ransoms, this sort of art theft will continue."[24]

Police put a surveillance team on Petrov when he next left the prison to meet with his attorney. They spotted him with the missing Nordström outside the lawyer's office. The two split up, and Nordström, who was carrying a bag, was arrested. In his sack police found more Polaroid photos of the stolen Renoirs.

The group of robbers and coconspirators who had so deftly handled the actual heist proved to be wildly clumsy, indiscreet, and undisciplined in its aftermath. Petrov was also arrested after his fingerprints were found on Nordström's Polaroids. A Filofax datebook found in a cellar frequented by their ring was filled with exact details about the crime. Most of the outfit—there were a dozen or so conspirators—was rounded up. Although police never determined which three men stormed the museum, they were certain that they had the gang and its leaders. Petrov was sentenced to eight years in prison, Nordström to six, and the others received various shorter terms. They were also a bit laughingly ordered to pay damages to the museum of about $4.5 million.

Despite the prosecutorial success, the major question remained: Where were the paintings? Museum officials must have feared the art was far underground and well beyond reach—otherwise the gang members would surely have given it up in exchange for leniency. Anxious and puzzled, they went about shoring up museum security and dealing with recriminations, with no sense that a major break was at hand.

Just months after the trials, news of the art began to percolate in the Swedish underworld.[25] Boija said police started receiving tips that Renoir's *The Conversation* was up for sale. They deployed an agent to arrange a buy that might net the paintings and the arrests of more thieves.

An undercover man infiltrated the crime ring, and soon enough he had arranged a meeting with the "sellers" at a Stockholm café. The mole set up the get-together on the pretext that he had a buyer for *The Conversation* standing by and needed to affirm that the real painting was available. He was startled when the criminals holding the Renoir showed up at the café with the actual painting in a costume case and revealed it to the undercover man in the café's bathroom. After making a show of examining it under a magnifying glass, the agent told them, "I have a buyer, and he will buy this painting."[26] Pleased, the suspects left the café, only to be busted with the art a few blocks away. Cops soon swept up the rest of the gang—among them Alexander "Sasha" Lindgren, son of Boris Kostov, as well as Baha Kadhum and three of his brothers. They found no other stolen paintings, and only one of the suspects, a Swede, went to jail. The others were let off after claiming entrapment. Not a whisper had yet arisen about the missing Rembrandt *Self-Portrait*.

*   *   *

Some four and a half years later, and a quarter of the world away, the FBI's organized-crime squad was looking into a group of Bulgarian criminals operating in the Los Angeles area. The bureau's focus was on hard drugs, but fine art is what it would find.

Based on wiretap information, agents learned that Renoir's *Young Parisian* was in the control of local Bulgarian drug dealers. One of those Bulgarians had even entered the United States illegally from Sweden in the late 1990s.[27] The investigation took on urgency in March 2005, when the FBI learned that the Bulgarians hoped to move *Young Parisian* out of Los Angeles, and the bureau caught a break. Agents listening to wire-tapped conversations intercepted a call from one of the gang's top figures, Boris Kostov. They heard him speak not just of the Renoir, but also of a Rembrandt. They staked out Kostov's house and spotted him putting a package about the size of *Young Parisian* in his trunk. The agents rolled up on him, but the item turned out to be his dry cleaning. Nonetheless, Kostov was taken into custody on drug charges. He broke after a few hours of grilling when he learned the extent of the wiretap evidence against him and realized that, at 66, he was now likely to die in prison.[28]

Keen on a deal, Kostov said the Renoir had been smuggled to him from Sweden. He promptly led the authorities to *Young Parisian*—stashed in a local pawnshop's basement. According to FBI agent Jonathan Mosser, "It was in good condition, considering that it had been sitting against a wall of this business for the last four-and-a-half years. It was actually stored in an art folio case wrapped in a couple towels and some Ralph's grocery bags."[29]

Kostov's assistance would become more valuable when the FBI turned its focus to the Rembrandt. Wheeling and dealing for leniency, the burly Bulgarian said he had a contact in Sweden who knew of its whereabouts. That source was none other than Alexander "Sasha" Lindgren, arrested but never imprisoned four years earlier in connection with the National Museum case, and still living in Sweden. Lindgren was Kostov's son.

While the FBI was squeezing Kostov in Los Angeles, his son was feeling the pressure from two criminal associates—Baha and Dieya Kadhum—to sell off the hot Rembrandt. Kostov wasted no time in agreeing to incriminate his own son to evade prison. The bureau asked

Swedish police to put Lindgren and the two Kadhums under surveillance, and tapped the phone Lindgren was using to speak with his father in the United States.[30] Confident that the trio had grown serious about selling the Rembrandt, the FBI summoned its most reliable closer in matters of art theft: special agent Robert K. Wittman.

Wittman was in the midst of a storied career. He was the creative force behind the FBI's Art Crime Team, and had years of success posing as a crooked art expert, typically masquerading as a buyer for organized crime. Part scholar, part daredevil, Wittman had managed stings in Paris, Philadelphia, Rio de Janeiro, Miami, and Madrid. He had recovered works by Degas, Rodin, Goya, and Dali, as well as hundreds more American and international treasures and heirlooms. The total value of his recoveries has been pegged at $200 million.

Wittman's *nom de guerre* for such exploits? Bob Clay.

*   *   *

And so it came about that Bob Clay found himself in Copenhagen, Denmark, meeting with Boris Kostov's son, Sasha Lindgren, in September 2005. To convince Lindgren that he meant business, Clay showed him a quarter of a million dollars in U.S. currency (supplied and marked by the FBI). Kostov hovered about approvingly as his son took Clay's bait. The money was enough to persuade Lindgren and his Iraqi partners across the border in Sweden that they had a serious buyer on the hook. The Kadhum brothers agreed to travel to Copenhagen with the Rembrandt and close the deal with Lindgren, Kostov, and Clay.

The tricky cross-border gambit was a necessary step in reeling in the Iraqis. Kostov had told them he was a wanted man in Sweden—which was true—and could travel only as close as Denmark. This outlaw status raised his estimation in the eyes of the Iraqis. So when Kostov suggested that they all gather with Clay in Copenhagen, five hours away from Stockholm by train, the idea seemed sound. The Kadhum brothers made the trip, tailed by cops from both nations. Even though the Iraqis had a bag in their possession that could have contained the

Rembrandt, police did not move to arrest them. Possession of the stolen object was not enough of a charge; they wanted to catch them in the act of selling it.

Anyone with intergovernmental experience, or with experience trying to manage an operation between separate law enforcement agencies, knows how gnarly the turf battles can be. The annals of criminal investigations are replete with tales of suspects who got away with little or no justice because of breakdowns in communication and cooperation between agencies. Given that reality, the bruised Swedish police showed admirable equanimity during the sting. Keeping their eyes fixed on the recovery of the *Self-Portrait,* they put their trust in Danish authorities and an FBI undercover agent, allowing them to run the show.

On the evening of September 15, Clay and Kostov awaited the three targets in the lobby of the Scandic Hotel. When the men arrived, Clay outlined how the transfer would take place. His cash was in one room, but the swap would occur in a different room—one wired up for sound and video. Baha Kadhum followed Clay and Kostov to the money room, and avidly and carefully counted the cash. "That's when I knew I we had him," Wittman recalled. "Kadhum had the look, the one most criminals get when they believe they're going to get away with it, when they think their plan is going to work."[31]

Clay instructed Kadhum to retrieve the Rembrandt and deliver it to the wired room. "Bring it back to me. I'll look at it, I'll authenticate it, and if everything's right, then we'll do the deal," Clay told him.[32]

Satisfied, Kadhum left the room, ostensibly to fetch the Rembrandt from his brother and Lindgren, who were still in the lobby holding a bag. But the trio surprised the lawmen by abruptly leaving the hotel. All the preparation and hard work seemed to have gone sour. Had their cover been blown? One of Wittman's undercover colleagues called him on his cell phone to discuss the dispiriting turn of events.

As it turned out, Kadhum and his confederates had a clever gambit of their own. The bag they had been carrying was a decoy, intended to draw out any overeager police. Now, pleased with the sight of a quarter-million in cash, and convinced that the deal was genuine, they retrieved the real bag. Kadhum returned to Clay's wired-up transfer room bearing the velvet satchel that would prove so difficult to open. He knocked. Clay closed his cell phone and reached for the door latch. As the cameras rolled, Kadhum entered with the missing Rembrandt.

Clay examined the painting closely, but more for show. He knew right away that it was the real thing, based on what he had been told about the back of the painting—that it bore three Swedish Museum stickers and several deep gouges. Clay spotted them immediately.

Bob Clay then officially became Bob Wittman. As Danish SWAT team officers stood by, Wittman spoke the code words necessary to launch their raid on the room: "This is good. We've got a done deal." He then stepped into the hotel room bathroom cradling the framed copper self-portrait to his chest, prepared to duck and cover in the bathtub should shots be fired. But there was no gunplay. The SWAT team quickly overwhelmed the stupefied suspects. The arrests of Baha Kadhum, his brother Dieya, and the betrayed Lindgren went off without a hitch.

Asked to describe his emotions after the successful sting, Wittman said this: "Nothing quite compares to the feeling an art investigator gets when he finally holds the object of his long pursuit. It is a 'eureka!' moment. I liken it to how I felt when my children were born. It is that feeling of elation and your feet don't touch the ground, but the difference is, it only lasts for a few moments as compared to children, which lasts for years. That was how it felt when I finally held the 1630 Rembrandt *Self-Portrait* close to my chest in my arms."[33]

The painting was quickly returned to the National Museum, which was about to host an exhibition titled "The Dutch Golden Age: Rembrandt, Frans Hals and Their Contemporaries." With the story of the sting and recovery an international sensation, the museum's head of collections, Torsten Gunnarsson, found a silver lining in the five-year ordeal.

"The new exhibit is already attracting a lot of attention, but we are especially happy to have the missing link back in place," he said. "The timing is unbelievable."[34] Cynics might wonder whether a theft helps put a museum on the international map.

When the exhibition opened, the Rembrandt got the *Mona Lisa* treatment. It was displayed behind a glass window, with a specially assigned security guard standing by its side. "Now that we have gotten this piece back, we want to make it clear that we have good security and we are taking extra good care of it," said security chief Jan Birkenhorn.

But, he added, "I don't think you can ever protect yourself from an armed robbery. If you are threatened with a gun, you just have to stand aside."[35]

POSTSCRIPT

The Kadhum brothers and Alexander Lindgren were convicted of receiving stolen goods. Their sentences were overturned by a Swedish appeals court, which ruled they were "provoked" into the crime by American and Swedish police. They are still living in Sweden.

Robert K. Wittman has retired from the FBI and coauthored a book on his exploits, *Priceless: How I Went Undercover to Rescue the World's Stolen Treasures*. His coauthor is journalist John Shiffman.

The government of Sweden has augmented art security since the 2000 blitz and a 2004 armed assault on the Edvard Munch Museum in Oslo, Norway, during which thieves stole *The Scream* and other works. When a 1635 Rembrandt, *Minerva in Her Study*, was put on sale in Stockholm in late 2004 by its Canadian owner, security included armed guards, bulletproof glass, and 24-hour video surveillance. It is rare for a Rembrandt to go on sale, and the asking price for this one, depicting the Roman goddess of wisdom, was $42 million.

That prompted Dr. Bob van den Boogert, curator of the Rembrandt House Museum in Amsterdam, to remark: "Anyone who wants to buy one should do it now. If a Rembrandt painting gets into a museum collection, it will never get out again."[36]

Sadly, many a thief will come along with ambitions to challenge that.

CHAPTER EIGHT

The Rembrandt that Wasn't

Timing is everything—in life, in art, and in art theft. Rembrandt was born into the Dutch Golden Age, a brief and supercharged epoch in which the Netherlands and the city of Amsterdam in particular were the economic, scientific, and cultural crossroads of the world. The seventeenth-century Dutch created the first stock exchange, multinational corporations, and central banking system. They were a shipping, trading, and colonial juggernaut who far outstripped England and France in global reach, and were on par with the rival Spanish on the high seas. With innovations in hydraulics, windmill power, and peat-based energy farming, and inventions like the sawmill, they led the world in shipping to Asia, India, and Africa, and in the array of goods hauled about the earth. A stroll along the Amsterdam piers was like a short sally around the globe. Free Africans and persecuted European Jews and Protestants mixed with Flemish dockworkers and high and mighty Calvinist officeholders and officials from the power-ful and profitable Dutch East India Company. Warehouses were flush with pepper, nutmeg, silk, salt, ice, wool, exotic woods, beer barrels, tobacco, malts and barley, and plants, herbs, and flowers from places like Congo, Japan, Indonesia, and North and South America. It would not have been unusual to see a circus elephant or two roaming about (Rembrandt drew several of them). The Dutch guilder was an accepted currency worldwide. Even as fearless Dutch explorers sought toeholds from China to the Arctic Circle, eager European workers migrated to a land that embraced exotic voyagers and offered unmatched levels of religious tolerance. Thinkers like Descartes and Spinoza resided in Holland, marveling at the pioneering work of microbiologist Anton van Leeuwenhoek and land reclamation engineer Jan Leeghwater, among others. Holland was the world's foremost book publisher, and pamphleteering and newspapering were common. Any individual with energy and ambition could find a route to comfort, even prosperity, in what can only be described as the Manhattan of its day. The seeds of egalitarianism that grew into the American Constitution and other great democratic documents were nurtured in Golden Age soil, and Rembrandt was a sharp observer of this cosmopolitan era. Had he been born into a more suffocating monarchical or religious system, it is hard to imagine his work and life would have been so varied, illuminating, and interesting. The timing of his career was a gift for the ages to come.

At a more mundane level, timing is often critical to the success of a Rembrandt heist. Thieves are very apt to commit them on or near holidays, when security measures seem to loosen up and owners and overseers are more distracted. Law enforcement knows this, and holi-days typically strain patrols, delaying 911 and alarm-system responses. Museums, which always require security around-the-clock, can be especially hard-hit.

A glaring case is the March 18, 1990, theft from the Isabella Stewart Gardner Museum, when thieves made their entrance into the building at 1:24 A.M. Though the clock said St. Patrick's Day had ended, there were plenty of beery celebrations throughout the city. It is natural to speculate that the robbery was planned for a night that the Boston police would be stretched thin. Additionally, the ploy used by the thieves—disguising themselves as police officers "responding to a disturbance"—was all the more effective on a night known for boisterous partying.

While the Gardner thieves' plot worked all too well, the holiday that seems to hold a special appeal for art thieves—especially Rembrandt thieves—is Christmas. The 1973 theft of two Rembrandt portraits from Cincinnati's Taft Museum, the theft of a self-portrait from Stockholm in 2000, and the first heist of the bedeviled "Takeaway Rembrandt" from the Dulwich Picture Gallery in 1966 all took place within a week of Christmas Day. And on Christmas Eve, 1978, thieves made their way into the M. H. de Young Memorial Museum in San Francisco with a Rembrandt as their target. Their timing proved to be impeccable.

*   *   *

Many aspects of the de Young heist—foremost the identities of the perpetrators—remain unsolved more than three decades years later. No one knows how many thieves entered the museum, or what time they did so. Based on security patrols in place that holiday night, investigators can say only that the robbery occurred between midnight and dawn. The crime wasn't discovered until morning, after a guard making his rounds through the museum's Dutch gallery spotted broken glass on the floor. When he looked up, he found a gaping hole in the skylight. Within seconds, he saw that four paintings were gone from the Dutch gallery's walls.[1] They were Rembrandt's *Portrait of a Rabbi* (1657), along with works by the Dutch artists Eglon van der Neer (*River Scene at Night*), Willem van de Velde, the Younger (*Harbor Scene*), and Anthonie de Lorme (*Interior of St. Lawrence Church in Rotterdam*).

The de Young was not built with security in mind. The building featured skylights situated above the room holding the Rembrandt.

(In this way it is similar to the Dulwich Picture Gallery in London, home to the Takeaway Rembrandt.) The de Young thieves climbed the exterior wall of the museum to access the roof. Investigators speculated that the thieves used rope ladders to scale the building. Once on top, they deactivated an alarm and cut through the skylight to access the Dutch gallery. They removed the four paintings and used an antique wooden Dutch chest to climb out of the museum and back onto the roof.[2] Curiously, the thieves removed five paintings from the walls but left one of those behind, Rembrandt's *Joris de Caullerie* (1632), which was found on the floor of the Dutch gallery. Experts valued *Joris de Caullerie* at more than $1 million, at least as valuable as *Portrait of a Rabbi*.

Based on the size and weight of the paintings taken from the de Young and the effort needed to lift them through the skylight, investigators surmised that at least two thieves entered the museum. Beyond this, investigators were left with no real leads or clues.

The de Young was not viewed as a soft target in the museum community. It had recently been awarded the popular traveling King Tut exhibit in part because of its robust security posture. One episode stood out, though. An armed thief had forced his way into the museum about four months earlier, in August 1979, subdued a museum guard, and attempted to steal *Portrait of a Rabbi*. He was thwarted by the arrival of a second watchman. The museum immediately upped its contingent of gallery guards.[3] After the Christmas theft of the four pieces, museum officials spent $1.2 million more to overhaul security in anticipation of the Tut show.[4]

Even though the successful Christmas heist of *Portrait of a Rabbi* marked the second time in a short span that thieves had targeted the 31-inch-by-25½-inch Rembrandt, no solid leads emerged. Ian White, the de Young's director, told the media that the theft "might have been an inside job," adding, "There was a certain awareness of the skylights and where they were located."[5] No secret dossier was necessary to realize that a skylight was situated above the Dutch room, or that one could break away enough glass to slip bodily into the building. But the thieves also knew about the alarm on the skylight and had an idea of how it functioned. Without this information, the thieves would not have been able to disable the alarm with such ease. Although the theft took place while the guards were in the building, the event did not trigger the museum's monitoring systems. Further, the thieves seemed to know the guards' movements during closing hours. They entered the museum at a time when watchmen were not conducting rounds in or around the Dutch gallery. Had he been near the break-in area, surely a security guard would have heard the cracking of glass, the lifting of five frames from the walls, the removal of two paintings from frames, the movement of the heavy wooden Dutch cabinet across the floor to aid in the escape, and the tricky business of passing the art through the busted skylight. Police also perceived the incident as an inside job.

The use of insider information in art theft is the norm. According to former assistant United States attorney Robert Goldman, who worked with the FBI's Art Crime Team, about 80 percent of museum art thefts are inside jobs.[6] The complicity of an insider is a key element in a successful theft. While anyone can repeatedly visit a museum to plot out a theoretical heist and getaway, knowing the finer points of the museum's alert system and its sentry procedures is the game-changer. And while it is straightforward enough to determine how many guards are stationed near the entrance to a museum when the facility is open, one would need the insider to learn what procedures and technologies are used to thwart a daylight "blitz" theft. Are the guards armed? Are they equipped with duress buttons that allow for instantaneous alerting of the police? How forcefully are the paintings secured to the walls? Would the removal of a piece trigger a noisy or a silent alarm? Are there alternate paths to escape, such as fire-escapes that must by law be accessible to the public?

Beyond the obvious questions lurk the uncertainties. Thieves planning overnight entries can benefit from data such as the schedule guards keep while doing their late rounds; the means by which the guards contact emergency responders; the number of staff on duty overnight; and museum policy for allowing access after business hours.

(Pizza deliveries should be out of the question.) While it seems that the ideal setup for a thief is one in which a museum guard is complicit, this is not necessarily so. Criminals also know that whenever security is compromised, the first targets of interrogation are the watchmen. It takes an extraordinary mix of bravado and sangfroid for a colluding insider to shed all suspicion. If the person breaks under questioning, or if a connection between him and known criminals can be drawn, the thieves are in rapid jeopardy of being caught. A far better resource for thieves is the inside information that comes from a loose-lipped or inebriated staffer, a person who cannot resist telling friends or acquaintances or barstool buddies about security details or weaknesses. That sort of connection is almost impossible for investigators to trace. It is maddening as well, since clues that suggest the use of insider information force investigators to focus attention and resources on former and current employees who had nothing to do with organizing a heist.

*   *   *

The thieves who made off with *Portrait of a Rabbi* must have thought themselves adept given their clean getaway and the lack of clues. The art stolen from the de Young made its way onto INTERPOL's global list of "Twelve Most Wanted Works of Art," yet police were nowhere near getting a bead on the robbers. But the thieves had little idea of the troubles that awaited them as owners of a stolen Rembrandt. First, they apparently decided that *Rabbi* and another of their pilfered pieces (*Interior of the Church of Saint Lawrence, Rotterdam*) would sell better after a bit of cleaning. Clearly, they were not trained conservators, as evidenced by the fact that their efforts harmed both paintings.[7] De Young curator Lynn Orr later described finding a "milky rectangle" on *Rabbi*.[8] Such damage surely decreased the value of the works (art conservation and restoration are among the most exacting practices on earth). But *Portrait of a Rabbi*'s value wasn't undercut nearly as much by criminal damage as it would be by the work of scholars. Ten years before it was stolen, the Rembrandt scholar Horst Gerson questioned the painting's attribution. He said of *Rabbi*, "I am not convinced at all that [it] is the real original Rembrandt."[9] The de Young thieves made off with the painting while it was still being hailed as authentic, at least by laymen. But doubts about the work had begun to spread.

It is hard to say whether the de Young bandits knew that questions about their now-purported Rembrandt were percolating as it sat in their possession. But from what history teaches us about art thieves, it is unlikely. While they are adept at removing paintings from their perches, they are far less competent at moving them for profit. And due primarily to ignorance, they frequently bypass more valuable pieces during their capers. When the culprits took *Portrait of a Rabbi*, they snared a valuable painting by a recognizable name—or at least that was the case on that night. But the aesthetic beauty and dollar value of their haul paled when compared with Rembrandt's *Joris de Caullerie*, the painting they left behind. One cannot criticize them too heavily. Ongoing scholarly discussions about the attribution of particular artworks—even those by the great masters—are not typical fodder for media coverage. One would have had to monitor the more obscure and technical art history publications and scholarly conferences to have a true idea of the market value of *Portrait of a Rabbi* in 1978. Today the task is far simpler, thanks to the work of cataloguers like Frank J. Seinstra, a computer engineer and senior researcher with the Faculty of Science at the University of Amsterdam. His online photographic catalogue of Rembrandt paintings is hailed as the most complete and well-thought-out online resource of its kind. It separates a total of 742 works linked to Rembrandt into three categories: Category I paintings, which are "generally accepted" as authentic (that tally is 253); Category II paintings, those that are "disputed or doubted" (that tally is 119); and Category III paintings, those now "widely rejected" or confirmed to be the work of other artists (that tally is 370). Today's Rembrandt thieves could easily familiarize themselves with targets that are legitimate.

*   *   *

Portrait of a Rabbi is a somber oil on canvas that Rembrandt was believed to have completed in 1657. The pensive subject has a long brown beard, sidelocks, and shaved upper cheeks, and wears a plush red cap. The hat and a heavy golden chain around the subject's neck give the otherwise morose portrait some sense of life and hope. The rabbi is depicted to the torso, with his head and body turned slightly to the viewer's right. His identity, like that of his thieves, remains unknown.

Rembrandt painted and drew many depictions of Jews and everyday Jewish life during his career, in part because Amsterdam was a magnet for Jews escaping persecution elsewhere in Europe. The city of 120,000 had about 15,000 Jews in Rembrandt's time, and the artist lived in a heavily Jewish quarter. One of the homes neighboring his was owned by Portuguese Jews. Popular myth suggests that Holland was a starkly Calvinist federation, but it was in fact far more tolerant of religious diversity than the early English colonies in North America. Many prominent seventeenth-century Dutch painters and draftsmen found inspiration in Jewish subjects, from the biblical to the mundane. The demonization and grotesque caricatures often seen in depictions of Jews during the Middle Ages and the Renaissance are generally absent from Dutch art in the Golden Age. One of Rembrandt's most beloved works is *The Jewish Bride* (1665), illustrating a moment of tender intimacy between a newly married husband and wife. Van Gogh praised it, calling it an "infinitely sympathetic picture" painted with "a hand on fire."[10]

The *Rabbi* painting, executed on a canvas, hung at the de Young in a heavy gilded wood frame. Like *Joris de Caullerie*, the painting was acquired by the de Young in the 1940s. But within 30 years it was losing its masterpiece luster. The minutes from a December 9, 1999, report to the executive committee of what is today known as the Fine Arts Museums of San Francisco, the entity that oversees the de Young, quote European-paintings curator Lynn Orr as saying, "Before the theft leading Rembrandt scholars voiced concerns about whether *Portrait of a Rabbi* was actually a work by a Rembrandt follower."[11]

In 2000, Steven Nash, chief curator of the Fine Arts Museums, told the media that the Rembrandt Research Project had spent a decade reviewing photos of the painting while it was missing and concluded that the work was probably by one of the master's students, and that the subject could not even be conclusively authenticated as a rabbi.[12]

Back in 1978, however, when *Portrait of a Rabbi* was stolen, its status as a Rembrandt was not such an open question. "A Rembrandt Is Among 4 Works Stolen on Coast," announced a front-page headline in the *New York Times* on Christmas day of that year. But while the thieves might have read that the museum valued the painting at more than $1 million, their options for profit had been narrowed by word from the authorities that none of the paintings was insured. Absent insurance, the possibility of a large ransom all but disappeared. Perhaps they could use the paintings to negotiate a reduced jail sentence for themselves or a criminal associate, as Myles J. Connor Jr. had done in Massachusetts three years earlier. Or maybe they could use the art as collateral in some other sort of black-market trafficking. That would depend on whether the robbers were usefully connected to the underworld. But leveraging their crime into a million-dollar-plus payday would now be impossible. The sole offer from the museum was a reward of $50,000, less than 5 percent of the stated value.[13] It is unlikely that the thieves were enticed by such a small jackpot given the risk and complexity of the robbery and the perils of executing an exchange. So they folded their hand, sitting on the art for decades and leaving the de Young mystified and violated.

*   *   *

The man who gave his name to the museum, Michael Harry de Young (1849–1925), was a prominent news executive and arts patron whose family, coincidentally, was of Dutch-Jewish descent. Much like Rembrandt, whose household brimmed with curios and oddities from around the globe, de Young came of age with "a great desire to acquire curious things."[14] Beginning with a collection of stuffed extinct birds that he began as a young man, de Young grew into a collector of Chinese wood carvings, pre-Columbian skulls, and other exotic objects. When he was unable to store them any longer, he sought to donate them to the

San Francisco Parks Commission, which declined his offer. He then sold his collection for $26. Later in life he said of this episode, "I have never forgotten that sale and the pang it gave me when I thought my little treasures had been thrown away."[15] In 1894, de Young, by now a wealthy and influential editor and owner of the *Daily Dramatic Chronicle* (the predecessor of the *San Francisco Chronicle*), became the driving force behind the city's Mid-Winter Exposition, a five-month-long West Coast version of the World's Fair. The exposition made a good profit, and with $75,000 and, at last, a hard-won approval from the president of the Parks Commission, de Young began to create his museum. On March 23, 1895, he presented it to the public "with the understanding that it was to remain in Golden Gate Park under the title of the Memorial Museum and to be open free every day in the week."[16] The Memorial Museum was badly damaged during the infamous 1906 earthquake and fire that ravaged San Francisco. As a result of the calamity, and because the collection was now outgrowing the building, de Young provided funds to build a new wing in 1917.

De Young's life as a businessman and civic leader was marked by other notable episodes. In addition to his founding of the *Chronicle* and the museum, he worked for two decades as director of The Associated Press. He also fell victim to a would-be assassin. The man, Adolph Spreckels, was the son of a Caribbean sugar magnate. Angered by a negative article in the *Chronicle*, Spreckels lay in wait in de Young's office and shot the editor twice as he entered. De Young was critically injured but pulled through.[17] In the notorious attempted-murder trial that ensued, Spreckels was acquitted by a jury that accepted his temporary insanity defense.[18] In an odd twist, Spreckels would later donate the California Palace of the Legion of Honor to the city of San Francisco. Today that building is incorporated along with the de Young into the Fine Arts Museums of San Francisco.

A year after de Young's death in 1925 (he outlived Spreckels by a year), his original building was condemned as unsafe and a third wing, formally named the M. H. de Young Memorial Museum, was built in 1931. After that, the de Young enjoyed a generally sleepy existence for nearly a half-century, slowly acquiring anthropological holdings from Peru and Africa, early-American decorative arts, and European oil paintings such as *Rabbi*. Wandering into the museum 80 years ago, one would have encountered Aztec spears and masks, vigilante hanging ropes, two-headed snakes kept in jars, marble sculptures, stuffed canaries, early California landscape paintings, Civil War tent pegs, and the skin of a flying squirrel. For a time the de Young was dubbed "the city's attic."

Then in 1978, the museum received a burst of publicity after the John D. Rockefeller family gave it 140 paintings, drawings, and sculptures. This multimillion-dollar gift likely drew the attention of some of the thieves who infiltrated the de Young that year.

Another misfortune befell the de Young Museum 11 years after its "Rembrandt" was stolen. In October 1989, the Loma Prieta earthquake struck San Francisco. Although the de Young and Palace of the Legion of Honor suffered remarkably little damage given the severity of the earthquake, four marble sculptures at the de Young were badly damaged. The building's structure was also hurt by the quake, forcing the construction of a new museum building. Today, the rebuilt de Young Museum is a gleaming piece of architecture designed by the Swiss firm of Herzog & de Meuron. A year after the opening of the new de Young in 2000, the firm was awarded the Pritzker Architecture Prize. Still, in 1999, the museum bore the blemish of a long-unsolved robbery.

*   *   *

On November 2, 1999, the William Doyle Galleries in New York City was conducting one of its popular "Walk-in-Tuesdays." These are days in which the public is invited to visit with the gallery's experts without an appointment to have their art evaluated free of charge. Walk-in-Tuesdays were a popular event at the Doyle Galleries, and were well attended by members of the public, perhaps inspired by the valuable finds they saw on PBS's successful *Antiques Roadshow* series. Gallery personnel estimate that up to 100 people attended these special days. On this particular

Tuesday, a nondescript man reportedly wearing a wig entered the gallery with a crate and, unbeknownst to Doyle personnel, left without it. The crate caught no one's attention until, a bit later, the gallery received an anonymous telephone call. Alan Fausel, one of the Doyle's experts on duty that day, was instructed by the unknown caller to look for the crate. Doyle vice president Louis Webre and his staff decided that since they did not know the crate's contents, law enforcement should be alerted in case it contained something dangerous. Soon, the New York Police Department and the Federal Bureau of Investigation were on the scene, and the crate was opened. Fausel recognized the items inside as three of the paintings missing from the de Young. Only *Harbor Scene,* by Willem van de Velde, the Younger, was not there. Because no one got a good look at the man bearing the crate, investigators were again stymied.[19]

As is often the case in an art recovery, museum and law enforcement officials held back on announcing the news. The FBI needed to examine the crate and the art and take confidential steps. The art would also have to be transported to San Francisco, where museum experts could evaluate it. The delay prompted questions about the Doyle's ethics from the unlikeliest of sources: the people behind the heist. On November 5, 1999, a man identifying himself as "Carl La Fung"[20] called the offices of the International Foundation for Art Research (IFAR) and said he was the person who had left the crate at Doyle's. La Fung said he received the art from the men who committed the heist and had returned the three paintings in such a manner as to avoid arrest and prosecution. He asked to meet with IFAR executive director Sharon Flescher in New York's Bryant Park. Surprised that he had not seen headlines announcing the return of the paintings, La Fung wanted Flescher to know that they had been dropped off. He also accused the Doyle Galleries of subterfuge. Flescher received the message, and La Fung was also advised to contact the Art Loss Register, the London-based organization that maintains a database of stolen art as well as a registration service for art owners wishing to safeguard their collections. La Fung did so, and both IFAR and the Art Loss Register contacted the FBI, which already knew about the art.

By November 11, the story of the recovery hit the worldwide media, and La Fung was satisfied that any wrongdoing had ended with him. He called IFAR a second time and told Flescher, "I guess it's okay now." He added that he believed he had done "the right thing." Although the identity of the caller was never determined, he knew his way around the art world. His decision to first contact IFAR indicates he had done some homework. Unlike the Art Loss Register, IFAR is a nonprofit organization that does provenance research and is the first organization to distribute important and immediate details about stolen art to a wide audience. A relatively small organization with limited resources, IFAR has arguably done more over the last three decades to get the word out about the problem of art crime, and to help prompt recoveries, than organizations many times its size. Nevertheless, the organization is not a household name, and it's doubtful that "Carl La Fung" simply got lucky in choosing to contact the small, reputable organization.

This was not the first time IFAR helped the authorities recover stolen art. Located in New York City, where "a lot of art does turn up," according to a former IFAR director, the group has aided the FBI and police on both coasts. In one instance, IFAR was asked to provide the FBI with an informal appraisal of works by Rembrandt, Rubens, Chagall, Van Gogh, Renoir, and Degas that had been purchased by a professor for less than $10,000. It took IFAR's staff little time to identify problems with all the works and determine them to be inauthentic. IFAR has often been able to give an expert opinion to investigators quickly enough to bring a case of art fraud or misidentification to a close.[21]

Naturally, the recovery of the stolen de Young art was met with excitement by the museum and the art community. "The art market has been beleaguered with so many stories of art thefts that we're so happy to be part of the solution," said Louis Webre of the Doyle Galleries.[22] Wanda Corn, chair of the art history department at Stanford University, said, "I think it's wonderful that we have our paintings back. It shows that someone felt guilty or desperate to get rid of the hot property."[23] Those who are still awaiting the return or recovery of stolen works, like the Isabella Stewart Gardner Museum in Boston or the Montreal Museum of Fine Arts (which lost millions in art and jewels, including a Rembrandt in 1972), were encouraged that works lost for long periods could make their way home. "This occurrence should hearten those who want to see the artworks returned, all the officials at the Gardner and other who have worked so hard on this case all these years," said Brien O'Connor, a former assistant U.S. attorney who handled the investigation of the Gardner heist from 1992 until May 2000.

*   *   *

When the paintings arrived at the de Young Museum, a spokesperson told the media, "We're thrilled to have them back and we're grateful that they were returned."[24] Harry Parker, the director of the Fine Arts Museums of San Francisco, expressed relief at the recovery because it closed an "embarrassing" episode in the museum's history.[25] "We're very pleased to have them recovered," he said, "but it's not all euphoria."[26] By the time of the recovery, *Portrait of a Rabbi* was all but rejected as a Rembrandt—a fact made plain in media coverage. In its lead article announcing the reappearance of the stolen art, the *San Francisco Examiner* described *Rabbi* as "one whose original status as a Rembrandt is in some doubt."[27] Museum officials did little to contest the idea. Parker told the world: "The Rembrandt may not be as advertised. This may not be the great art recovery of the century."[28] While the vice president of the Doyle Galleries was quick to note that *Portrait of a Rabbi* was "still very valuable,"[29] Parker talked down its value, saying it was "worth less than the $1 million we thought it was worth when it was stolen."[30] The de Young's true Rembrandt, *Joris de Caullerie,* was by now worth $25 million to $30 million.[31]

To determine the authenticity of *Rabbi*, curators made plans to study it with all modern tools available. But in a sign of its doubts, the de Young began calling the painting *Portrait of a Man with a Red Cap and Gold Chain.* The museum's curator of European art, Lynn Orr, was blunt. Noting that paintings by Rembrandt pupils and followers like Govaert Flinck, Ferdinand Bol, and Willem Drost are well-respected works of art, she said *Man with a Red Cap and Gold Chain* "will probably turn out to be by a lesser hand."[32] She cited the lack of "tonal subtleties, personality characteristics and spatial development" in the work.[33] The painting was proving to be an embarrassment to the de Young twice over. The theft called into question its safeguards in the late 1970s, and the misattribution meant a painting that was once considered a jewel was now significant largely for having been stolen and mistaken for a Rembrandt. Nash, the associate director and chief curator of the Fine Arts Museums of San Francisco, put it nicely: "The painting's value is in somewhat of a downward spiral."[34] Rembrandt expert Gary Schwartz, author of *Rembrandt's Universe: His Life, His Art, His Work* (Thames & Hudson, 2006), says: "My own take on it would be that the museum misled the public in 1979 by going along with the Rembrandt hype and not issuing a press release referring to scholarly opinion concerning the attribution."

Though a museum's foremost interest when a painting is stolen is recovery, it is galling when no one is arrested or prosecuted. In this case those who stole four Dutch paintings from a museum and kept them from public view for more than two decades walked away without punishment. One piece remains missing, and the three pieces returned to the museum were seriously damaged. Van der Neer's *River Scene at Night*, a painted wood panel, was returned in three pieces. *Man with a Red Cap and Gold Chain,* as well as De Lorme's *Interior of the Church of Saint Lawrence, Rotterdam,* suffered the alarming "cleaning damage."[35] As Fine Arts Museums director Harry Parker said, "That's what's so sad. These paintings have not been cared for."[36] Aside from the rectangular blemish on *Man with a Red Cap and Gold Chain*, the painting had begun to separate from its lining, probably due to the poor environment in which it was kept. Mold on the back of the painting indicated it had been kept in an area where humidity fluctuated greatly.[37] And little can be said for the manner in which the art was hauled about. The movement of fine art, especially priceless centuries-old paintings, is a precise affair. Today, a Rembrandt would be transported primarily for one of three reasons: (1) when on loan to another institution for a special exhibition; (2) when being moved to an off-site lab for conservation; or (3) upon the completion of an auction or sale.

* * *

The industry standard for moving a Rembrandt painting (etchings and drawings are handled differently) would begin with a careful, white-gloved removal of the painting from its wall or display area. Conservators would place the art in a specially made case, typically built to order from wood and egg-crate-foam packing material by a professional known in the museum world as a preparator. The case would then be securely closed. If the piece were being moved off-site, it would be transported by a certified art-movement firm. Because such work is technical and precise, very few firms provide such a service. In the case of a Rembrandt, a courier and security professional would travel with the art at all times. The place where the art is headed would be secured and cleared before the painting left its originating building. Once loaded onto a truck, the art crate would be tightly strapped into place. The moving firm's vehicle (which would carry the art, the movers, and the courier or security person together) might be followed by contracted armed guards in a "chase car." The vehicles and likely the crate would have GPS devices. If the art were traveling by air, a courier would oversee the movement of the art through airport security and customs. It would be accompanied the entire trip and handled with similar delicacy on its arrival. Anyone who imagines that art thieves would take such precautions is mistaken. Stolen Rembrandts have been tossed into car trunks, stored outdoors in sub-freezing barns and shacks, carried about in plastic shopping bags, and hidden under beds.

To cope with the damage to *Rabbi*, which had darkened considerably, the de Young took a novel approach. While they were committed to applying all necessary conservation techniques to return it to its original state, a process that would take about a year, the Fine Arts Museums made a bold decision. They would create an exhibition that featured the stolen art in exactly the condition in which it was returned. On February 12, 2000, the paintings were put on view to the public in the crates in which they were recovered by the FBI. Even the heavy Dutch chest used by the thieves to get out of the gallery through the skylight was put on display. Director Parker said the exhibition presented a "wonderful education opportunity for the public to see what happens when old master paintings are neglected. When they see their current state, they might understand why museums are uptight about people touching pictures, about temperature and humidity levels, about why we might want to build new museums that can better protect works of art."[38] Curator Orr took it a step further, adding that the exhibition "shows that a museum is a functioning institution, that there's a whole lot of activity that goes on beyond exhibitions."[39] Such equanimity in the face of art theft is rare. Few museums would flaunt such an episode, although the public often finds tales of art heists as alluring as the art itself. Curators also displayed the recovered *Portrait of a Rabbi* alongside *Joris*, the museum's firmly authenticated Rembrandt, "so people can have an idea why it was discredited as a genuine Rembrandt."

The de Young episode is further evidence that a Rembrandt, real or imagined, is far harder to sell than it is to steal, especially if it has suffered deterioration due to poor handling. As for the *Portrait of a Man with a Red Cap and Gold Chain*, the painting has now been put into storage at Adolph Spreckels's Legion of Honor museum. One could say the deattributed Rembrandt serves as a fitting final "gift" from M. H. de Young to his would-be assassin.

CHAPTER NINE

Rembrandt's Stolen Etchings

Georgia Christy had a problem on her hands. It was January 15, 2010, and a business associate she knew only as Freddy was on the phone complaining. Two years earlier, he had bought a Rembrandt etching, *The Return of the Prodigal Son* (1636), from Christy and her husband, Hugh. Now, Freddy said, new information led him to suspect that it was a stolen item.

Christy, also known as Monica Natti, said she was shocked. To her knowledge, she told her client, the etching was acquired legitimately. She explained that her husband had obtained it a few months before selling it by swapping a 1932 Chevrolet. Freddy accepted her assurances but was only briefly placated.

Five days later, on January 20, he called back Christy with firmer information. The etching, Freddy said, was definitely hot, and the collector he had sold it to wanted his $5,000 purchase price refunded.

Freddy sounded worried about how to handle the hot etching once he gave back the money. "What should I do?" he asked.

"Morally it should go back [to its rightful owner]," was Christy's initial answer, according to federal prosecution records. But her subsequent instructions were far less ethical, and illegal, the government alleges: She reputedly urged Freddy to resell the Rembrandt, and then admonished him: "We never had this conversation."

Christy was stepping into a trap set by the FBI's Art Crime Team. Freddy was in fact working for the bureau as an informant, trying to get Christy to say something incriminating. The federal government has since alleged that Georgia Christy and her husband, Jerry "Hugh" Christy (a.k.a Nick Natti), knew all along that the Rembrandt etching was stolen property. On November 24, 2007, they say, *Prodigal Son* was taken from a home in Sammamish, Washington, during a burglary. The thief got away clean, and an insurance company paid the owner a claim of $20,000. But losing the art was surely a dreadful blow. Few residents of tiny Northwest villages can boast of owning an authentic Rembrandt.

In a May 2010 complaint, FBI special agent Wesley C. Floyd alleges that in January 2008, at Hugh Christy's urging, Georgia Christy drove what she knew to be the stolen Sammamish etching from Granite Falls, Washington, to Freddy's location outside Portland, Oregon, and took $5,000 in payment for it. For her trouble, she stands accused of what is today a severe crime—interstate trafficking in stolen art. Her husband was also arrested and charged.

While no one yet knows who stole the Rembrandt from the private home, the government also notes in its complaint that Hugh Christy is an ex-convict with ten felony convictions on his rap sheet, many for burglarizing private homes in the state of Washington. The FBI states as well that he shared a cell at Washington State Prison in Monroe in 2007 with a notorious regional art thief and swindler named Kurt Lidtke. Lidtke is also charged in the 2010 complaint, accused of having "gone into business" paying professional burglars like Christy to rob specific items of art from private homes.

"I can say, 'Hey, go get that painting for me,' you know, and they do," Lidtke reportedly told an undercover agent, the complaint alleges. Lidtke would either share the loot with the thief or sell it himself and pay his burglar a commission, the complaint says. Lidtke knew where to steal the best art because he was once a trusted art gallery owner in Seattle—before fleecing his clients for $400,000 and spending 40 months in jail.[1]

*   *   *

Given the millions at stake when dealing with a single Rembrandt painting, it might seem a high-risk, short-money waste of time for alleged art criminals like the Christys and Lidtke to dabble in the lesser realm of his prints and etchings. But it can be a lucrative area when targeted properly. Kurt Lidtke lived the high life for years thanks to his swindles. Many other small-time art dealers, shady middlemen, and low-rent con artists scratch out a few dollars hawking and trading at the lower end of the art theft world. Time and again the alluring name they toss around is "Rembrandt."

Rembrandt prints are bought, sought, displayed, and collected across a wide swath of the art community. They can be viewed in museums and libraries, and purchased in private galleries, through dealers, or at auction. Some command prices in the hundreds of thousands of dollars. Others are worth a couple of thousand or less. But because there is much confusion over how to value them, chiselers and bottom-feeding antiques dealers can cash in on public confusion. "Eventually all early impressions of Rembrandt etchings will be datable," says historian Gary D. Schwartz, the editor of *The Complete Etchings of Rembrandt: Reproduced in the Original Size* (Dover, 1994). "The chief factors in value are: quality of the printing, trimming of the paper, condition, and absence of doubt concerning a printing date in the 17th century."

There should be little confusion today about new prints run off the metal plates originally etched by Rembrandt, because the paper and ink are not dated to his time. Plate owners have every right to make the copies, and will sell them in person or over the Internet, which is why owning an original plate is so desirable. Buyers need to be aware that they are not getting a "real" Rembrandt print, merely a modern copy of something he etched long ago. On Rembrandt's death, about 150 of his plates entered general circulation, and many of their new owners made and sold prints. In his book *Rembrandt as an Etcher: The Practice of Production and Distribution,* Dr. Erik Hinterding further points to evidence that some of Rembrandt's copper plates passed out of his possession while he was still alive and could have been used by others during his lifetime to print etchings.[2] All this makes it almost impossible to know whether Rembrandt performed the printing on many of the etchings that are unquestionably dated to his time. (In a sad irony, one of the best indicators that a print might have been pressed by Rembrandt rather than a subsequent owner is that the original metal plate is lost.) Many unscrupulous print dealers will try to persuade customers that newer prints are highly valuable, when the opposite is the case. Some plate owners will ply the seas in cruise ships and print and sell Rembrandt pressings on the spot. The buyers will imagine they are getting something immensely valuable—after all, the plate was created by Rembrandt—and will pay $5,000 to $10,000 for this "fresh" print. But among connoisseurs, such prints are valued in the $100 to $200 range. They would much rather have pressings that are more than three-and-a-half centuries old.

One of the many reasons that Rembrandt is esteemed so highly is his command not just of painting and drawing, but of the fine art of etching. The Italian painter Guercino (1591–1666) wrote, "I have seen a number of his printed works which have appeared in these parts; they are very beautiful, engraved in good taste and in a good manner. . . . I frankly consider him to be a great virtuoso."[3] The number of etchings produced by the master has been a topic of debate for many decades. The first catalogue raisonné of Rembrandt's etchings, compiled by Edmé-François Gersaint in 1751, put the number at 341. Half a century later, Adam Bartsch wrote a renowned catalogue in which he put the number at 375 etchings. Today, however, art historians accept about 290 etchings to be authentic Rembrandts, with this body of work created almost entirely in a period that began in 1628 and ended abruptly in 1661.[4] Remarkably, but not surprisingly, even his earliest etchings, created when he was 22, show him to be uniquely talented in the medium. Rembrandt's body of work as an etcher differs from his painterly output because it shows a far wider range of topics and interests. Beyond Bible scenes, personal and self-portraits, and historical depictions, his etchings feature landscapes, still lifes, animals, and many random and unexpected studies of daily life.

Rembrandt's technique for creating etchings is known as "drypoint," an approach he is credited with pioneering. Drypoint involves the use of a special needle rather than the "burin" used by engravers. The needle creates what is known as a "burr," yielding a richer impression on the metal plate that will be used to make prints. Rembrandt etchings scholar Holm Bevers wrote that he "used the needle as if it were a paintbrush, and in doing so became the first artist to maximize the aesthetic possibilities of the medium."[5]

The nature of etchings affects their overall availability. Because etchings are pressed onto paper from an inked plate, the artist can produce multiple originals of the same (or at least close to the same) image. For instance, when Rembrandt etched his *Self-Portrait* of 1634, he printed multiple versions of this work. One of these versions was stolen from the Isabella Stewart Gardner Museum two times, most recently in 1990. The museum has worked hard over the years to keep its likeness in the public eye to help recover the precious piece. Sharp-eyed art lovers visiting other museums, like the one at the University of Texas at Austin, will spot pieces that are nearly identical to the missing Gardner etching. Identical, that is, but for slight differences in lines made during the application of the plate to paper. Much of the art of making prints from etchings involves the artist's skill in drawing up the ink from the plate. With each pressing, small forensic differences are created. Many of these differences are noticeable only upon close examination. While the Gardner receives many calls about etchings that resemble its stolen item, the search for the museum's true etching continues.

Another useful example involves Rembrandt's etching *The Print-Dealer Clement de Jonghe*. The etching, made in 1651, depicts the dealer seated square to the viewer in a three-quarter-length rendering. He wears a wide-brimmed hat and a cloak, and on his left hand, which is prominently displayed, a glove—the sign of a nobleman. Rembrandt created the work in six separate but very similar states. In November 1946, one of the *Clement de Jonghe* etchings was taken when burglars struck the art galleries of Arthur H. Harlow & Company near Park Avenue in New York. Other valued Rembrandt etchings, including *The Gold Weigher's Field, Beggars at the Door of a House*, and *Jan Silvius*, were stolen as well. The thieves had clearly targeted etchings. They left behind all the paintings while removing etchings by Dürer, Whistler, Schongauer, Meryon, and Zorn, among others. While the thieves exhibited discriminating taste by focusing solely on etchings, they bypassed some that were far more valuable. And they ignored the second story of the gallery, where an exhibition of additional Rembrandt and Dürer etchings hung. Investigators believe this might have been because the exhibition gallery could be seen from the street by passersby. Had they looted that gallery as well, Mr. Harlow would have been left with very little to sell. After 65 years, nothing is known about the fate of the etchings. They could easily have been bought by novices unaware that they were stolen. However, collectors and specialists would know if they had one of the Harlow items.

Eight months after the Harlow Galleries theft, police thought they had found the culprit. On July 15, 1947, New York City police arrested Dante Forzano, a 31-year-old Bronx resident, as he and his wife, Gilda, strolled along White Plains Avenue. Under his arm, Forzano carried a package that police said contained 26 etchings by Zorn, Millet, Dürer, and, of course, Rembrandt. Unfortunately for Mr. Harlow, the etchings were not from his gallery, but they were valuable nonetheless. At his arraignment, Forzano expressed shock when he heard police tell the magistrate that the batch was worth $10,000, making for a grand larceny charge. Although he had stolen the etchings from various galleries, Forzano told investigators he thought they were worth $5 or $10 apiece.

Three years later and 45 miles away, more Rembrandt etchings went missing, this time from Princeton University. Coincidentally, the two pilfered Rembrandts were *The Print-Dealer Clement de Jonghe* and *The Gold Weigher's Field*, although they were not the same etchings stolen from the Harlow Gallery. Universities have long been ripe targets for etching thievery. In 1965, Rembrandt's *Death of the Virgin* (1639) was lifted from the Falvey Memorial Library on the campus of Villanova University. The piece, which measured 12 by 14 inches, was quickly returned, and the story behind its disappearance was kept secret.

Rembrandt's etchings are almost always smaller than his paintings, and devoid of color. Bona fide etchings by the master have sold in recent years for as little as $5,000 and as much as $1,000,000. According to Australian gallery director Josef Lebovic, an authority on works on paper dating back to the fifteenth century, the value of Rembrandt etchings varies widely depending on the condition of the print, the quality of the impression, and the authenticity of the attribution. As a result, he tells us, "You can buy them for 500 bucks or $50,000."[6] Forgers have long gotten in on the act, aware that passing off a fake etching is far easier than passing off a fake painting.

In July 1983, a man calling himself Dr. Thomas Cruz visited Syracuse University's George Agents Research Library to gather information for a book on Rembrandt. Carrying a pencil, notebook, and magnifying glass, and appearing the very model of an academic, Cruz presented his New York State driver's license as identification. Library staffers should have realized something was amiss because the license was expired; instead, they granted the charming researcher full access to their collection. Librarians recall Dr. Cruz taking careful notes and handling all materials with white gloves. Though the gloved approach seemed overly cautious to library personnel, it helped sell the scam. Dr. Cruz visited the library five times between July and August that year.

Dr. Cruz chose the next two months, September and October, to visit the National Gallery of Canada in Ottawa. There, he met with Douglas Druick, the print curator. Druick remembered Cruz as "a respectable, serious-minded academic type." Again, Cruz brought only a magnifying glass, pencil, and paper when he examined etchings in the gallery's Prints and Drawings Room.

The day after Dr. Cruz's final visit in Ottawa, Druick went to look over the Rembrandt etchings for a research project of his own. "When I removed the semi-opaque paper, I discovered that something was not right. The paper looked dead. I took it out to the light, and indeed it was wrong." Inspecting the paper on which an etching is printed is an important clue in determining authenticity. Hand-woven paper from Rembrandt's time is starkly different from today's stock, which is made by machine. The latter is far more uniform and the differences are often visible to the naked eye. To his horror, Druick found that Cruz had lifted two Rembrandt etchings: 1654's *Presentation in the Temple in the Dark Manner* and, as in Manhattan and at Princeton, *The Print-Dealer Clement de Jonghe*. He had replaced them with mediocre reproductions. Investigators discovered that Cruz had used his early visits to examine the size of the etchings and the method by which they were stored. He was then able to filch those etchings that he could hide inside the pages of his notebook, and smuggle in copies that would fit perfectly into the real binders.

Druick's discovery blew the top off Cruz's scheme. Soon, the librarians in Syracuse determined that he had also taken three of their Rembrandt etchings: *Faust, Samuel Manasseh,* and *Jan Antonides van der Linden.* According to Mark Weimer, a rare-book librarian at Syracuse University, the three etchings were worth $25,000. The two taken in Ottawa were valued at $100,000 apiece. Interestingly, the FBI announced the value of the five prints to be $500,000, more than twice the owners' estimates.

Dr. Cruz, whoever he was, must have feared being identified and arrested. He had clearly intended his flimflam to go unnoticed for a long time. A month after the theft in Ottawa, an anonymous man contacted the aforementioned International Foundation for Art Research (IFAR) in New York City. A small but robust nonprofit organization staffed by passionate art experts, IFAR was at the forefront of art-theft investigation before such crimes became commonplace. IFAR was the force behind the *Stolen Art Alert*, an early publication that announced thefts to the world. Today, IFAR publishes the *IFAR Journal*, which includes a section dedicated to thefts and recoveries. The caller reached staff member Linda Ketchum and told her the etchings from both thefts were stored at Grand Central Terminal in New York City. "You know what I'm talking about, right?" he asked. She told him she did indeed and requested his name. "That doesn't matter now" was the abrupt answer.[7]

Ketchum notified authorities and accompanied them to Grand Central. In locker No. 137, they found two large yellow envelopes containing the five prints, all in good condition.

*   *   *

Trying to fob off counterfeit etchings has become routine in Rembrandt crimes, and the photocopier is now the medium of choice. In 2000, two con men in western Massachusetts produced a replica of the Gardner's missing Rembrandt etching using opaque white paper and the ubiquitous office machine. After copying the etching, they "aged" it by dunking it in home-brewed tea, then presented it to ABC News as the real deal. They went so far as to lay a photo of the etching, hostage style, atop a current issue of the *Boston Herald,* alongside a ruler intended to "demonstrate" that it was the correct dimensions. ABC reported on it with a mix of hype and skepticism, and an aspiring mobster from Rhode Island named Rocco, intrigued by the report, foolishly forked over $250,000 for the fake. Why so much money for an item that, even if real, would fetch far less than that on the open market? Rhode Island Rocco convinced himself that the "etching" would help lead him to all the Gardner masterpieces stolen in 1990, and leave him in a position to reap the museum's $5 million reward. (Soon after being taken in by the scam, Rocco was convicted in federal court for tax evasion related to other art deals.)

In a wonderfully ironic twist, it turned out that Rocco asked none other than the Worcester Art Museum's 1972 Rembrandt villain,

Florian "Al" Monday (see Chapter 2), to be his intermediary. Monday met with the two con men along a Massachusetts highway and swapped Rocco's cash for the phony etching. The forgers made off with the money and Monday delivered the fake to its gullible new owner, who must have blanched when the *Herald* immediately exposed the item as a crude forgery. The episode is instructive because it shows how far petty criminals and lowlifes will stoop to insinuate themselves into an unsolved art theft if they smell reward money. Monday says he was just going along for the ride.

Rembrandt etchings are owned by a wide range of collectors and have been stolen from galleries, universities, warehouses, museums, and private homes. As far back as 1936, on Good Friday no less, a thief entered the Provincial Museum in Segovia, Spain, apparently using a key, and stole an etching by Rembrandt depicting *Christ's Descent from the Cross*. A rather rude act just before Easter.

Rembrandt etchings cropped up in a massive interstate fencing roundup in 1978 dubbed Operation Flytrap. Fifteen undercover officers broke up a ring that extended from Boston, Massachusetts, to Wilmington, Delaware. They set up a phony fencing business north of Wilmington, and the criminals were drawn like flies. So many stolen items were hand-delivered by thieves that the arrest bookings took two days to complete. The operation netted 1,700 stolen items valued at $409,000. These included a Cadillac Seville and a bulldozer along with a selection of Rembrandt etchings.

The theft of Rembrandt etchings remains an active criminal sideline. In May 2007, a middle-aged couple walked into the Hilligoss Gallery on Chicago's "Miracle Mile" and headed for its opulent preview room. The blond-haired woman and her short, stocky male companion homed in on Rembrandt's *Fall of Man* (1638), a 9-inch-by-6-inch framed etching. One Hilligoss employee said of the couple, "They went straight into the preview room. They didn't linger. They didn't look."[8] Staff members recalled seeing the pair on previous occasions, and the speed and swiftness with which they acted showed that they had planned carefully. They were in and out in less that three minutes, having lifted the $60,000 etching, which had been consigned to gallery owner Tom Hilligoss by a friend.

Fall of Man is a unique piece. Rembrandt has filled the work with great detail, including a small elephant in the background that can only be studied with a magnifying glass. Prints and drawings curator Suzanna Fold McCullagh of the Art Institute of Chicago describes the print as "quite a shocker in its day" because of its unflattering portrayal of Adam and Eve.

Hilligoss called it a "significant piece of significant quality," and added: "It's not really hard to find a home for it." The second part of Hilligoss's statement is a departure from what is typically said by owners of valuable art. Usually, the fact that the piece is famous is cited by a museum or gallery official as the key reason why it cannot be sold off. But Hilligoss was being candid. Because there are multiple authentic printings of each etching, moving a filched print can succeed in the legitimate market. *Fall of Man* remains missing.

The theft of Rembrandt etchings from private homes is also a bit of a plague. In the southeastern Australian town of Mount Eliza, in December 2003, burglars entered a home featuring two etchings by Rembrandt that had been family heirlooms for seven generations. The criminals were likely motivated by the sale of a Rembrandt etching earlier that month that netted 7,000 Australian pounds. The stolen etchings, a self-portrait and a portrait of Rembrandt's mother, had been insured for $700,000 some ten years earlier. They are still missing.

The unsolved Mount Eliza theft is a tragic tale, but some thefts of Rembrandt's etchings are marked by comic bungling. In 2006, James Otis Denham broke into the home of Barbara Dorney of Broken Arrow, Oklahoma. Dorney had previously hired Denham to do some handyman work. He made off with a dramatic depiction of *The Raising of Lazarus*, etched by Rembrandt around 1632, as well as its ownership papers. *The Raising of Lazarus* is accepted by Rembrandt scholars as an important and authentic work, and at 14 by 10 inches was the largest etching he had made to that date. The work shows Lazarus struggling to sit up in his grave while onlookers watch in amazement. It is a riveting and action-packed scene in which witnesses gape as Christ, barefoot and shown from the rear, gestures theatrically with his left had, commanding the prone and desiccated Lazarus to rise.

Denham proved to be as inept as any art thief could be. In a scene that evokes the films of the Coen Brothers, he met an art collector at Torchy's Legends, a grill and beer joint in Broken Arrow. There, over burgers, he showed her the etching and the ownership papers. Fortunately for Dorney, the collector had the smarts to ask to hold onto the documentation and the scruples to contact Dorney, whose name was on the paperwork. Dorney learned only then that her etching, valued at $6,000, was gone. The collector also notified police and agreed to take part in a mini sting, telling Denham by phone that she was ready to pay $1,500 for the Rembrandt. Police seized Denham as he made his way to her home, the goods in his hands. Sergeant J. D. Martin of the Broken Arrow Police Department enjoyed the rare Rembrandt recovery ruse. "We're going to have to develop a fine-arts group within the department," he jested. Dorney called the honorable (and anonymous) collector her "angel from heaven." Her words for Denham were less glowing. "At least he was stupid and I got it back," she said. Dorney's own acquisition of the etching had been unconventional: She won it during a blind auction aboard a passenger ship. After bidding $3,200 for an item that she hadn't seen, she was elated to find that her prize was a certified Rembrandt. "It was the highlight of my cruise," she told the press. Of course anything sold as a Rembrandt on a cruise ship bears exacting scrutiny.

While the Broken Arrow episode has a disarming quirkiness, few Rembrandt capers of any sort can compare with the bizarre case of Angelo Amadio and Dr. Ralph Kennaugh of Pebble Beach, California. The two self-described art collectors initially told authorities that on September 25, 2009, their rented home in Monterey County was burglarized. Among what they described as $27 million in stolen art were two Rembrandt etchings, *St. Jerome Praying* and *Woman Making Water,* the latter a work world famous for its scrupulously rendered subject matter.

(They also claimed to have lost paintings by Miró, Pollock, Renoir, and others.) The value affixed to the missing art made the burglary one of the largest thefts from a private home in American history. If, that is, there was any theft at all. Not long after the initial media reports of the crime, investigators found problems with the duo's story.

First, there was the issue of provenance—proof that the men indeed had owned such fabulous works. Amadio and Kennaugh told the media and police that all their ownership documentation had also been stolen, a rare feat in such a large-scale theft. Next, they told authorities they found a ransom note in their home a full four days after the break-in. Police met this claim with something approaching jeering skepticism because they had originally searched the home for evidence "with a fine-tooth comb."[9] To make matters worse, police then announced that the pair had stopped cooperating with their investigation. All these oddities led the commander of the Monterey sheriff's office, Mike Richards, to issue this statement: "There have been untruthful and inconsistent statements presented to us by Mr. Amadio.... We're actively pursuing this on face value and the fact is that it seems like a hoax right now."

A "hoax" in which the name Rembrandt was invoked once again to grab the imagination of a captivated public.

Our Debt to Rembrandt

The vast majority of thefts discussed in this book have endings in which priceless and important works by the great Rembrandt van Rijn are recovered and returned to the waiting walls of their relieved owners. In this we are fortunate. Unlike the theft of money or jewels, cars, and other collectibles, the theft of a singular work by an artistic virtuoso is truly a crime against all of us. When a Rembrandt (or any other great object) goes missing, we are denied a chance to see it in person and experience the awe and pleasure it gives. Isabella Stewart Gardner Museum director Anne Hawley sums it up well when she likens the theft of a masterpiece to the loss of a symphony by Beethoven, a play by Shakespeare, or a jazz recording by Louis Armstrong. To see such beauty ripped from the public sphere, never to be enjoyed again, is a tragedy.

Sadly, the unimaginable is forced on us again and again. Art theft continues at an alarming rate the world over. We see it in the looting of antiquities in the Americas, Asia, and the Middle East and in the continuing plague of thefts from museums, galleries, and private homes.

Important works stolen decades ago remain lost or in limbo, including far too many paintings by Rembrandt, arguably the most famous name in all of art.

The most notable missing Rembrandt is *The Storm on the Sea of Galilee*. Taken by thieves more than 20 years ago in the infamous 1990 heist at the Gardner, *The Storm* is a work of particular importance. While Rembrandt's oeuvre contains a large number of portraits, landscapes, and historical and religious compositions, *The Storm* stands as his only known seascape. Painted in 1633, it depicts the moment that Christ is awakened by the Apostles, who fear that their small boat will capsize. His serenity, as all around him seem to lose their heads, is gloriously rendered. It could serve as a lesson to those who must react to the crisis brought on by a museum theft. *The Storm* was not the only Rembrandt stolen on that grievous night in Boston. *A Lady and Gentleman in Black*, also completed in 1633, was, like *The Storm*, cut from its frame and spirited away, as was a postage-stamp-sized self-portrait etching. The thieves also made off with *Landscape with an Obelisk*, an oil painting on oak panel by Govaert Flinck, a student of Rembrandt's. (Until the 1970s, the painting had been misattributed to Rembrandt himself.) Horrifyingly, the Gardner thieves meant to take the museum's fourth and final Rembrandt, his 1629 *Self-Portrait* on a wooden panel. For reasons known only to them, the thieves left this exquisite work behind. Police and museum personnel found the self-portrait leaning against a chest, the back of the panel facing outward. Perhaps the thieves found the oak panel too heavy to transport. Perhaps they simply forgot to carry it off. Perhaps they were typical of many Rembrandt robbers: they did not know what they had on their hands. Regardless, we are fortunate. The self-portrait, among Rembrandt's very best, still hangs in the Gardner's majestic Dutch Room, allowing visitors a mesmerizing glimpse at the young face of one of the greatest artists of all time.

The absence of *The Storm on the Sea of Galilee* and *A Lady and Gentleman in Black*, both large and commanding paintings, has inspired one of the art world's most fitting and moving tributes to stolen masterworks. The ornate gilded frames that held the art now hang empty in the spaces that the paintings once occupied. While some view the frames as a symbol of mourning, the Gardner Museum sees them as placeholders for works that they trust will be returned. They are an important reminder to us to remain steadfast in the face of crimes against cultural property.

The belief that the Gardner art will be recovered is not based on foolish optimism or wishful thinking. Art theft expert and former FBI agent Robert K. Wittman (Chapter 7) has said art is usually recovered either soon after a theft, or after a generation has passed. Data on art theft suggest that while the recovery rate for stolen art in general is low, the rate of recovery for masterpieces is high, with some estimates near 80 percent. Whatever the rate, it is important not to concentrate too much on data, because every theft is different and those who end up with stolen Rembrandts are unpredictable.

The lost Gardner Rembrandts stand out, and the work put into locating them will not slacken, but there are less heralded cases that deserve renewed vigor. In 1972, three hooded men slipped into the Montreal Museum of Fine Arts around 1:30 A.M., descending through a skylight that was in the midst of repair. The armed men quickly subdued three security guards. The team fanned out into the galleries, snatching dozens of great works. They also fired shots into the museum's ceiling to let the captured guards know they meant business. All told, they made off with 18 paintings, the most notable being a Rembrandt oil on wood panel titled *The Farm* (and also known as *Evening Landscape with Cottages*), which was painted in 1654. Also taken were paintings by Breughel, Courbet, Daumier, Delacroix, Gainsborough, Millet, and Corot, as well as jewelry from the seventeenth, eighteenth, and nineteenth centuries.[1] The interlopers seemed prepared to take 18 more paintings. They appear to have abandoned those because an alarm sounded when a side entrance door was opened. Among the spared works were paintings by El Greco, Picasso, Tintoretto, and Rembrandt.

The Canadian press likened the robbery to the 1964 film *Topkapi*, in which thieves disable an alarm to steal jewels.[2] The disabled alarms were a major issue in the investigation. It was determined that museum workers had placed a layer of plastic over them, which had interfered with the signal. Whether the placement of the plastic was inadvertent or willful has never been determined, and the possibility that an insider was in cahoots with the gang cannot be dismissed.[3] The Montreal MFA had been robbed in 1964 as well, when Rembrandt's drawing *The Death of Jacob* was removed from a gallery wall in broad daylight. It has not been recovered.

Nearly four decades have passed since the Montreal Museum of Fine Arts was so badly denuded, and no progress has been made in the hunt for its art. That much time away from the sharp eyes and gloved hands of professionals is a severe threat to the lifespan of the paintings. Renowned paintings conservator Gianfranco Pocobene describes his greatest fear as the damage that can occur to a work of art when it falls into the wrong hands. While canvas tears or flaked paint can be repaired, the original work is altered. "Ultimately," he says, "we have less of the artist's work than we had before, and thus our appreciation and understanding of the artist's creation is diminished."[4]

The Federal Bureau of Investigation's National Stolen Art File lists 11 missing Rembrandts, including the etchings *The Return of the Prodigal Son*, *The Adoration of the Christ Child*, *The Holy Virgin with the People*, *The Artist's Mother Seated at a Table*, *The Goldsmith*, and *The Descent from the Cross*; and the paintings *Portrait of an Old Man* and *Portrait of a Young Girl*.[5] INTERPOL, too, has an online (members only) database of stolen art. Their list includes several other Rembrandts: *Battle Scene*, *Child with a Soap Bubble*, *Judas and Soldiers Arriving in the Garden*, *Portrait of Rembrandt's Father*, *Portrait of Rembrandt's Mother*, *Landscape with Cottages*, and two works that both have the title *Portrait of an Old Man*. INTERPOL also lists a drawing titled *Three Men Walking*, as well as 11 etchings. Combined with the missing works we do not know about, this amounts to a global crisis in the arts community.

Rembrandt left the world some 2,000 works. This is a gift for the ages, and while far too much is missing, most of his output is safe and properly cared for. Rembrandt poured his heart and soul into his work, labored over every last detail, and put art above life. He knew full well that he was handing his essence to posterity. As temporary caretakers, it is our duty to make sure his works get handed down yet again, and only to those who would first do no harm. We hope that this book drives home the folly of art theft, a crime that costs us dearly and certainly does not pay, and that it inspires some to come forward with the whereabouts of these irreplaceable and unrivaled treasures.

TARGET REMBRANDT: A LIST OF KNOWN AND REPORTED THEFTS

The following list has been compiled by the authors using original research, news reports, academic journals, and law enforcement databases. It identifies reported thefts of Rembrandt's paintings, etchings, and drawings during the past century, and is a first accounting of its kind. While incomplete, because thefts are often not made public, this tally of 80-odd cases shows the alarming breadth of the phenomenon. Thefts that appear in law enforcement databases are marked with an asterisk (*). (*This list does not include works looted by the Nazis during World War II. In some cases, the stolen work was not an authentic Rembrandt.*)

Christ Healing the Sick (oil painting)
Stolen 1920 from an unidentified warehouse in New York City

Man Wearing Red Skull Cap (oil painting)
Stolen 1921 from Galerie Weber, Hamburg, Germany

St. Paul in Prison (oil painting)
Stolen 1922 from the Staatsgalerie, Stuttgart, Germany

Portrait of Christ (oil painting)
Stolen 1927 from the Moscow Museum of Fine Arts

The Head of an Old Man (oil painting)
Stolen 1929 from Massimo Palace, Rome

The Reformer (oil painting)
Stolen 1930 from the Carlton House Galleries, London

Leonardo da Vinci (oil painting)
Stolen 1930 from the Carlton House Galleries, London

An Old Beggar (oil painting)
Stolen 1930 from the Carlton House Galleries, London

Jeremiah Mourning Over the Destruction of Jerusalem (oil painting)
Stolen 1933 from the home of M. Herman Rasch, Stockholm

Descent from the Cross (etching)
Stolen 1936 from The Provincial Museum, Segovia, Spain

Woman Carrying a Child (drawing)
Stolen 1937 from the Fogg Art Museum, Cambridge, Mass.

Children Playing Rummel-Pot (drawing)
Stolen 1937 from the Fogg Art Museum, Cambridge, Mass.

Old Man with a Fur Cap (oil painting)
Stolen 1938 from the home of George R. Cobham, New York

Oil painting first identified as *Saskia at Her Toilet,* but likely *Bathsheba*
Stolen 1938 from the Chilham Castle, Kent, England

Portrait of a Meditating Philosopher (unsigned oil painting)*
Stolen 1938 from The Royal Museums of Fine Arts, Brussels

Clement de Jonghe (etching)*
Stolen 1946 from the Arthur Harlow & Co. Gallery, New York

The Gold Weigher's Field (etching)*
Stolen 1946 from the Arthur Harlow & Co. Gallery, New York

Beggars at the Door of a House (etching)
Stolen 1946 from the Arthur Harlow & Co. Gallery, New York

Jan Silvius (etching)
Stolen 1946 from the Arthur Harlow & Co. Gallery, New York

Dr. Faustus (etching)
Stolen 1946 from the Arthur Harlow & Co. Gallery, New York

The Gold Weigher's Field (etching)*
Stolen 1949 from the Art Museum of Princeton University

The Print-Dealer Clement de Jonghe (etching)
Stolen 1949 from the Art Museum of Princeton University

Portrait of a Lady with a Lap Dog (oil painting)
Stolen 1959 from the Toronto Art Gallery

Portrait of a Lady with a Handkerchief (oil painting)
Stolen 1959 from the Toronto Art Gallery

Study of the Head of Christ (oil painting)
Stolen 1959 from the Gemäldegalerie, Dahlem, West Berlin

Unidentified Rembrandt oil painting
Stolen 1962 from the home of Jonkheer John H. Loudon, Holland

The Death of Jacob (drawing)
Stolen 1964 from the Montreal Museum of Fine Arts

Death of the Virgin (etching)
Stolen 1965 from the Falvey Memorial Library, Villanova University, Philadelphia

Portrait of Jacob de Gheyn III (oil painting)
Stolen 1966, 1973, 1981, and 1983 from the Dulwich Picture Gallery, London

Portait of Titus (oil painting)
Stolen 1966 from the Dulwich Picture Gallery, London

Girl at a Window (oil painting)
Stolen 1966 from the Dulwich Picture Gallery, London

Unidentified Rembrandt drawing
Stolen 1966 from the Museum of Fine Arts, Besançon, France

Portrait of Rembrandt's Mother (oil on wood panel)
Stolen 1968 from the Museum of Art and History, Geneva

Portrait of a Young Man (oil painting)
Stolen 1968 from the Eastman House, Rochester, New York

Unidentified Rembrandt oil painting
Stolen 1969 from the Cumberland House, Portsmouth, England

Unidentified Rembrandt painting (disputed)
Stolen 1971 from a gallery, Zagreb, Yugoslavia

The Rabbi (oil painting)
Stolen 1971 from the Basque Museum, Bayonne, France

Self-Portrait (oil painting)*
Stolen 1971 in Milan, Italy

Flight of the Holy Family to Egypt (oil painting)
Stolen 1972 from the Museum of Fine Arts, Tours, France

Evening Landscape with Cottages (oil painting)*
Stolen 1972 from the Montreal Museum of Fine Arts

St. Bartholomew (oil painting)*
Stolen 1972 from the Worcester Art Museum, Worcester, Mass.

Portrait of an Elderly Woman (oil painting)
Stolen 1972 from the Taft Museum, Cincinnati, Ohio

Man Leaning on a Sill (oil painting; recovered and deattributed)
Stolen 1972 from the Taft Museum, Cincinnati, Ohio

Portrait of Elisabeth van Rijn (oil painting; later called *Portrait of a Young Woman*)
Stolen 1975 from the Museum of Fine Arts, Boston

Self-Portrait (oil painting)
Stolen 1976 from the Granet Museum, Aix-en-Provence, France

Portrait of a Lady (oil painting)*
Stolen 1978 from the home of Arthur C. Herrington, Cohasset, Mass.

Portrait of a Rabbi (oil painting; deattributed)
Stolen 1978 from the M. H. de Young Memorial Museum, San Francisco

Saskia and Rombartus (two-sided drawing)*
Stolen 1979 from the Rembrandt House Museum, Amsterdam

Battle Scene (oil painting)*
Stolen 1980 from Ordan-Laroque, France

Judas and Soldiers Arriving in the Garden (oil on wood)*
Stolen 1982 in Brussels

Unidentified Rembrandt oil painting
Stolen 1982 from a gallery in Oslo, Norway

The Goldsmith (etching)*
Stolen 1983 in Cumberland, Canada

Old Woman Sitting at a Table (etching)*
Stolen 1983 in Cumberland, Canada

*The Angel Appearing to Tobias**
Stolen 1983 in Rome, Italy

Faust (etching)*
Stolen 1983 from the George Arents Research Library, Syracuse University

Menasseh ben Israel (etching; also called *Samuel Manasseh*)*
Stolen 1983 from the George Arents Research Library, Syracuse University

Clement de Jonghe (etching)*
Stolen 1983 from the National Art Museum of Canada, Ottawa

Presentation in the Temple in the Dark Manner (etching)
Stolen 1983 from the National Art Museum of Canada, Ottawa

Circumcision in the Stable (etching)*
Stolen 1989 in Vienna

Deposition from the Cross (etching)*
Stolen 1989 in Vienna

The Return of the Prodigal Son (etching)*
Stolen 1989 in Vienna

St. Hieronymus Kneeling in Prayer (etching; also *St. Jerome Kneeling in Prayer*)*
Stolen 1989 in Vienna

Landscape with Three Gabled Huts at a Road (etching)*
Stolen 1989 in Vienna

The Storm on the Sea of Galilee (painting)*
Stolen 1990 from the Isabella Stewart Gardner Museum, Boston

Portrait of a Lady and Gentleman in Black (painting)*
Stolen 1990 from the Isabella Stewart Gardner Museum, Boston

Self-Portrait (1634) (etching)*
Stolen 1970, 1990 from the Isabella Stewart Gardner Museum, Boston

Portrait of an Old Man (etching)*
Stolen 1990 in Vancouver, Canada

Landscape with Boat (etching)*
Stolen 1991 in Bern, Switzerland

Three Men Walking to the Right (chalk on paper)*
Stolen 1992 in Amsterdam

Baptism of the Eunuch (etching)*
Stolen 1996 in Paris

Portrait of a Lady (oil painting)
Stolen 1999 from Nivaagaard Picture Gallery, Niva, Denmark

Child with a Soap Bubble (oil painting)*
Stolen 1999 from municipal museum, Draguignan, France

Self- Portrait (1630) (oil on copper)*
Stolen 2000 from the National Museum, Stockholm

Portrait of an Old Man (oil painting)*
Stolen 2002 in Torremolinos, Spain

Portrait of Rembrandt's Father (oil painting; deemed a fake)*
Stolen 2006 from Novi Sad City Museum, Serbia

The Raising of Lazarus (etching)*
Stolen 2006 from a private home in Broken Arrow, Oklahoma

The Return of the Prodigal Son (etching)*
Stolen 2007 from a private home in Sammamish, Wash.

Adam and Eve (etching)*
Stolen 2007 from the Hilligoss Gallery, Chicago

The Adoration of the Christ Child (etching)*
Stolen (date and place not provided by FBI)

Portrait of an Old Man (oil painting)*
Stolen (date and place not provided by FBI)

Portrait of a Young Girl (oil painting)*
Stolen (date and place not provided by FBI)

Please visit www.StealingRembrandts.com for available images, additional details, and updates.

ACKNOWLEDGMENTS

My sincere thanks go to the many people who supported me as I worked on this book, which I wrote during a difficult period in my life. I must start with Elena Pushak, whose support, patience, and encouragement—and daily reminders to write—led to the completion of this book. Thanks to the people at the Worcester Art Museum, especially museum director James A. Welu, Deborah Aframe, and Francis Pedone. Much of the detail in the Worcester chapter was due to the work of WAM conservator Birgit Straehle, and I owe her a debt of gratitude. The interview granted by Florian "Al" Monday was more than enlightening; it was a key launching point for the chapter. Cincinnati police department officers Lt. Stephen R. Kramer (ret.) and Lt. Thomas Oberschmidt (ret.), who both now serve via the Greater Cincinnati Police Historical Society Museum, worked to provide us with important information about the investigation into the Taft Museum heist. You can help support the police museum by visiting their website at www.gcphs.com. Thanks are in order to Michael H. Peters at Chilham Castle, who helped me tremendously, and to Michael Foight at Villanova University. I'd also like to thank Noah Charney, Mark Durney, Catherine Sezgin, and Derek Fincham at the Association for Research into Crimes Against Art (ARCA); Sharon Flescher and the good people at the International Foundation for Art Research (www.ifar. org); and the Art Loss Register. Thanks to Geoff Kelly of the Federal Bureau of Investigation and Brian Kelly and Rob Fisher of the Office of the U.S. Attorney for Massachusetts for their work on the "GTTF." To Jurek "Rocky" Rokoszynski for trusting me enough to share his best advice about work and life, thank you. Thanks also to Robert Wittman, whose assistance was "priceless." I'm indebted to Derek Fisher, Ricky MacKinnon, and Peter Crowley for letting me vent to them countless times, and to all my friends and family, especially my sister Lori. Thank you to our agent, Sharlene Martin, and to our patient editorial team of Luba Ostashevsky, Laura Lancaster, Donna Cherry, and Daniel Seidel. And, of course, thanks are due to my coauthor, Tom Mashberg, an artist whose medium is the written word.

Finally, many thanks to the people of the Isabella Stewart Gardner Museum, especially our inspirational director Anne Hawley, trustees Barbara Hostetter and Stephen Kidder, chief operating officer Peter Bryant, conservators Gianfranco Pocobene, Valentine Talland, and Holly Salmon, Shana McKenna, Jennifer DePrizio, Paula Lyon Green, Joseph Saravo, Katherine Armstrong-Layton, Rob Zeiller, and Erica Ruane. Special thanks to Annemarie Healey, whose formidable research skills and artistic talents helped this project immeasurably, and Natalie Williams, a walking thesaurus and trusted proofreader who taught me the correct pronunciation of "Dulwich."

—A. A.

I echo all of Anthony's "thank you's," with particular emphasis on our loyal book agent, Sharlene, and the superb people at Palgrave Macmillan named above. I would like to extend my sincerest thanks as well to the following people for making this book come to pass: My patient and wise wife, Barbara Pattison, and my good friend Lawrence Edelman, both exceptional editors; Rembrandt expert Gary Schwartz, whose precision guidance rescued us again and again; Carl Horsley, George Warrington, and newsman Allan White in Cincinnati; Myles J. Connor Jr., Florian "Al" Monday, attorney Martin K. Leppo, Al Dotoli, as well as several old hands who wish to remain anonymous, all in Massachusetts; Sean Kelly, Maile Meloy, Jennifer Simington, and Beth Teitell for invaluable feedback; Vivette Porges, Annie Mashberg, and Alexandra Lack Gross for aid and comfort; and Anthony M. Amore, who suffers for his own art—the art of recovery.

—T. M.

NOTES

INTRODUCTION

1. Special correspondent, "Rochefort Tells How Americans Buy Art Fakes," *The New York Times,* September 24, 1911, SM2.
2. "The Legend and the Man," in *The World of Rembrandt: 1606–1669,* edited by Walter Wallace (New York: Time-Life Library of Art, 1968), 20–21. Excerpt available at http://www.rembrandt-painting.net/rembrandt_van_rijn_legend_and_man.htm.
3. Cynthia P. Schneider, an expert on Rembrandt landscapes, was the first scholar to re-attribute the work. She published her findings in "A New Look at *The Landscape With an Obelisk,*" Fenway Court, Isabella Stewart Gardner Museum (1985).

CHAPTER ONE

1. During his conquests in Europe in the early nineteenth century, Napoleon and his commanders organized the removal of paintings from Italy, Holland, Germany, and Austria to the Louvre and elsewhere on the continent. Among these was Rembrandt's *Descent from the Cross* (1634) from Germany. It hangs now in The Hermitage Museum in St. Petersburg.
2. Hugh McLeave, *Rogues in the Gallery: The Modern Plague of Art Theft* (Boston: David R. Godine, 1981), 8.
3. Ibid., 66.
4. For a superb account of this and similar wantonness through the centuries, see *Art as Plunder: The Ancient Origins of the Debate About Cultural Property* (Cambridge: Cambridge University Press, 2008), by Margaret M. Miles, professor of art history and classics at the University of California at Irvine.

5. "Agreement Between the National Park Service, North Atlantic Regional Office, and Boston Office, Federal Bureau of Investigation for the Recovery of Two Stolen Paintings," dated and signed March 13, 1995. Obtained via Freedom of Information Act request of October 7, 2007.
6. Nigel Reynolds, *The Telegraph, London,* November 5, 2005, 1.
7. Jack Malvern, *The Times of London,* December 21, 2005, B1.
8. Robert Sullivan, "Russborough Art Robberies—A Major Collection," *The Irish Letter* (quarterly letter), May 2005.
9. See bibliography for some of the many titles. It is fair to say this has become a genre, if not an industry.

CHAPTER TWO

1. Noah Charney, ed., *Art and Crime: Exploring the Dark Side of the Art World* (Santa Barbara, CA: Praeger, 2009), 136.
2. Pronounced WOOS-ter.
3. Milton Esterow, "Rush to Art Turning into a Stampede," *The New York Times,* May 14, 1966, 1.
4. S. Lane Faison, *The Art Museums of New England* (Boston: David R. Godine, 1982), 8–9.
5. "Sadness in Maine over a Van Gogh," *The New York Times,* October 4, 1987, B9.
6. Editorial, "Art Theft Is Best in Daylight," *Boston Globe,* May 18, 1972, 22.
7. United Press International, "2 Shoot a Museum Guard and Flee with 4 Paintings," *New York Times,* May 19, 1972, 1.
8. Ibid.
9. Peter Donker, "More Than a Gun Hurt Museum Guard," *Worcester Telegram,* May 30, 1982, 14A.

CHAPTER THREE

1. Alan Riding, "Your Stolen Art? I Threw Them Away, Dear," *The New York Times,* May 17, 2002, C1.

2. W. Granger Blair, "Stolen Art Found by Scotland Yard," *New York Times*, January 4, 1967; and W. Granger Blair, "$5 Million in London Art Stolen," *The New York Times*, December 31, 1966.

3. Blair, "$5 Million in London Art Stolen."

4. Blair, "Stolen Art Found by Scotland Yard."

5. From Hugh McLeave, *Rogues in the Gallery* (Raleigh, NC: Boson Books, 2003), 104.

6. Ibid., 105.

7. Ibid., 105–106.

8. Ibid., 107; and Associated Press, "Art Found in Thieves' Lair," *New York Times*, January 4, 1967.

9. McLeave, *Rogues in the Gallery,* 107; Blair, "Stolen Art Found by Scotland Yard."

10. Blair, "Stolen Art Found by Scotland Yard."

11. Constantijn Huygens, "Constantijn Huygens on Rembrandt," in *Rembrandt Creates Rembrandt: Art and Ambition in Leiden, 1629–1631*, edited by Alan Chong (Zwolle: Waanders, 2000), 135.

12. Michael Zell, "The Gift Among Friends: Rembrandt's Art in the Network of His Patronal and Social Relations," in *Rethinking Rembrandt*, edited by Alan Chong and Michael Zell (Zwolle: Waanders Publishers, 2002).

13. Simon Schama, *Rembrandt's Eyes* (New York: Alfred A. Knopf, 1999), 29.

14. Schama, *Rembrandt's Eyes,* and *The Rembrandt Book* (New York: Abrams, 2006), by Gary Schwartz, an American scholar living in Maarssen, the Netherlands, are unsurpassed explorations of the great painter.

15. Schwartz, *The Rembrandt Book,* and others.

16. Christopher White, *Rembrandt* (London: Thames and Hudson, 1984), 24.

17. Stichting Foundation Rembrandt Research Project, *A Corpus of Rembrandt Paintings: Volume II: 1631–1634*, edited by J. Bruyn, B. Haak, S. H. Levie, and P. J. J. van Thiel (New York: Springer, 1986).

18. Ibid.

19. Terry Trucco, "The Gallery: Dulwich's Disappearing Rembrandt," *Wall Street Journal,* July 17, 1987; Geraldine Norman, "Takeaway

Rembrandt Stays Hidden/Dulwich Gallery Keeps Recently-Recovered Painting at Secret Location," *The Times of London*, October 10, 1986; and "3 million pounds 'takeaway Rembrandt' found in left luggage locker/West German Police recovers stolen printing in Munich," *The Times of London*, October 9, 1986.

20. Trucco, "The Gallery: Dulwich's Disappearing Rembrandt."

21. Trucco, "The Gallery: Dulwich's Disappearing Rembrandt"; Norman, "Takeaway Rembrandt Stays Hidden/Dulwich Gallery Keeps Recently-Recovered Painting at Secret Location"; and "3 million pounds 'takeaway Rembrandt' found in left luggage locker/West German Police recovers stolen printing in Munich"; UPI, "Painting by Rembrandt Is Recovered in London," *The New York Times*, September 3, 1981; and "Charges Laid Over Theft of Painting," *The Globe and Mail* (Reuters), September 7, 1981.

22. Trucco, "The Gallery: Dulwich's Disappearing Rembrandt."

23. Ibid.

24. Ibid.

25. Norman, "Takeaway Rembrandt Stays Hidden/Dulwich Gallery Keeps Recently-Recovered Painting at Secret Location."

26. Ibid.

27. Trucco, "The Gallery: Dulwich's Disappearing Rembrandt."

28. Ibid.

29. Ibid.

CHAPTER FOUR

1. This account of the crime and its aftermath is based on multiple newspaper, broadcast, and wire service reports from the time, supplemented by interviews conducted by the authors with primary sources, as noted in the text. The news media sources are as follows: WCPO-TV (Channel 9) in Cincinnati; the *Cincinnati Enquirer*; the *Cincinnati Post*; and the Associated Press. These are supplemented with written records from the Cincinnati Police Museum, the United States Federal District Court for the Southern District of Ohio, and John W. Warrington's "Report to Literary Club of Cincinnati," October 2, 1978.

2. Stichting Foundation Rembrandt Research Project, *A Corpus of Rembrandt Paintings: Volume II: 1631–1634,* edited by J. Bruyn, B. Haak, S. H. Levie, and P. J. J. van Thiel (New York: Springer, 1986), 390.

3. Ibid.

4. The Metropolitan Museum of Art, Works of Art Collection Database, gallery label, available at http://www.metmuseum.org/works_ of_art/collection_database/european_paintings/portrait_0f_a_ young_woman_with_a_fan_rembrandt_rembrandt_van_rijn/ objectview.aspx?collID=11&OID=110001841.

5. Wilhelm Bode, *The Complete Work of Rembrandt,* VIII vols. (Vol. II; Paris: Charles Sedelmeyer, 1897), 80.

6. "Chas. P. Taft Gets Famous Rembrandt," Special Cable to the *New York Times,* August 8, 1909.

7. Ibid.

8. Taft Museum of Art website, http://www.taftmuseum.org/pages/ museumhistory.php.

9. Maurice W. Brockwell, *A Catalogue of Paintings in the Collection of Mr. and Mrs. Charles P. Taft* (New York: privately printed, 1920), 55–56.

10. Schichting Foundation Rembrandt Research Project, *A Corpus of Rembrandt Paintings, Vol. IV: Self Portraits,* edited by Ernst van de Wetering (New York: Springer, 2005), 406.

11. For this book, Horsley consented to his first and only interview about the theft.

12. Warrington's recollections are included in a short monograph he wrote about the case for the Cincinnati Literary Club, "Report to Literary Club of Cincinnati," dated October 2, 1978. His son, George, provided a copy to the authors, as well as private footage of Warrington discussing the episode.

13. Ibid.

CHAPTER FIVE

1. *International Herald Tribune,* October 11, 1994, 2.

2. Paul Zumthor, *Daily Life in Rembrandt's Holland* (New York: Macmillan, 1963), 246.

3. Melanie D. G. Kaplan, "FBI Art Crime Team says residences are biggest target," March 2, 2010, available at http://www.smartplanet.com/people/blog/pure-genius/fbi-art-crime-team-says-residences-are-biggest-target/2156/.

4. "A Rembrandt Work Stolen in Stockholm," *The New York Times*, November 15, 1933.

5. Alan Chong, "The Myth of Young Genius: Understanding Rembrandt's Early Career," in *Rembrandt Creates Rembrandt: Art and Ambition in Leiden, 1629–1631,* edited by Alan Chong (Zwolle: Waanders, 2000), 79.

6. "Stolen Rembrandt is Found," *The New York Times*, November 16, 1933.

7. "$26,500 in Art Stolen from Critic's Home; painting by Rembrandt is Among the Loot," *The New York Times*, September 10, 1938.

8. Ibid.

9. Associated Press, "Priceless Paintings Found Buried in Moscow; Rembrandt, Titian and 3 Others Stolen in 1927," *The New York Times,* November 18, 1931, 1.

10. Information from Chilham Castle official website, available at http://www.chilham-castle.co.uk/history.aspx?id=8.

11. "Art: Knaves with Knives," *Time*, May 2, 1938, available at http://www.time.com/time/magazine/article/0,9171,848914,00.html#ixzz14FuvAzpk.

12. *Arts Magazine*, vol. 12 (perhaps incorrectly listed as a 1937 document by *Art Digest*).

13. "£100,000 Paintings Stolen in England," *The New York Times*, April 24, 1938.

14. "$100,000 Paintings Stolen in England," *The New York Times,* April 24, 1938, 1.

15. Ibid.

16. "Four Paintings Stolen," *The New York Times*, October 12, 1959.

17. "Stolen Rembrandt Recovered," *The New York Times*, August 10, 1962.

18. Quoted in Robert Lacey, *Sotheby's: Bidding for Class* (New York: Little Brown & Co, 1998). Originally from Sotheby's Corporate History

19. *New York Herald Tribune,* October 17, 1958, 11.

20. "Art Worth $600,000 Is Stolen in Toronto," *The New York Times*, September 16, 1959, 1.

21. "Stolen Paintings Found in Toronto: Art Insured for $640,000 Is Little Damage." *The New York Times*, October 6, 1959, 1.

22. Will and Codicil of Isabella Stewart Gardner, probated July 23, 1924, in the Probate Court of Suffolk County, Commonwealth of Massachusetts.

23. "A Rembrandt Stolen in Rochester," *The New York Times*, February 1, 1968.

24. "Police Set Trap, Recover Stolen Rembrandt Upstate," *The New York Times*, October 17, 1968.

25. "5 Jailed in Buffalo Art Theft Plot," *The New York Times*, October 25, 1968.

26. The story of the Herrington theft consists of reports from the following articles: "13 Year Term in Art Theft," *Boston Globe*, January 16, 1980; William M. Carley, "Easel Pickings: For this Art Collector, Priceless Paintings are Get out of Jail Cards," *Wall Street Journal*, September 29, 1997; and Associated Press, "$1 million in Stolen Art is Recovered in Boston," *The New York Times*, August 16, 1979; and Stephen M. Shepherd, "Cohasset Art Worth $3M is Recovered," *Patriot Ledger*, August 16, 1979.

27. "Rembrandt Copy is Stolen," *The New York Times*, December 13, 1962.

28. "Rembrandt is Recovered," *The New York Times*, August 9, 1976.

29. Barry James, " 'Rembrandt' Needed a Night Watchman," *International Herald Tribune*, October 11, 1994, 2.

30. Facts about the recovery of the double-sided drawing are from Rita Reif, "A Stolen Rembrandt Drawing is Identified," *The New York Times*, July 20, 1989.

CHAPTER SIX

1. Connor has written a longer, slightly different account of the robbery in his memoirs, *The Art of the Heist: Confessions of a Master Thief* (New York: Collins, 2009). This account is drawn from multiple one-on-one interviews with him conducted several years earlier. The small variations in the versions do not in any case alter the basic sequence of events.

2. Stichting Foundation Rembrandt Research Project, *A Corpus of Rembrandt Paintings: Volume II: 1631–1634,* edited by J. Bruyn, B. Haak, S. H. Levie, and P. J. J. van Thiel (New York: Springer, 1986), 166–167.
3. Paul Zumthor, *Daily Life in Rembrandt's Holland* (New York: Macmillan, 1963), 239.

CHAPTER SEVEN

1. Edward Dolnich, *The Rescue Artist: A True Story of Art, Thieves, and the Hunt for a Missing Masterpiece* (New York: Harper Collins, 2005).
2. Ibid.
3. Stephan Nasstrom, "Stolen Rembrandt spirited off in speedboat," *The Guardian of London,* December 23, 2000, 3.
4. Robert K. Wittman and John Shiffman, *Priceless: How I Went Undercover to Rescue the World's Stolen Art Treasures* (New York: Crown, 2010), 219.
5. This account of the crime and its aftermath is based on multiple newspaper, broadcast, and wire service reports from the time, supplemented by interviews conducted by the authors with primary sources, as noted in the text. Sources include: *The Guardian of London;* The Associated Press; *The Stockholm News; The Times of London; Art of the Heist: The Big Sting,* video by the BBC in association with the Art Loss Register (2007); the Aftonbladet daily newspaper, and FBI officials and sources.
6. Many of its Old Master works were acquired under the auspices of Louisa Ulrika of Prussia, queen consort of Sweden between 1751 and 1771. She was the wife of Sweden's King Adolf Frederick and sister to Prussia's King Frederick the Great. Her son, Gustav III, shared his mother's love for art and is credited with greatly expanding the museum and its Old Masters Gallery. (He also founded the Swedish Academy in 1786. Today, it awards the Nobel Prizes.) The National Museum also houses a world-class collection of eighteenth-century French Masters, among them François Boucher's *Birth of Venus* (1740).

7. The painting features an absurdly crowned one-eyed Roman-era Batavian chieftain. (The Dutch revere the Batavians as their valiant, independence-minded forebears.) He is demanding oaths of allegiance from his vassals at sword points. The great Rembrandt scholar Sir Christopher White of Yale described them as "ruffianly conspirators gathered together at [a] strange barbaric rite" (Christopher White, *Rembrandt* [London: Thames and Hudson, 1984], 192).

8. Mariet Westermann, "Making a Mark in Rembrandt's Leiden," in *Rembrandt Creates Rembrandt: Art and Ambition in Leiden, 1629–1631,* edited by Alan Chong (Zwolle: Waanders, 2000), 25.

9. Alan Chong, ed., *Rembrandt Creates Rembrandt: Art and Ambition in Leiden, 1629–1631* (Zwolle: Waanders, 2000), 11.

10. Christopher White, "Rembrandt's Technique during the Leiden Years," in *Rembrandt Creates Rembrandt: Art and Ambition in Leiden, 1629–1631,* edited by Alan Chong (Zwolle: Waanders, 2000).

11. Stichting Foundation Rembrandt Research Project, *A Corpus of Rembrandt Paintings: Volume I: 1625–1631,* edited by J. Bruyn, B. Haak, S. H. Levie, P. J. J. Van Thief, and E. Van de Wetering (New York: Springer, 1982), 426. The Rembrandt Research Project cited the possibility that the condition of the painting might be the cause of their inability to make a positive attribution to Rembrandt. They refer throughout their report to noticeable wear on the surface paint, to the point where some of the underlying gold leaf shone through.

12. Cullen Murphy, "Defining Rembrandt: Art historians are still trying to establish which paintings are by the master and which ones are not," *The Atlantic* 257 (May 1986), 116.

13. Kenneth Clark, *An Introduction to Rembrandt* (New York: Harper & Row, 1978), 11.

14. As Clark notes on page 14: "All his life Rembrandt's deepest ambition was to give visible form to human feelings; and this at first meant simply making faces." (Clark, *An Introduction to Rembrandt.*)

15. Christopher White, *Rembrandt* (London: Thames and Hudson, 1984).

16. Ibid.
17. Stichting Foundation Rembrandt Research Project, *A Corpus of Rembrandt Paintings: Volume I.*
18. Ibid.
19. The provenance of the 1630 *Self-Portrait* comes from Stichting Foundation Rembrandt Research Project, *A Corpus of Rembrandt Paintings: Volume I,* 426.
20. Interview with Görel Cavalli-Björkman, excerpted from "The Big Sting," episode from the BBC television series *The Art of the Heist* (2007), produced by Electric Sky Productions in association with The Art Loss Register (UK).
21. Interview with Pär Lundmark excerpted from "The Big Sting," episode from the BBC television series *The Art of the Heist* (2007), produced by Electric Sky Productions in association with The Art Loss Register (UK).
22. The caper somewhat resembled a 1955 French film noir classic, *Rififi,* except the movie features a jewelry heist.
23. Interview with Anders Fellenius, in "The Big Sting," episode from the BBC television series *The Art of the Heist* (2007), produced by Electric Sky Productions in association with The Art Loss Register (UK).
24. Julian Isherwood, "Swedes Will Not Pay Art Ransom: One Rembrandt, Two Renoirs Worth $45M Stolen during Daring Heist," *The Daily Telegraph,* January 2, 2001, 3.
25. Sweden is still considered a low-crime nation. But a decade-long influx of Russians, Bulgarians, Serbs, and others from the former Soviet bloc had altered things. Nowadays there are networks of international criminals to infiltrate and keep track of, hardened men aware of Sweden's traditional complacency toward lawbreakers.
26. From "The Big Sting."
27. Robert K. Wittman, with John Shiffman, *Priceless: How I went Undercover to Rescue the World's Stolen Treasures* (New York: Crown Publishers, 2010), 226–7.
28. Wittman, with Shiffman, *Priceless,* 222.
29. Interview with Jonathan Mosser, in *Art of the Heist.*
30. From "The Big Sting."
31. Wittman, with Shiffman, *Priceless,* 231.

32. From "The Big Sting."

33. Robert K. Wittman, interview with the authors.

34. Agence France-Presse, "Stolen Rembrandt on View again in Sweden as Suspects Detained," September 22, 2005.

35. Agence France-Presse, "Stolen Rembrandt on View again in Sweden as Suspects Detained," September 22, 2005.

36. Karen Mattias, "Historic Painting, Historic Price Tag amid Tight Security, Rembrandt Work Goes on Sale for $46 Million," Associated Press, September 25, 2005.

CHAPTER EIGHT

1. Pranay Gupte, "A Rembrandt is Among 4 Works Stolen on Coast," *The New York Times*, December 25, 1978.

2. Ibid.

3. Ibid.

4. Ray Delgado, "Paintings from '78 heist Reappear," *San Francisco Examiner*, November 11, 1999.

5. Gupte, "A Rembrandt is Among 4 Works Stolen on Coast."

6. Clare Morgan, "$1.4 million Cavalier Art Theft Probably an Inside Job," *The Age*, June 15, 2007, available at http://www.theage.com.au/news/national/14m-cavalier-art-theft-probably-an-inside-job/2007/06/14/1181414466910.html.

7. Delgado, "Paintings from '78 heist Reappear."

8. Sharon Flescher, "Three Stolen Paintings Back at the De Young Museum After 21 Years," *IFAR Journal* (winter 1999/2000), 8.

9. Ibid.

10. Letter no. 426 (to Theo), October 10/11, 1885, in Vincent van Gogh, *Complete Letters of Vincent van Gogh, Vol. 2* (New York: Bulfinch, 2000).

11. Minutes from the Fine Arts Museums of San Francisco Executive Committee Board of Trustees, "Report on Recovered Dutch Paintings Stolen from the M.H. de Young Memorial Museum on December 24, 1978," December 9, 1999.

12. Joshua Brandt, "Stolen Rembrandt is no Rembrandt and Perhaps not a Rabbi, either," JWeekly.com, August 25, 2000.

13. Delgado, "Paintings from '78 Heist Reappear."

14. M. H. de Young, "Disappointment Created the Museum in Golden Gate Park," 1916, *California Living,* as reprinted at "The Virtual Museum of the City of San Francisco," available at http://www.sfmuseum.org/hist10/mhdeyoung.html.

15. Ibid.

16. Ibid.

17. "Mike De Young Shot," *The New York Times,* November 20, 1894.

18. Ellen McGarrahan, "Color It Gone," *San Francisco Weekly,* October 4, 1995, available at http://www.sfweekly.com/1995–10-04/news/color-it-gone/2/.

19. The story of the recovery comes from a variety of sources, including Jonathan Curiel and Stacy Finz, "San Francisco Art Treasures Recovered," *San Francisco Chronicle,* November 11, 1999; "Three Stolen Paintings Back at the De Young Museum After 21 Years," *IFAR Journal* (winter 1999/2000); and an interview with IFAR executive director Sharon Flescher with author (Anthony Amore) on October 20, 2010.

20. The presumed pseudonym "Carl La Fung" is the best guess at the name provided to IFAR staff during his November 4, 2010, phone call to that organization.

21. Michael Winerip, "Hot on the Trail of Missing Masterpieces," *The New York Times Magazine,* November 12, 1989.

22. Finz, "San Francisco Art Treasures Recovered."

23. Stacy Finz and Dan Levy, "Thieves Likely Couldn't Peddle Masterpieces," *San Francisco Chronicle,* November 12, 1999.

24. Chuck Squatriglia, "Stolen Paintings Return to de Young," *San Francisco Chronicle,* February 10, 2000.

25. Delgado, "Paintings from '78 Heist Reappear."

26. Finz, "San Francisco Art Treasures Recovered."

27. Delgado, "Paintings from '78 Heist Reappear."

28. Ibid.

29. Finz, "San Francisco Art Treasures Recovered."

30. Delgado, "Paintings from '78 Heist Reappear."

31. Finz, "San Francisco Art Treasures Recovered."

32. David Bonetti, "Recovered Paintings on View," *San Francisco Examiner,* February 11, 2000.

33. "Three Stolen Paintings Back at the De Young Museum After 21 Years."

34. Brandt, "Stolen 'Portrait' is no Rembrandt and perhaps not a rabbi, either."

35. Delgado, "Paintings from '78 Heist Reappear."

36. Finz, "San Francisco Art Treasures Recovered."

37. Bonetti, "Recovered Paintings on View."

38. Ibid.

39. "Three Stolen Paintings Back at the De Young Museum After 21 Years."

CHAPTER NINE

1. Mike Carter, "Thieving art dealer faces new charges," *Seattle Times,* May 12, 2010, A1.

2. Erik Hinterding, *Rembrandt as an Etcher: The Practice of Production and Distribution* (Atlanta, GA: Sound & Vision, 2006).

3. Holm Bevers, "Rembrandt as an Etcher," in *Rembrandt: The Master and His Workshop, Drawings and Etchings,* edited by Sally Salvesen (New Haven: Yale University Press, 1991), 160.

4. Ibid.

5. Ibid.

6. Gabriella Coslovich and Jamie Berry, "Rembrandt Raiders Hit Suburban Home," December 12, 2003, www.theage.com.au.

7. Seth Mydans, "Stolen Etchings Are Recovered in Manhattan; 5 Works Are Found in a Grand Central Locker," *The New York Times,* November 7, 1983, B2.

8. Associated Press, "17th Century Rembrandt Etching Stolen from Chicago Gallery," May 21, 2007.

9. Demian Bulwa, "Art Theft Smells Fishy, Investigators Say: Men reported $80 Million Heist from Pebble Beach Home," *San Francisco Chronicle,* October 7, 2009, B1.

EPILOGUE

1. "Montreal Museum Looted of Art Worth $2 Million," *The New York Times,* September 5, 1972, 1.

2. "2M Art Stolen at Montreal in a Topkapi Job," *Daily News,* September 5, 1972.

3. The work of Catherine Sezgin, who completed a master's thesis on the 1972 Montreal MFA heist, was invaluable in recounting this story.

4. Anthony Amore interview with Gianfranco Pocobene, November 8, 2010, Boston.

5. FBI Art Theft National Stolen Art File, available at http://www. fbi.gov/about-us/investigate/vc_majorthefts/arttheft/arttheft/@@ search-artcrimes?getCrimeCategory=&maker=rembrandt&Addi tionalCatalogedData=&TitleAndDescription=&period=&form. submitted=1&form.button.search=Search (accessed on November 8, 2010). Catherine Schofield Sezgin, "The Skylight Caper: The 1972 unsolved theft of the Montreal Museum of Fine Arts," MA thesis, Association for Research into Crimes Against Art, Amelia, Umbria, 2009.

SELECTED BIBLIOGRAPHY

Bailey, Anthony. *Rembrandt's House: Exploring the World of the Great Master*. Boston: Houghton Mifflin, 1978.

"The Big Sting." Episode from the BBC television series *The Art of the Heist* (2007). Produced by Electric Sky Productions in association with The Art Loss Register (UK).

Blankert, Albert. *Rembrandt: A Genius and His Impact*. Zwolle: Waanders, 2006.

Bomford, David. *Art in the Making: Rembrandt*. New Haven: Yale University Press, 2006.

Brown, Christopher Leslie, Jan Kelch, and Pieter van Thiel. *Rembrandt: The Master and His Workshop*. New Haven: Yale University Press, 1991.

Burnham, Bonnie. *Art Theft: Its Scope, Its Impact, and Its Control*. New York, International Foundation for Art Research, 1978.

Charney, Noah, ed. *Art and Crime: Exploring the Dark Side of the Art World*. Santa Barbara: Praeger, 2009.

Chong, Alan, ed. *Rembrandt Creates Rembrandt: Art and Ambition in Leiden, 1629–1631*. Zwolle: Waanders, 2000.

Chong, Alan, and Michael Zell, eds. *Rethinking Rembrandt*. Zwolle: Wannders, 2002.

Clark, Kenneth. *An Introduction to Rembrandt*. London: John Murray/ Readers Union, 1978.

Connor Jr., Myles J., with Jenny Siler. *The Art of the Heist: Confessions of a Master Thief, Rock and Roller, and Prodigal Son*. New York: HarperCollins, 2009.

Crenshaw, Paul. *Rembrandt's Bankruptcy: The Artist, His Patrons and the Art Market in Seventeenth-Century Netherlands*. Cambridge: Cambridge University Press, 2006.

Esterow, Milton. *The Art Stealers*. New York: Macmillan, 1966.

Houpt, Simon. *Museum of the Missing: A History of Art Theft*. New York: Sterling, 2006.

Kloss, William. *The Dutch Masters*. Washington: Smithsonian Associates, 2006.

McLeave, Hugh. *Rogues in the Gallery: The Modern Plague of Art Thefts*. Raleigh: Boson Books, 2009.

Mee Jr., Charles L. *Rembrandt's Portrait: A Biography*. New York: Simon & Schuster, 1988.

Middlemas, Keith. *The Double Market: Art Theft and Art Thieves*. Toronto: Saxon House, 1975.

Miles, Margaret M. *Art as Plunder: The Ancient Origins of the Debate about Cultural Property*. Cambridge: Cambridge University Press, 2008.

Pescio, Claudio. *Rembrandt*. Minneapolis: The Oliver Press Inc., 2008.

Schama, Simon. *Rembrandt's Eyes*. New York: Alfred A. Knopf, 2001.

Schwartz, Gary. *The Rembrandt Book*. New York: Abrams, 2006.

———. *Rembrandt: His Life, His Paintings*. Amsterdam: Viking, 1985.

Shorto, Russell. *The Island at the Center of the World*. New York: Vintage, 2005.

Stichting Foundation Rembrandt Research Project. *A Corpus of Rembrandt Paintings: Volume I: 1625–1631*. Edited by E. van de Wetering, J. Bruyn, B. Haak, S. H. Levie, and P. J. J. van Thiel. New York: Springer, 1982.

———. *A Corpus of Rembrandt Paintings: Volume II: 1631–1634*. Edited by J. Bruyn, B. Haak, S. H. Levie, and P. J. J. van Thiel. New York: Springer, 1986.

———. *A Corpus of Rembrandt Paintings: Volume III: 1635–1642*. Edited by E. van de Wetering, J. Bruyn, B. Haak, S. H. Levie, and P. J. J. van Thiel. New York: Springer, 1990.

———. *A Corpus of Rembrandt Paintings: Volume IV: Self Portraits*. Edited by E. Van de Wetering. New York: Springer, 2005.

Van Loon, Hendrik Willem. *R. v. R.: The Life and Times of Rembrandt van Rijn*. New York: Garden City Publishing Co., 1930.

White, Christopher. *Rembrandt*. London: Thames and Hudson, 1984.

Wittman, Robert K., with John Shiffman. *Priceless: How I Went Undercover to Rescue the World's Stolen Treasures.* New York: Crown Publishers, 2010.

Zell, Michael. *Reframing Rembrandt: Jews and the Christian Image in Seventeenth-Century Amsterdam.* Berkeley: University of California Press, 2002.

Zumthor, Paul. *Daily Life in Rembrandt's Holland.* New York: Macmillan, 1963.

INDEX